DERBY LIFE

● ● ● ●

DERBY LIFE

● ● ● ●

A CRASH COURSE
IN THE INCREDIBLE SPORT OF
ROLLER DERBY

Margot Atwell
AKA
Em Dash

GUTPUNCH PRESS

Cover Photo: TJ Chase

Cover Design: Zak Deardoff

Editing: Ali Lemer, Lisa Williams

Book Design: Jamie Kerry of Belle Étoile Studios

Wanna get in touch? Drop us a line at info@gutpunchpress.com.

Gutpunch Press
Brooklyn, New York
www.gutpunchpress.com

Trade paperback ISBN: 978-1-943316-00-7
ePub ISBN: 978-1-943316-01-4
Kindle Mobi ISBN: 978-1-943316-02-1
PDF ebook ISBN 978-1-943316-02-1

To Manhattan Mayhem, my derby family
for teaching me everything that's worth knowing

To Mom, Dad, and Zak
for always being there to cheer me on

CONTENTS

INTRODUCTION

ROLLER DERBY IS A SPORT UNLIKE any other. It can be chaotic, complex, fierce, and graceful. Almost nobody grows up playing roller derby. You don't learn the rules in grade school gym class. Most people have never even seen a bout. In spite of its long, unusual history, it's still a young sport that is finding its way and building itself as it goes along.

This book is an introduction to the sport and a guide for those who want to play derby or become part of the community. There is useful information for skaters at every level, from the freshest of fresh meat to the most seasoned veteran.

This book can't teach you how to skate, but I try to cover everything else. You'll find chapters on the history and culture of roller derby, how to get up and rolling, what gear you'll need, rules and strategy, taking your game to the next level, how to deal with injuries, and many other subjects.

Roller derby is a team sport, so it didn't feel right for this book to be an individual effort. I have called on some of the smartest, strongest, most talented skaters, coaches, and trainers in the sport to share their wisdom in these pages. If you don't recognize their names, check the Contributors section in the back for more information about them.

I have also included other derby people's advice and stories in this book to introduce readers to a range of personalities and possibilities. The interviews I've done and the stories I've chosen can't represent all of the voices and experiences in the sport, but these many voices have helped me create a richer picture of roller derby than I could have created on my own.

You'll also notice stunning photography throughout the book. Some of the greatest unsung heroes of this sport are the photographers and videographers who literally put their bodies on the line (or near the lines) to capture what we're doing for posterity. These photographers aren't just artists, they're artists who have to deal with skaters careening off the track at them right as they're about to capture the perfect shot. So keep that in mind as you enjoy their work!

Who Am I?

I have been playing, watching, and writing about roller derby for a long time. I started playing in 2007 with the fledgling Suburbia Roller Derby, then joined Gotham Girls Roller Derby in 2008, when I was named Gotham's Rookie of the Year. Between 2009 and 2012, I traveled all over the country skating for the GGRD All Stars. In 2009 I was nominated for Rookie of the Year in Derby News Network's annual reader poll and won Gotham's league award for most points scored. In 2012 I was co-captain of my home team, Manhattan Mayhem, when we won the team's first-ever league championship victory. I co-captained Gotham's B-team, the Wall Street Traitors, in 2014. I have coached Gotham's league practices, rec league, and juniors, and have been a visiting coach for other leagues. In 2015 I was formally elected to the Gotham Coaching Committee. Over the years I've played as a blocker, jammer, and pivot. This year, 2015, marks my eighth full season in the sport.

I've also been very involved in roller derby off the track. I helmed Gotham's PR Committee for two years and the Finance Committee for one. I began working with Derby News Network in 2009 and cofounded Derbylife.com in 2011, taking over as editor-in-chief in 2012. I've written about roller derby for both of those websites, as well as for *fiveonfive magazine*, *Derby Central*, and some mainstream publications as well. My thoughts on roller derby have also been featured in Ellen Parnevelas' book *The Roller Derby Athlete* and in Dr. Lynn F. Hellerstein's book *50 Tips to Improve Your Sports Performance*.

Roller derby has been an important and transformative part of my life for almost a decade, and in the last few years, I've wanted to give back to the community in a new way. With *Derby Life*, I've tried to write the book I wish I had found when I first discovered the sport.

Historical Record

I have spent months researching the history of roller derby, reading dozens of books and articles, and doing numerous interviews. Chapter 2, which focuses on the history of the sport, is my best effort at piecing it together. There are some facts about roller derby that everyone agrees on, and many others that are disputed or simply lost to the ravages of time. I have tried to find more than one source for each fact whenever possible, and I've included my references in the back. If you're interested in the history of roller derby, there are a few wonderful books and articles in the Additional Resources section at the end of this book that can provide a more detailed look at the fascinating past of this colorful sport.

A Note on Pronouns

In this book I have used female pronouns as the default. Roller derby is currently an overwhelmingly female sport, though there are many fantastic and talented male, transgender, and intersex individuals playing, and this book's usage is not intended to undervalue or ignore their contributions and participation. But modern roller derby is the only sport I can think of where the default implies female—the common phrases are "roller derby" and "men's roller derby." There are enough sports in the world where male pronouns and participation are the standard (NBA as opposed to WNBA, for example) that I thought it would be nice to flip the script and go with female pronouns in this book.

So, What Now?

In the upcoming chapters, I'll talk more about how to get involved, what you need to know to play, and many other aspects of derby life. You can read straight through or skip to the section that's most interesting or relevant to you. This book should be a resource for you as you begin your roller derby journey.

I'm glad to be on this journey with you!

Margot Atwell
AKA Em Dash

Goldie the Grinder, photo by Dave Wood

CHAPTER 1

WHAT IS ROLLER DERBY?

ROLLER DERBY IS AN AMERICAN-BORN FULL-CONTACT sport played on roller skates. It is also a DIY movement, a lifestyle, and a worldwide community.

The sport of roller derby has had a fascinating history since its birth in 1935. It's so intriguing that I dedicated a whole chapter to it, so skip ahead to Chapter 2 if you want to learn more about the sport's roots.

Modern roller derby was born in 2001 with a scrappy, punk-rock, do-it-yourself vibe that continues to inform the aesthetic and the attitude of the sport today. It's generally a very open, welcoming, and inclusive sport, though in the early days of the revival, men's roller derby struggled to find a foothold and faced opposition from some folks in the derby world. However, over time, even some of the most die-hard former critics of men's derby seem to have adopted the belief that roller derby is for everyone.

The modern version of the sport grew from a crazy idea to an international phenomenon in about a decade. Though these statistics will already be out of date by the time you read this, by some tallies there are currently 1,847 leagues worldwide [1], with skaters in far-flung locations such as Prague, Cairo, and Tokyo, along with hundreds of cities and towns in the United States.

Who Can Play Roller Derby?

Anyone who is interested in playing a full-contact sport can play roller derby. Though the modern sport was started by adult women, the men quickly got into the action, and now there are more than a hundred men's leagues worldwide. As derby's popularity increased, younger people also fell in love with the sport, and there are now over 260 junior leagues around the world as well. Most adult leagues are for skaters eighteen (or twenty-one) years and above, but junior leagues often accept skaters as young as eight or nine years old. The Junior Roller Derby Association (JRDA) does not have a stated minimum age, so each junior league will have its own rules about how old skaters must be to be eligible to play.

On the other end of the spectrum, the maximum age for skating is really up to the individual skater. There are no age caps in any ruleset I have seen, so it depends on the skater's fitness and comfort level. I've known great players in their late fifties, and I wouldn't be surprised to meet skaters in their sixties.

What Makes a Good Derby Player?

Almost nobody these days grows up playing roller derby, or even skating on quad roller skates, which is great! That means everyone is starting from a fairly equal place, and even the veterans in your local league who are so awesome now can probably remember what it was like a few years ago when they were as wobbly as Bambi on ice.

Having an athletic background can help you become good at roller derby, but I've known many fine skaters who were band or theater geeks in school and never touched a pair of skates or cleats. Some skills from other sports do translate, but even derby players with athletic backgrounds still have areas where they struggle.

Being physically fit is helpful, but I definitely wasn't a gym rat when I started! The process of learning to skate and practicing will help you get in shape if you aren't already.

So, what do you need to be good at derby? Some traits are part of a skater's personality, such as:

- Passion for the sport
- Burning desire to improve
- Ability to take instruction
- Willingness to work hard

But others can be developed over time:

- Toughness (both physical and mental)
- A good understanding of the rules and strategies
- The ability to take a deep breath and get back up when you fall

I talk about how to build up these skills later in the book.

Why People Play Roller Derby

Roller derby is a great sport, and there are probably as many reasons to play as there are players. Here are just a few.

To get fit and stay in shape

I hate working out at the gym and have a hard time motivating myself to go on my own. It's so easy to find an excuse not to go on any given day. But with roller derby, you have a team of people relying on you, so you can't skip practice just because you don't feel like going. Plus, it's way more fun than running on a treadmill; two hours skating will pass in a flash, even though twenty minutes on a treadmill feels like *forever*.

To make new friends

Roller derby opens up a whole world of strong, confident, smart, fabulous women and men who spend a few nights a week together. It can be very intense, which goes a long way toward creating a powerful bond of friendship. Don't be surprised if you find yourself hanging out mostly with derby people on your off nights as well!

To learn new things

I have learned an incredible amount both on and off the track. My first season, I volunteered to head our Public Relations committee, in spite of not knowing that much about PR. The skills I learned and the connections I made have helped me in my professional and personal life ever since.

To travel

Traveling for roller derby isn't required, but there are many opportunities to travel—with your league's travel teams, to local tournaments, even to RollerCon and the World Cup! There are tons of big events to travel to in derby, and frequently you can even stay with local skaters to keep costs down and make some new friends. If you don't want to travel or can't afford it, consider hosting skaters who visit your town and traveling vicariously through them.

To feel like part of something

Being part of a team and working hard to accomplish something together is a unique experience, one that many adults don't have the opportunity to enjoy. The success of every jam, every bout, every team, and every league depends on each skater. The sport of roller derby is something we create together.

To express yourself

Roller derby offers many ways for you to express yourself—from your derby name to what you choose to wear for a bout to the persona you adopt on the track. That said, you don't *have* to make up a new name or wear outlandish outfits—it's totally up to you. But having an excuse to wear outfits or makeup that are totally different than what you'd normally wear can be very fun and empowering!

To prove how tough you are

Maybe you feel like you're just a normal person, maybe even a little small or weak. But when you play roller derby, you get to feel how capable and powerful you are. Feeling physically strong gives you great confidence, and that can carry over to other areas of your life as well.

Because it's awesome

When you're seventy years old, nobody is going to want to hear the story about how you *didn't* play roller derby. Playing derby will open up doors, give you a new sense of yourself, put you in touch with your body in new ways, astound your in-laws, impress people at cocktail parties, and take over your life in ways you could never have expected!

April Ritzenthaler, one of the founders of modern roller derby, says, "It's always been, for me, a spiritual practice, the whole entire time. Even when I wanted to give up, I didn't, because I was like: This makes people happier. It breaks them open. They become something more than they ever were. And there's really no other point in life."

If this resonates with you, then you should definitely get involved in roller derby! It's hard, and it's time-consuming, and you will sometimes cry with frustration, but you'll get to spend your time doing something really fun and rewarding with an incredible group of people. Basically, if you love the sport and you're willing to put in the work, roller derby is for you! The rest will come with time.

How to Get Involved

You can find a league in your area by checking out the Derby Listing website[2] which lists over 1,800 leagues all around the world. Once you've found the closest league (or leagues), check their website to see if it mentions anything about open skates, skills nights, recreational leagues, or tryouts. Every league has a different policy for how new skaters join, so it's important to connect with your nearby league to figure out who is eligible to play and what the process is. I talk more about this in Chapter 4.

If there's an upcoming bout or event, you should definitely attend. You might also consider volunteering to help out. Volunteering to work a bout or an event is a great way to meet skaters and learn a lot about the culture of the sport and your local league. Derby leagues are always grateful to have an extra pair of hands. Plus, you can often get a free ticket to the bout!

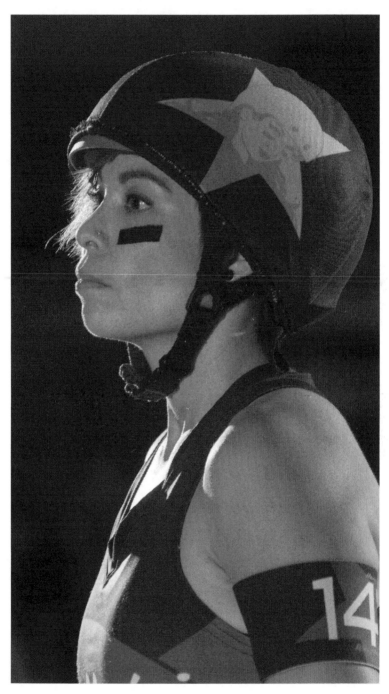

Havoc, photo by Dave Wood

CHAPTER 2

THE HISTORY OF ROLLER DERBY

THE ROLLER SKATE WAS INVENTED IN the eighteenth century by a Belgian, John Joseph Merlin, who created what was essentially an ice skate with wheels where the blade would be—all in a line, similar to modern Rollerblades. However, people (including Merlin himself) found these very difficult to control. He once wore his newfangled skates to a fancy masquerade party at Carlisle House in London, playing his violin while skating around the party. Unfortunately, he wasn't terribly good at skating, and he crashed into a huge, expensive mirror, which shattered, breaking Merlin's violin and injuring him rather badly.[4]

Roller skating didn't become popular until after 1863, when a New Yorker, James Leonard Plimpton, invented a four-wheeled roller skate which was capable of turning when the wearer shifted his or her weight, creating the pattern for the quad skate that is still worn today.[5] These skates were made of metal and would be strapped over the wearer's shoes. Early skate wheels were made of hard wood, or sometimes metal or rubber.

Delighted with his invention, Plimpton built a wooden skating floor in the office of the New York City furniture business he owned and rented skates to people who wanted to try them out. He went on to found the New York Roller Skating Association to promote the developing sport. He even opened the first public roller rink in 1866, a year after the Civil War, transforming the dining room of a swanky hotel in Newport, Rhode Island, into a rink with rental skates available to the public.[6]

A Dangerous Evil

Even in the very early days of roller skating, there was a whiff of impropriety associated with it. Stodgy folks who apparently didn't have anything better to do with their time were scandalized by this coed pursuit, which one detractor called the "most mischievous form of public entertainment ever produced" and "a dangerous evil."[7] This same critic, in a December 1884 editorial published in the *Lowell Sun*, asked, "Does it improve a young girl's modesty or morals to fall in a heap on a skating rink floor, in the gaze of hundreds, with perhaps her feet in the air and her clothes tossed over her head? Is it good for her proper training to see other females in such plight?"

In spite of, or perhaps because of, the questionable moral underpinnings of roller skating, the pastime increased in popularity, and other roller rinks opened all over the country. At the end of the nineteenth century, manufacturers began mass-producing roller skates that improved on Plimpton's design. These skates were much more affordable, significantly increasing the popularity of roller skating among people of all classes.[8]

Dance Marathons

In the early twentieth century, Americans were hungry for new forms of entertainment. Born from "an early-1920s, giddy, jazz-age fad for competitions such as flagpole sitting and six-day bicycle races,"[9] dance marathons, also called walkathons, became popular spectacles of human endurance. Coed couples would dance together for hundreds of hours, sometimes over the course of a month or two. The last couple standing would earn prize money. As America sank into the Great Depression, these walkathons increased in popularity, providing the participants food, a temporary place to stay, and a chance to win some money. Spectators enjoyed the inexpensive form of entertainment, as they could watch a walkathon for as long as they wanted for just a quarter.

These walkathons (so named because social dancing was still considered slightly disreputable) were a mix of genuine endurance contests and staged spectacles with vaudeville roots. Nearly every American city of 50,000 people or more hosted at least one of these dance marathons.[10]

A man named Leo Seltzer, who operated three movie theaters in Oregon, thought walkathons sounded like a great idea for bringing in spectators, and he decided to produce one. Once he got going, he ended up running walkathons all across the country for five years.

But a repetitive form of entertainment based on novelty can't hold people's interest forever. In 1935, on the heels of a disappointing turnout for a walkathon at the Chicago Coliseum, Seltzer began to brainstorm other ideas for events that would bring crowds to the huge venue.

The Transcontinental Roller Derby

Seltzer was inspired by a magazine article that mentioned that 97 percent of Americans had roller skated at some point, a pretty unbelievable statistic. Based on that, he decided to create a new type of endurance marathon on roller skates. He designed an event called the Transcontinental Roller Derby, in which coed pairs would attempt to be the first team to skate four thousand miles, or about 57,000 laps, meant to represent the distance between New York and San Diego. On August 13, 1935, Seltzer's first roller skating marathon attracted 20,000 fans to the Chicago Coliseum.[11]

Following this success, Seltzer took his attraction on the road. The crowd loved it when skaters "stole laps," so he retooled the rules, phasing out the map showing skaters' progress between two cities and instead granting skaters points for passing one another.

Seltzer also realized that skaters could go faster if the track slanted up on the outside, so he created the banked track that became synonymous with roller derby for most of the sport's history. He continued to retool the rules to try to produce a sport that was most appealing to fans.

In 1936 skater Joe Laurey claimed, "I threw a couple of guys over the railing. They fined me $25 and disqualified me, so I threw my skates on the track and left. Everyone else was pushing, so I thought, 'What the hell?' People loved it."[12] Although roller derby eventually became known for its brutal hits, contact between skaters continued to be illegal until 1937, when during a particularly heated bout, Seltzer instructed the referees to stop penalizing the pushing and hitting, to see what happened.[13]

Damon Runyon, a popular sportswriter and essayist for the *New Yorker*, whose stories formed the basis for the musical *Guys and Dolls*, happened to be sitting in the crowd that night. Enthralled by the rough-and-tumble action on the track, Runyon later sat with Seltzer and helped create the rules that have, with some minor changes, continued to govern the sport ever since.

Each team would have five skaters on the track at a time. Jammers—the point scorers—would try to fight their way through the pack past blockers, who would try to hold them back or knock them down. On the jammers' second lap through the pack, and any subsequent ones, they would score one point for each opponent they passed. The jammer who was in front, called the lead jammer, could call off the jam. Otherwise, the jam would run for a preset length of time (originally one minute); then a fresh set of skaters would take the track, and the next jam would begin.

Women in Roller Derby

From the very beginning of the sport, when it still consisted of teams of two skaters racking up laps with a long-distance goal, women were an equal part of it. Even as the rules changed, women still had their place. Each team included men and women, who would compete in alternating "jams" or longer periods—men against men and women against women. Jerry Seltzer, Leo's son, said, "My father felt that women should be represented in the sport," which might have helped account for the fact that even early on, audiences were at least half female. At that time, women had few opportunities to participate in *any* sports, let alone contact sports, which made roller derby unique.

According to Jerry, Leo Seltzer "was so criticized—and so was I. I had the men skaters come—especially when we were doing so well—and say 'We don't need the women anymore.' I said, 'You don't.' The women were part of roller derby, and they always would be, and that was pretty much it."

The novelty of women playing a sport—and a contact sport, at that—fascinated some sportswriters. However, the inclusion of women and the theatricality of the sport led other papers to cover it in the entertainment section rather than on the sports pages, a struggle that roller derby faces even to this day.

There was no doubt about how Leo Seltzer viewed roller derby. In his letters, he called it "a game which I think will be the greatest spectator sport of all."[14]

Tragedy Strikes the Derby

The sport was dealt an almost fatal blow in 1937, when a bus carrying skaters from St. Louis to Cincinnati "blew a tire, crashed, and exploded in flames, killing twenty-two performers.... Claiming the lives of virtually all of Leo's two squads, the wrenching accident came close to ending the entire attraction on the spot."[15] This tragedy prompted some of the first national exposure the sport ever received.

Leo Seltzer managed to find other skaters to fill in, and roller derby continued, against all odds. To honor the skaters who died, the number 1 was retired, and no skater in the Seltzers' derby ever wore the number again. Many modern skaters continue to observe this tradition.

Roller Derby on the Rise

In spite of the tragic setback, roller derby continued to grow and thrive, attracting audiences around the country. Leo Seltzer would book venues all over the country for single-night stands, and after skating, the players would pile into cars and trucks and drive to the next destination, sometimes covering hundreds of miles in a night. Skaters would sleep in shifts until they got to the next town. To earn extra money, some skaters would even help break down the track and load it into a truck before hitting the road. The mobile attraction of roller derby had a lot in common with the traveling circus, another beloved American tradition.

Seltzer tried to combat the shady associations people had with roller derby by enforcing strict moral standards on the skaters. There was a set of "Rules Governing Skater Members of the Transcontinental Roller Derby Association," which included the general requirement that skaters' "conduct and appearance must always be beyond reproach."

At first Seltzer tried to prevent fraternizing between male and female skaters, but he quickly realized that relationships between skaters could actually be a good thing, as "civilian" spouses might try to convince his players to stop skating and stay in one place. Numerous marriages between derby players have taken place, including one between Gene Gammon and Gerry Murray, who explained that sharing the sport was part of the attraction: "You marry a skater and they understand your moods, what you're going through. Something happens on the track, you get upset about it, they understand it."[16]

Retaining talent was incredibly important to Seltzer, who put a lot of energy into recruiting and training skaters. It was especially difficult to find female skaters. To improve his chances of finding talented women to play, when he held tryouts at local roller rinks, he'd insist that any man who wanted a crack at playing roller derby had to bring along a woman who would also agree to try out.

Roller Derby Comes to Television

In the 1940s the new technology of television began to spread, though very few people had their own sets. According to Jerry Seltzer, "At this point, television was very expensive; very few were in homes. They were in bars or the front of radio stores, where people would gather at night and look in the window."

Grasping the power of the new medium, Leo began trying to televise his roller derby games. Though he couldn't interest any networks in roller derby at first, in November 1948 he scheduled seventeen games at the 69th Regiment Armory in New York City. Leo's previous attempts to put on roller derby games in New York had flopped badly and lost money for him. But in spite of the dismal ticket sales for that first game—around two hundred paid admissions—the game also aired on CBS.

As Jerry Seltzer tells it:

> My dad and my stepmother went back to their apartment in New York, very disheartened, saying, "How do you think it went?" When they walked in, the phone was ringing, which meant the other five lines at the office were busy. There's nobody there—nobody thought to put operators on during the telecast. Belle Seltzer picked up the phone, and they said, "Is this where you make reservations for roller derby?" She took them until two o'clock in the morning.

The next day a line wound around the block at the armory, and police on horseback had to be summoned to manage the crowd. A few days later a sell-out crowd of 5,300 turned up there. Roller derby also got loads of press attention, appearing on the front pages of newspapers and getting coverage in national magazines.

What followed was a "lovefest" with roller derby in New York, according to Jerry Seltzer. By June 1949, roller derby was played at Madison Square Garden, with 55,000 tickets sold for a five-day-long World Series of roller derby.[17]

Leo signed a long-term contract with ABC. The network broadcast derby three times a week, and it became the most popular show on the network. But the contract specified that derby had to be played year-round, which is quite unusual for a sport. The day after the championship, the next season would start.

According to some estimates, in the three years after the first televised game, roller derby earned more than $2.5 million. Buoyed by that success, Leo thought he could negotiate a great new deal with another network and so declined to renew the ABC contract. But like its forebear, the walkathon, roller derby had been overexposed, and Seltzer didn't find any takers.

Derby Hits the Skids

Leo Seltzer moved heaven and earth trying to find a new television deal that would replace the ABC contract, but he didn't succeed. Though the 1951 roller derby World Series sold 82,000 tickets for its five-day run at Madison Square Garden, crowds soon began to shrink, and the finances of roller derby began hurting. By December of that year, Leo Seltzer couldn't even afford to pay the skaters, though many agreed to keep skating in exchange for room and board.

In 1952 Leo Seltzer decided to move the roller derby to California, but the westward move wasn't able to turn around the fortunes of the sport, which continued to falter.

In 1958 Leo asked his son, Jerry, if he'd announce the games. Although Jerry had grown up watching games at the Chicago Coliseum, he'd never really considered being involved. But Leo was offering to pay him $25 a night, and Jerry wanted to support his father's enterprise, so he decided to give it a shot.

After more than twenty years of running the sport, Leo Seltzer was tired and demoralized. He decided to shut down roller derby at the end of 1958.

Jerry Seltzer Takes Over

Roller derby is in the Seltzer blood, it seems. Jerry Seltzer recounted a conversation he had with his father. "I said, 'Hey, what if I could run it?' He said 'Well, I can't put any investment in, or anything, but you can certainly use the track and make a deal with the skaters,' which I did. The next thing I knew, every manager was gone, and I was running it at twenty-six years of age."

Jerry's approach to roller derby was quite different than Leo's had been, though both inspired respect and loyalty from the skaters. Roller derby had been Leo's dream, and he had always wanted it to be respected.

Jerry was less concerned with the image of roller derby than with the practical matter of selling tickets. He had watched Leo run the operation for two decades, and developed a different approach. Though Jerry would never predetermine the outcome of a game, he didn't discourage skaters' theatrics. According to skater Joanie Weston, "He said he wanted a game that was exciting and something you could hold your head up about. I mean, as far as predetermining the outcome or scores, no way. 'Color,' now that was something else."[18]

Another way he played up the entertainment value of the sport was by actively courting press off the sports pages. He'd send a press release with a few photos to local papers near where a derby game was going to be played and submit an ad to be run in the entertainment section as well.

Back on the Small Screen

Videotape was a seemingly small development that had a huge impact on the fortunes of roller derby. For the first time, you could air a game some time after it was played instead of only showing it live as it was happening. There was not a lot of videotaped content on television at that time, a fact that gave roller derby an edge.

Jerry recounted that at the beginning of his time running roller derby,

> KTVU Channel 2 came on the air at that time, and we were able to make a contract with them to televise one game a week. We televised every week and built the schedule of one-nighters around California, which involved moving the banked track,

setting it up, tearing it down for each one. They wanted to reshow the last hour each Saturday, which we did, and before you knew it, we were starting to syndicate that show. Eventually it was on 120 stations around the country. We started this pattern of skating in the Bay Area in the spring and summer, shipping the last-hour tapes—nobody knew what date they were; it didn't mean anything.

Jerry Seltzer was a very savvy marketer, using the taped roller derby games to turn TV viewers into fans who would buy tickets to live events. He also offered to send copies of the rules to anyone who wrote in to request them, using this as a way to build an opt-in mailing list. He also had a mailing list signup available at live derby games. (One star skater, Lou Donovan, who was apparently quite a joker, signed the list every time he saw it.[19])

Roller derby returned to its roots as a traveling spectacle. According to Jerry Seltzer,

> We would drop television spots in, and we'd set up the tour, and we were just far more successful than we ever thought we would be, selling out every major arena in America—Madison Square Garden; we played high schools, we played Notre Dame, we played University of New Hampshire—and we did that for fifteen years.

The Personalities of Roller Derby

Though the sport remained hard-hitting and athletic, some superstars began to gain attention—not just for their skating skills, but also for their personas. Skaters such as Charlie O'Connell, Ann Calvello, Joanie Weston, Buddy Atkinson, Jr., and Ronnie Robinson (son of the boxer Sugar Ray Robinson) were some of the main public faces of roller derby, and fans responded to them and bought tickets specifically to see them play.

Derby's Star Is Back on the Rise

In 1968 a journalist named Frank Deford hung around the roller derby and its skaters for part of the road tour. Deford managed to connect with the skaters and published a long behind-the-scenes piece about roller derby in *Sports Illustrated* in 1969. An expanded version of the article, titled *Five Strides on the Banked Track*, was published as a book by Little, Brown and Company in 1971.

Following the publication of Deford's article, roller derby started to gain more traction and coverage in national publications, and its scores were even included in Reuters wire service, which was syndicated in newspapers nationwide. Jerry Seltzer expanded his roller derby, tripling the size of the league between 1969 and the 1971–1972 season.

Money Trouble

In spite of the growth of the sport and its surge in popularity, roller derby was still struggling financially. Jerry Seltzer said, "We never got past that initial $500 that I started the company with. So we would always start the next season based on the revenue we received from our fall and winter. We had six teams, which were always fully paid. We had profit sharing with them, which was unique at the time." Most skaters were paid modestly—between $5,000 and $10,000 a year, though superstars like Charlie O'Connell and Joanie Weston made $50,000 a year.

In 1972, worn out by constant touring and frustrated by a lack of salary increases, among other concerns, a group of skaters went on strike, carrying picket signs as they skated around the Kaiser Center in Oakland, California. Jerry Seltzer was willing to hear their demands, but, unfortunately, the money just wasn't there to pay them more. It had rained a lot that year, and attendance had been down. A few skaters went to a different roller derby outfit, called Roller Games, which was run by Bill Griffiths, Sr. and Jerry Hill, but most rejoined

Jerry Seltzer's roller derby. Divisions and hurt feelings remained, however.

That May a fiasco marred the Roller Derby Gold Cup at New York's Shea Stadium. The Ticketron sales system was down for the three days leading up to the event, which should have been the biggest sales days. Jerry Seltzer was not informed of this problem at the time, so he couldn't do anything about it. In spite of strong initial sales, the event did not sell out, and Jerry's roller derby was cash-strapped.

But the biggest challenge derby faced was completely unpredictable, and it had huge consequences. When the oil crisis hit in 1973, the price of gas skyrocketed and its availability became limited. The Federal Energy Office instituted gas rationing, which meant that in many places consumers could buy gas only every other day. Sometimes, there was no gas available to buy. For a sport that relied on driving long distances between nightly engagements, this was a disaster.

Even worse, the roller derby typically spent the winter playing in the Northeast, as the TV ratings were highest then. However, it started to become too expensive to heat the stadiums where derby thrived. According to Jerry, "They would cancel us. Just plain cancel us. They couldn't heat the buildings in winter."

The Wheels Stop Rolling

Ultimately, between the oil crisis, the ongoing financial problems, and the lingering bad feelings from the skater strike, Jerry Seltzer decided it was time to stop. "Around the tenth of October, we made the decision we just had to shut down. We just wanted to make sure we had enough money to pay the skaters. And then, you know, that was it." Jerry told the players after the game on December 7, 1973.

He recalled, "Once we did close down, most skaters were surprised—they thought the profit sharing was a scam, but they got between $5,000 and $60,000, depending on how long they'd been skating, and what they were paid."

Just like the first time around, roller derby had suffered insurmountable setbacks right on the heels of great success, a whiplash reversal of fortune that must have been as hard on Jerry Seltzer as it had been on his father. Still, Jerry summarizes his experiences in roller derby by saying, "It was a wonderful ride for fifteen years."

Roller Games

From 1960 to 1975 a competing enterprise provided an alternative to Jerry Seltzer's roller derby. It was founded by former skater Herb Roberts, who sold it in 1961 to Bill Griffiths, Sr. and Jerry Hill. Because Seltzer owned a trademark on the term "Roller Derby," it was known as Roller Games. The two "outfits," as they were called, sometimes traded skaters or competed against each other but mostly left each other alone and did their own thing. Roller Games did not survive long after Jerry Seltzer's roller derby shut down.

Over the years, roller derby popped up again in different places with different rules and approaches, including Roller Games Japan in the 1980s. The property was briefly revived in 1989 for a televised run featuring some of the old skaters. It featured a figure-eight track and cheesy obstacles such as the "Wall of Death" and, inexplicably, an alligator pit. It also included hyped-up storylines and controversy about the skaters.

Though the ratings were quite good, beating out *American Gladiators*, the *RollerGames* show lasted only a single season. It inspired a video game of the same name, which was released in arcades and for the NES console in 1990.

Following the cancellation of the show, Griffiths kept a Roller Games league active under the name Roller Games International, which has occasionally played since then.

RollerJam

In 1997 the beloved roller derby star Joanie Weston died of Creutzfeldt-Jakob disease, at age sixty-two. An affectionate obituary was published in the *New York Times*, prompting many recollections of roller derby and attracting the attention of television producer Stephen Land. He reached out to a very skeptical Jerry Seltzer to find out what he would need to create his own version of roller derby for television.

Over the course of conversations, Land won Seltzer over, and he agreed to collaborate on the project and act as Commissioner of the new World Skating League. The show, called *RollerJam*, was picked up by TNN. It featured Spandex-clad skaters wearing inline skates instead of the traditional quad skates that Seltzer advocated, and which a few sentimental skaters wore. It also featured WWE-style characters and storylines, which took precedence over the actual skating, angering old-school derby fans. In spite of the resources and high production values, the show ran for only two seasons, from January 1999 to January 2001.

Something Stirring in Austin

At almost exactly the same time as RollerJam was throwing in the towel and once again relinquishing roller derby to the dustheap of history, a larger-than-life character named Devil Dan (aka Daniel Policarpo) was inspired to create his own version of roller derby.

Policarpo had just stopped playing guitar with his band, Arson. The band had been very interested in putting on illegal shows that were focused as much on creating a spectacle as on the music. When he moved to Austin, Texas, in 2000, he wanted to branch out from music. He said:

> I decided I wanted to put together something a little far-ranging. I wasn't sure exactly what it was going to be, but I knew it was going to be something that involved some sort of pop culture paradigm, and reinfuse that with new information, and do

it from the ground up. That was important. Something that anybody could really do. A plan that was able to be transferred. I was thinking about the circus, or a cult. A media cult, not a religious cult. Something that had more of a sense of humor to it. But I also wanted to cause trouble.

The idea of the audience was really important, too. My idea was to mic up the audience so people's conversations would be rebroadcast over the PA, so it was about the whole sonic atmosphere that would be created; the lighting, the announcers. Everything was open for reinterpretation or reuse. Roller derby just seemed to incorporate all the elements I was interested in at the time—visually, culturally.

He was familiar with roller derby, having grown up in the 1970s, and he had seen *RollerGames* on TV late at night. He was also inspired by Lisa Suckdog's *Rollerderby* zine. However, he didn't envision creating roller derby as a sport. He was more interested in creating "performance art, using sport as the catalyst. I didn't consider roller derby the central aspect; I considered it more of a cultural event."

In January 2001 Dan called a meeting at the Casino El Camino bar in Austin. His initial meeting in December had drawn only about nine interested women, but he was undaunted. He posted signs all over town advertising his vision for an over-the-top spectacle that included roller derby.

In spite of Policarpo's bizarre spin on the classic American sport, almost fifty women gathered at the bar on Sunday, January 21, 2001, to talk about a new version of roller derby with a punk/rockabilly aesthetic inspired by the fashions popular in Austin's Sixth Avenue bars. Four teams were born that night, with names and themes inspired by local bars. Team captains were chosen from among the women in attendance. April Ritzenthaler led the Putas del Fuego, a name derived from the decor of the Camino. Amanda Hardison stepped up to lead the Holy Rollers, a team themed after naughty Catholic schoolgirls. Anya Jack, who already had an appropriate cowgirl tattoo, was a natural fit for the Rhinestone Cowgirls; and Nancy Haggerty, an ironworker, became captain of the hotrod-themed Hellcats.

What's in a Name?

One prominent difference from the original sport was that the players all took skater names. When I asked April Ritzenthaler where derby names came from, she said:

> A lot of that was me. I was really influenced by drag queens. Divine was my absolute hero. Grace Jones was my other absolute, out-of-this world influencer.
>
> Part of it, for me, was that I was in a pretty degraded environment—with my relationship, with friends. I didn't have a whole lot of what made me a powerful person left, even though I was in fight training. I did Muay Thai, I boxed. I had all this energy I had to get out of me because I was so deeply unhappy.
>
> So April couldn't go out there and be a badass, but Queen Destroyer could go out there and f***ing kick some ass. It was a way to play a character until I could become that person. Of course, I didn't have all this articulated; I was more like, "Yeah, we get stage names!" Immediately, everyone gave themselves names. The teams already had outrageous names.

Policarpo, who had started going by "Devil Dan" slightly before his arrival in Austin, liked "the idea of having characters, and adopting a roller derby name. People reinventing themselves, the idea of people having a mask to show who they really are. In the rock world, and especially punk rock, that was always a popular thing, to have people have stage names. That just seemed like a natural fit."

Exit Stage Left

According to Ritzenthaler, Devil Dan made a lot of promises to the women in attendance about getting them skates and sponsorships, and they all enthusiastically pitched in to raise money to make their roller derby dream a reality. They found early support from a few local bars and businesses, and in March they decided to throw a huge fundraiser featuring local bands, paid for with the seed money they had raised so far. The event was planned for March 11, 2001, at the Mexican American Cultural Center.

Ritzenthaler and Policarpo have different accounts of his role, his involvement, and how he ultimately came to leave the sport. In several published accounts, he spent the league's money and took off, leaving the league in the lurch. Policarpo contends that the league never raised more than a couple hundred dollars and that, in fact, he lost about $400 putting on the fundraiser that March, as the skaters who were meant to be selling tickets and collecting the money for them just gave the tickets away. However, both Ritzenthaler and Policarpo agree that the fundraiser was a disaster.

Policarpo said:

> I started hearing "We don't need him, he didn't really come up with the idea." I could see the problems in the road ahead, and I was like, "If this is the way this is going to be every day, it's going to be a problem." From what I heard, those girls had a lot of problems for a long time. A lot of really bitter problems. There were relationship problems among the girls that I had no idea about.
>
> There was no official end, I knew they would be happy for me to step aside. Already, it was a women's empowerment thing. I just quietly stepped aside. I thought about marshaling my resources to start roller derby in another city, but at that point, there was already talk going on—the people I had talked to in California, Chicago, Washington, D.C., Houston, and Denver were already doing it themselves. They didn't need me at that point.

By all accounts, by May of 2001, Devil Dan had permanently parted ways with roller derby.

Rolling Solo

The exit of the man with the plan could have been the end, but the team captains and the other women were hooked by then, so they decided to soldier on without him. What they lacked in skating skills they made up for in enthusiasm.

This excitement was necessary as they did all the hard work to reinvent the sport almost from scratch. Drawing on memories of old televised derby bouts, the Raquel Welch film *Kansas City Bomber*, and skating skills co-opted from figure skating, jam skating, and hockey, the group made slow progress translating their more grounded vision into an actual sport.

To prevent another contentious situation like they'd faced with Devil Dan, the four team captains (with Heather Burdick replacing Amanda Hardison as captain of the Holy Rollers) created a business structure for the league. The captains created a company called Bad Girl, Good Woman Productions (BGGW) and declared themselves "She-E-Os."

Over the year and a half between the first meeting and the first bout, the skaters spent hours practicing skating and inventing the rules. There were very few sources of information available, so they relied on internet searches, a section Xeroxed from Frank Deford's *Five Strides on the Banked Track*, and their own ingenuity to cobble together a set of rules that made sense to them.

Ritzenthaler describes the process:

> Sparkle Plenty and I were the rules committee, along with another girl. I had never done team sports, so Sparkle Plenty did all the work on the rules. She was going to UT, and she found derby on videocassette in the library, so she taped it and brought it, and we watched it on this little VCR in the corner of Skate World. Up until that time, the way we read the rules, we thought there were two jammers per team. So for months, we practiced with two jammers per team. And then we see the video, and she says "Notice anything?" I'm like, "Oh my god, there's only one jammer!"

Other elements of the sport were similarly slapdash. Jams were extended to two minutes from roller derby's original one-minute length because, according to Ritzenthaler, "We literally could not get around the track in one minute and catch up to the pack. We always planned to move it back down to one minute." The track size was established based on the space available in their bouting venue after they set up the chairs for fans.

Style over Substance

The new version of the sport was even flashier than the original, with skaters taking on derby names such as La Muerta and Electra Blu, wearing bedazzled costumes instead of the practical uniforms of the old derby, and creating a Penalty Wheel with punishments such as pillow fights and "Spank Alley," where fans would line up to spank a skater who had broken the rules. When I asked April Ritzenthaler about these aspects of the new sport, she said, "The fighting was necessary, in our minds at least, because in our collective imagination, roller derby had a lot of fighting. We knew that we weren't that great at skating, so we knew we needed to up the production, so that's why I invented the Penalty Wheel. We had a band play. We basically just wanted people to show up."

The skaters improved and got more serious. Though fights on the track had originally been carefully planned, as skaters upped their game, they became more competitive. Skaters who were supposed to get taken down in a fight wouldn't let the other skater catch up to them. However, fighting did remain part of the sport. April explained that their philosophy was that fighting let skaters blow off steam and overcome off-track disputes: "Take it to the track, fight there. If it's real, make it look real. Inhabit your passions fully on the track."

League Split

The She-E-Os viewed roller derby as a business they owned. April recalls, "We were just like, this is awesome, I really like hitting people, I love roller skating, and we're going to have to make this a business if we want this to survive.

"We always asked for outside help. We would go to the free seminars with the Service Corps of Retired Executives. We did everything we could to make it a small business."

However, over time, a rift started to grow between the skaters and the owners, who had stopped skating to focus on running the business. Frustrated by perceived mismanagement by the She-E-Os, and disenfranchised without a vote or voice in leadership, most of the skaters left to form the Texas Rollergirls, a flat-track league. The remaining members of the BGGW organization formed the TXRD Lonestar Rollergirls, a banked-track league. This split was covered in the Crashcam Films documentary about the birth of the modern sport, *Hell on Wheels*[20].

Leagues United: The Birth of WFTDA

As the sport grew outside of Austin, teams from different areas became interested in playing each other. However, since the modern version of the sport was so new and DIY in nature, each league had created its own ruleset, so frequently, team captains would have to agree on the rules the night before a competition. It was also a challenge to start and run a sport that most people had never heard of.

To address this, in 2004 a handful of leagues founded the United Leagues Coalition, which started as a message board for networking and sharing ideas and information. In July 2005 representatives from twenty leagues met in Chicago to create a more formal organization. They voted to change the name to the Women's Flat Track Derby Association (WFTDA) and turn the organization into a real governing body for the fledgling sport. The representatives created a voting structure and set goals of creating a standardized track and ruleset.

In 2006 Tucson Roller Derby hosted the Dust Devil, the first WFTDA championship, with twenty leagues competing for the honor of being the first national champion of modern roller derby, a title won by the Texas Rollergirls. Later that year WFTDA created regionally based competitive divisions and a ranking system for tournament qualification. Eventually, as the sport spread even more, and WFTDA membership grew into the hundreds, they switched over to a playoffs model and a weighted ranking system, rather than one based on member voting. In 2013 WFTDA created a second competitive division to create opportunities for more teams to play in tournaments.

Men's Roller Derby

There were many male refs, coaches, and other volunteers interested in playing roller derby, but all of the competitors in the sport were women. Pioneer Valley Roller Derby in Massachusetts was the first league to have a men's team, which originally skated as "the Guys in Red from Massachusetts" before settling on the name the Dirty Dozen. In October 2006 a coed group of refs from Charm City, in Baltimore, invited the Dirty Dozen to play them in an exhibition bout, which the men of Pioneer Valley won. On April 29, 2007, the Dirty Dozen took on the newly formed New York Shock Exchange men's team in the first-ever men's bout in modern roller derby. The Shock Exchange took the day.

Male derby players faced a lot of criticism and mockery as they began establishing their teams. Many people thought of roller derby as exclusively a female sport. Some women who loved the fact that derby created a space for them to be tough and cool, to work hard and compete, were worried that men would show up and take over, making roller derby just one more sport where the women's version played second fiddle to the men's. Some people wore shirts with the slogan "There are no balls in roller derby." Some people thought it was emasculating and shameful for guys to play a "girl's sport" and heckled the men mercilessly. This was documented in the excellent film about men's roller derby, *This Is How I Roll*.

Over time, by continuing to show up, practice, improve, and expand their competition, male skaters and men's roller derby gained acceptance and even admiration among the broader derby world.

In 2007 three men's leagues created the Men's Derby Coalition, which gained members from across the United States and became the Men's Roller Derby Association (MRDA) in 2011. MRDA leagues began skating under WFTDA's ruleset, then collaborated with them to publish a gender-neutral version of the rules, and now have representation on the panel that determines the rules. The MRDA organized its first championship tournament in 2011, which the New York Shock Exchange won.

As more men's teams popped up in the United States, the rest of the world followed. In 2012, the first Men's European Cup was held in the United Kingdom, which was won by Southern Discomfort of England. The first-ever modern Men's Roller Derby World Cup took place in England in March 2014 and featured fifteen teams from all around the world. Team USA beat Team England in the final. The next Men's Roller Derby World Cup is scheduled for 2016 and will take place in Calgary, Canada.

Derby in the Media

In 2005 the A&E Network shot a reality show called *Rollergirls*, which followed the banked-track league in Austin; it aired in January 2006. It focused more on the drama off the track than on the skating and was canceled in March of its first season due to low ratings. However, it was the first major mainstream portrayal of the modern sport, and interest in roller derby rose sharply around the country in response.

Following that, many publications put out trend pieces focused on the fishnets and punk-rock flair, the offbeat names, and the skaters' day jobs. So many of these pieces featured variations on the phrase "By day, she's a mild-mannered editor, but by night, she straps on roller skates and fishnets and becomes Em Dash, a rough-and-tumble rollergirl" that some people in derby still laugh when you say it.

There were some better-written pieces as well. The *New York Times Magazine* published a multipage spread following the Gotham Girls Roller Derby All Stars to their first-ever WFTDA Nationals victory. But overall, coverage was spotty and inconsistent in quality. It also tended to live on the lifestyle pages, not the sports pages, just as the coverage of Jerry Seltzer's version of roller derby had.

In 2009 Ellen Page starred in Drew Barrymore's directorial debut, *Whip It*, a film about a girl in Austin, Texas, who discovers her own strength and a new family in roller derby. Though the film was fairly small compared to many of the blockbusters that are out there, it was completely world-changing for modern roller derby. It was effectively a multimillion-dollar ad campaign for the weird fringe sport we were all playing, which most people who grew up after the 1970s had never heard of. After *Whip It* people actually knew what roller derby was.

The film also brought a huge wave of attention and interest to the sport, which led to sell-out crowds and a big increase in new people trying out for leagues.

League Structures

Almost no modern leagues have owners—they are typically structured as skater-owned LLCs or not-for-profits. The tradition of skater ownership was established in the first few years of roller derby's revival, and that ethos has permeated the sport. WFTDA's governing principle, "by the skaters, for the skaters," isn't just a nice sentiment—it is the underpinning for the structure and bylaws of WFTDA and most modern leagues.

Roller Derby as a Career

Even though roller derby was originally a professional sport with paid skaters, the modern version is a completely amateur endeavor. A small number of top-level skaters receive sponsorship deals, mostly from equipment companies. Occasionally, there will be an expo bout or a tournament with a cash prize, but those are few and far between, and often the prizes don't even cover the travel costs for the teams.

Leagues can often negotiate sponsorships to cover some of their costs. These sponsorships are usually with local businesses such as bars, physical therapists, sports equipment stores, clothing boutiques, and restaurants. Sometimes these sponsorships offer skaters discounts or products instead of money.

A small number of skaters make a part-time or even full-time living related to roller derby. Great skaters can make some money as coaches, traveling to other leagues to teach them on the weekends, but this is usually just a supplement to whatever else they're doing.

There are also a number of derby-owned businesses, such as gear shops, equipment manufacturers, and apparel companies. These can make a living for the people running them, but the people I know who are making a living from derby businesses are working at it a lot more than forty hours a week.

Becoming Part of the Story

Now that you know more about the roots of the sport, you might have a better understanding of what you're getting yourself into. If you're still interested in becoming part of roller derby's fascinating story, turn the page and find out how.

Ty Fighter, photo by Manish Gosalia

CHAPTER 3

WHO'S WHO

There are many different ways to be involved in the roller derby community, in various roles such as skater, referee, non-skating official, manager, mascot, and volunteer. Each of these roles requires different skills and different time commitments, but all of them are vital to keeping a league going.

Skaters

Many people who fall in love with roller derby dream of becoming a skater—I know I did! This is one of the most time-intensive ways to be involved in derby. Being a skater requires athleticism and endurance, physical and mental toughness, the ability to take feedback and improve yourself, and a willingness to be part of a team and put the team's needs first. A lot of these are traits that you can develop over time, but all of them are necessary to be a good skater and teammate.

Typically, skaters are required to attend at least two or three practices each week, each of which can be two or three hours long. They must also do work to keep the league running, such as bout production, fundraising, and other important jobs, which I describe in detail in Chapter 9. There are usually bouts to work at or skate in at least once a month during the season, and more if you're on a travel team. Plus, many skaters also cross-train on non-practice days. Being a skater is not for the faint of heart or the terminally overbooked!

Some leagues have recreational skating options for people who want to learn and play the sport but don't have as much time to commit. There are also other ways to be involved in derby that aren't as time-intensive, which I describe below.

If you can handle all the tough parts, being a skater can be incredibly rewarding. It's a great way to make friends, stay in shape, and push yourself to do things that you might have thought were impossible for you. It will change you in so many ways, some of which you would never have predicted. Suzy Hotrod says, "I can't image life without the connection I share to so many wonderful different people. I love the spirit that is still at the heart of the sport. Even though roller derby has changed so much over the years, the women that play it are always diverse and incredibly unique."

Kamikaze Kitten says, "I love it for the person that it has made me and the experiences it has given me." And Wild Cherri relates, "I have been skating my whole life. I competed as a figure skater and enjoyed the individual sport, but being a part of a team means so much more. I love standing on a track, arms around my teammates as we are circled up for our team cheer. I love derby; it's perfect."

Referees

Referees are an essential part of the sport of roller derby. It's a hectic sport with a lot to pay attention to, so typically seven refs on skates preside over each bout. Roller derby refs skate around the inside and outside of the track, ensuring skaters obey the rules, counting points, and otherwise making sure the sport is safe and fair. There are different positions for refs, just as there are for skaters. These include head ref, jammer ref, inside pack ref, and others.

According to Judge Knot (aka Richie Frangiosa), the time commitment for referees "really depends on the official, and on the league policies. Some leagues have attendance policies for officials, and some officials set their own." You should ask refs at your local league what their policy is, but expect to practice between one and three times a week.

Refs might not compete on the track, but it's still important for them to be good skaters who can stop and start while paying attention to the action on the track. They should also be agile enough to avoid a skater who falls down or gets hit into the ref lane by an opponent. Judge Knot says:

> Too many refs come into this sport wanting to jump right into it without doing the necessary skating training. Many officials (even high-level ones) have learned to skate just enough to get the job done. In my mind, it's impossible to be a great (or good) official if you have to think even a little bit about your skating. You need to get into position, stay in position, pick your angles, see the action, all while blowing whistles, calling penalties, doing hand signals, sprinting, stopping, and communicating with the skaters and other officials. This is impossible without a firm skating base. Once you've established that, you can move on to the other fundamentals, like rules knowledge, decision-making, rapport, and the like.

Obviously, refs have to be smart and know the rules. Since roller derby is such a young sport, the rules can change every year, and sometimes there are even clarifications handed out mid-season, so a ref needs to be a quick study. It's also important to watch footage and stay current on the rules and the way they're commonly interpreted. Finally, refs should be unbiased about calls, and call things like they see them without letting any friendships or possible prejudices affect their calls. Judge Knot advises:

> You also need to be unflappable, or at least appear that way. I can't tell you how many times I've been nervous about a game, or a call, or a situation, and just had to exude confidence and hope it all worked out. I've come to learn that if you force yourself to look calm on the outside, it will become a reality on the inside.
>
> You are effectively putting yourself in a position to be scrutinized beyond what most people are comfortable with. I've had booing sections. I've had skaters call me all sorts of names and disagree with every whistle I blow. Coaches storming the center of the track to tell me what a poor job I'm

doing, and how I'm ruining the sport. You need to be able to use this scrutiny to become a better official, and not get caught up in the emotions it can evoke.

So what do you get in return for all that work? According to Judge Knot:

> I quickly realized that this was something I could pour my heart and energy into, and after about a year I began to find that I hadn't just joined a sport but a community of family and friends. I've had a unique opportunity to participate in many aspects of roller derby, from officiating to rules development, from training to tournament officiating. I've been able to effect positive change in a community I love. Officiating has given me the opportunity to help create something wonderful, and I can't think of anything more rewarding.
>
> Reffing is hard. Sometimes it's painful. And I've gone through many periods where I just wanted to up and quit. But if you love it, and stick with it, and give it everything you have, the rewards are immeasurable.

Non-skating Officials

If reffing sounds great, but you're not ready to hop on skates yet (or ever), leagues also need many non-skating officials (called NSOs) to carry out important official duties such as timing jams and penalties, tracking the score and other statistics, and many other critical jobs. Without NSOs, the game literally could not start, and nobody would know who won!

According to Julius Freezer:

> NSOs typically have practice once per week, though that can vary depending on the league and what their needs are. In my league, we have one night during the week that is designated as an officiating practice. On that night, we have classes on best practices, go over rules changes and clarifications, teach new positions, talk about upcoming games, and generally spend the time bonding as a crew. That night is usually a scrimmage night

as well, which gives us a chance to put into practice the things we've learned.

Outside of practice, I want the members of my crew to spend time studying the rules as well as the standardized procedures. The more we know both of these, the better we can be as officials.

Depending on the specific position they're in, NSOs don't need to know the rules as exhaustively as skating refs, but it's helpful for them to have a sense of the rules. Julius Freezer identified some other qualities that make people good at the job:

> If you have a passion for the sport, good attention to detail, and a willingness to learn new things every time you come out, you can be a great NSO. We are the nerds of the derby world, and immerse ourselves in all kinds of information to make ourselves better at our craft. Also, you have to be willing to quickly adapt to your surroundings. There can be last-minute changes to a roster, or a need to learn something new or train someone at the last minute.

The position can be challenging for other reasons as well. According to Julius Freezer, "there are times when the officials feel unappreciated, or even slighted. Officials volunteer for the sheer love of the game, with none of the glory associated with being a skater, so it can be easy to feel neglected by leagues at times."

But there are many factors that make it worthwhile, which Julius Freezer shared:

> To me, the most rewarding part of officiating is being part of a team that makes the sport run. There's a bond that develops there that's different than in other facets of derby. As officials, we are here for the sheer love of the sport, which is why we come out week after week. When an officiating crew all has that same feeling, games runs seamlessly, and that in and of itself is a huge motivator.

> Officiating crews are always on the lookout for new NSOs. If you want to join up, contact your local league or the league's Head of Officiating. Come to a practice and hang out with the crew at first. Watch everything going on; ask to try something if you feel comfortable. I guarantee they will be more than

accommodating and welcoming from your first visit onward. Be open-minded about trying new things. And be ready to inherit a new family as well. Much like the skaters, officials bond with each other when they are on a crew together, sharing the passion they all have for derby on common ground.

For someone who is new to derby and wants to be involved, this is a great way to try out the sport. You don't even have to buy gear or learn to skate, and you can still help the league, make friends, socialize with skaters, refs, and other NSOs, and be involved in a great community.

Managers

Each team typically has two managers. The managers can play different roles depending on what the team needs, but generally they lead the team during practices and bouts. The bench manager's job is to watch the action on the track, communicate with jammers, and request official reviews and timeouts as needed. The other manager (often called the lineup manager) will focus on the players and calling lineups. The job can be very intense and even stressful. Some players and teams can get heated during a close game (or one with lots of fouls), and a good manager will be able to defuse volatile situations and get the players focused on the game again. Managers might also lead practices and help decide on team strategies.

Not all managers know how to skate, but a manager who does skate can be helpful in demonstrating drills or even stepping into a drill if the numbers don't work out evenly for a group drill. Many managers have backgrounds in other sports as well, which can give them a different perspective on derby skills and strategies.

The requirements for managers depend greatly on what the team wants and the level of play. Some teams just expect managers to show up on bout day and to the occasional practice, while others require managers to attend one or two practices a week, watch footage, and attend meetings with the captains to talk about rosters and strategies. For All-Star teams and other traveling teams, the commitment can be even more intense.

Thor Olavsrud described the skills needed to be a good manager:

I suspect it's different for every manager. First and foremost for me, it's about keeping an even keel. A winning roller derby team is calm, focused, and communicative. But emotions can run hot during a bout, or even during a scrimmage. Skaters get fouled and the zebras may or may not see it. Some skaters may get a little dirty when they know the refs can't see it; other skaters get mouthy. When a skater gets angry (or worse, sullen) on the bench, it can become a contagion. If a manager is expressing those emotions, it's a disaster. Key skill number one: Keep calm and learn how to keep your skaters calm and focused.

The ability to project your voice is incredibly important. You may be telling the skaters on the track everything they need to know, but it won't do any good if they can't hear you over the noise of the crowd and the announcers. You need to get loud!

There are many other challenges associated with managing a roller derby team. Thor Olavsrud shared a few:

Aside from seeing a player get hurt, the toughest thing about being a manager is sometimes you have to be the bad guy. Sometimes you have to pull a really hard-working skater from a line during a bout because one of her teammates went to the penalty box. Sometimes, if your team is waterfalling to the box, it happens a lot. Sometimes a jammer is just struggling against a particular team and you need to readjust. It can lead to hurt feelings. Finding the right balance in those situations is hard.

In spite of the challenges, being a manager can be incredibly rewarding. According to Thor Olavsrud:

At its best, a roller derby team is like a family. You struggle together, win and lose together, celebrate together and sometimes cry together. Being a part of a family of amazing women—all of them striving to excel as athletes, teammates, and friends—is a tremendous privilege. I get the benefit of belonging to that family, all without having to do endurance drills like Suicides or Blood & Thunder!

And if you stick with it (and the team invites you to return), you get to see what all that striving buys. With each passing year, I get to see my friends grow in skill and confidence, overcome new and bigger challenges, and take on leadership and mentoring roles. As a manager I like to think my guidance and influence plays a role in that process, but all the really hard work comes from them.

Any past or present member of Manhattan Mayhem would tell you that I get a big smile on my face every practice when I get to make them do hard endurance drills. I'm sure most of them would say it's because I enjoy making them suffer. But that's not it. The truth is that I love asking them to do things that are hard—maybe even things they don't think they can do—and then seeing the realization on their faces that they can do it, they can kill it. That's the best thing.

Coaches

Coaches share many characteristics with managers, though they're focused on skating technique and training skaters to play roller derby rather than managing the team during bouts. Frequently, they are current or former skaters, though sometimes they come from a different background such as ice hockey or speed skating.

It's very helpful if coaches can demonstrate the skills and techniques they are teaching. At the very least, a coach should be able to observe a skater and provide specific constructive feedback about how to improve.

The time commitment for coaches is quite variable and depends on the needs of the team or league, and the coach's own schedule.

The rewards for coaching can be immense. Just like any sort of teacher, coaches help people learn and develop skills they desperately want.

Wild Cherri would likely agree: "I love sharing my knowledge of the sport and teaching people skills. I love watching the smile come out or the eyes light up when they finally have that 'aha' moment."

Cheerleaders & Mascots

Many leagues have mascots and cheerleaders (or "jeerleaders," in Gotham's case). They usually psych up the crowd, bringing signs, wearing costumes, and generally being upbeat and enthusiastic. Sometimes each team will have its own cheerleaders who wear the team's colors, and might even have a related name. (For example, my team, the prison-themed Manhattan Mayhem, has the Jailhouse Rockettes.)

Mascots and cheerleaders frequently dance or do cheer routines at halftime. They can also help out at fundraisers and other league events. This can be a great way to be involved in the sport if you're attracted to the culture and the flamboyant aspects but can't afford to get injured or aren't interested in learning to skate or officiate.

Photographers

Photographers have a special place in every derby player's heart. After playing in a tough bout, it's amazing to have visual evidence of all the hard work you did. Sometimes a photographer will capture an incredible hit or an apex jump, and it makes the skater feel like a superhero.

Photographers are usually independents who attend bouts and shoot pictures, which they'll usually share with the league and skaters. Leagues are grateful to have pictures to use to promote bouts and events, and sometimes they provide complimentary tickets to photographers. Even though most photographers are not formally part of the leagues they shoot, they are a beloved and vital part of the derby world.

The time commitment is really up to the individual photographer. The role is much more oriented toward attending bouts and events and doesn't usually involve going to practices. There can be a pretty steep learning curve for getting good at shooting roller derby, which is a very fast-paced sport with a lot going on at any one time. The more familiar a photographer is with the sport, the better able he or she will be to capture the action on the track.

Volunteers

Roller derby would not be possible without the legions of volunteers who help keep the leagues going. Volunteering can be as simple and limited as helping to lay track or sell tickets on the day of a bout, or as complex and time-consuming as running the video team or helping out as a bookkeeper or in another critical league role. There are many formal and informal ways that people volunteer.

Almost any professional skills can be valuable to a derby league. If you're great at construction, you might be exactly the person a league needs to help keep their practice space in good working shape. If you've got a fashion background, you might make an excellent merchandise committee member, or be able to design great uniforms. If you're a writer, you can write recaps of bouts for the league to post online or write up bouts for local newspapers or websites.

Sometimes skaters can be a little suspicious of people who volunteer to do a lot of work without taking on another role in the league such as skater, ref, or NSO, but if you prove yourself to be reliable, trustworthy, and a good person, I'm sure any league will welcome you with open arms.

If you love roller derby but aren't sure how you want to be involved, I'd recommend watching bouts, attending afterparties and fundraisers, and chatting with some current skaters or officials to learn more about your local league. Skaters are generally pretty friendly and approachable. They'll be able to tell you what it's like to be part of the league, and whether there are any burning needs that you might be able to fill.

If you decide you want to try out skating, the next chapter describes how you can get started.

Sugar Cookies, photo by Manish Gosalia

CHAPTER 4

HOW TO GET ROLLING

THE ONLY WAY TO GET GOOD at skating is to spend a lot of time on your skates. Nothing will help you become comfortable on skates faster than having them on your feet as much as possible. You might start out wobbly or get tired easily at first, but that's totally normal. Your body might be really uncomfortable about having wheels on your feet, but as you spend more time with your skates on, you'll learn what it takes to balance on them and recover when you do get off-balance.

Spending time on skates will also help you build up the muscles in your legs and core to support yourself and propel yourself forward. If your legs burn or you get out of breath quickly, that's OK. Everyone starts somewhere. Try pushing yourself more each time you skate: staying on skates a little longer, skating a little faster, or bending your knees more and getting lower.

If the weather is nice, try to skate outside every day. If you don't have a driveway, find a park with paved paths, a basketball court, a jogging track—any flat paved surface will do. You can even skate around when you do your chores. When I was getting comfortable on skates, I would sometimes skate to the local grocery store! I definitely got a few surprised looks, but there was no official rule against roller skating past the produce, and it forced me to have good control so I didn't knock anyone over.

If there's a roller rink nearby, awesome! It can be super fun to learn to roller skate to upbeat music, surrounded by other people.

You might even make some friends or meet other people who are interested in roller derby.

Equipment

If you've decided to try out skating, whether you want to become a roller derby skater or a ref, or just like the idea of rolling around, you'll need some equipment to keep you safe. Obviously, you'll need a pair of skates, but there are a few other things you'll need as well. Much of the information in this section was adapted from the Gotham Girls Roller Derby fresh meat welcome packet and materials created by Bonnie Thunders of Five Stride Skate Shop. There's a lot here, so feel free to skip over it if you already have your gear or you aren't ready to take the plunge yet.

Skates

You'll want a set of quad speed skates, which will look like sneakers with wheels on them, rather than dance skates, where the boots come up over your ankle. There are many boot styles, most of which come with stock wheels and bearings. These may be fine to start with. Wheels and bearings are easy to switch out and are most likely to be the things you'll want to upgrade or change later. You should make sure that the skates you have include plates and trucks that can be adjusted, not just plastic plates with straight axles fused to the bottom of the boot, which are very hard to skate in and can't be loosened to give you more flexibility. Popular skate brands for roller derby include Riedell, Brooklyn Skate Company, Bont, and Vanilla.

Skate sizing is different than shoe sizing, so you should look up a size conversion chart or call a skate shop to find out what size skate you wear. It's best to try on a pair of skates if you can, as sizing can run differently with each brand.

Wheels

For playing inside on a wooden floor, sport court, or polished concrete floor, you'll want indoor speed skate wheels, not outdoor wheels or indoor dance wheels. Speed wheels vary in durometer, which is a rating system for the hardness of the material. The higher the number, the harder—and more slippery—the wheel, while lower numbers are softer and therefore grippier. You may need to experiment to find what works best for you and the surfaces you skate on. Though many people (like me!) seek out grippy wheels for the control it gives them, Bonnie Thunders advises, "Don't be afraid of a little slide."

You should ask around to see what other people in your league are using. Many skaters will let you borrow their wheels to try them out before you commit to buying your own set, as they can be expensive: $80 to $120 for a full set of eight. Typically, wheels are sold in packs of four, so if you're buying online, make sure you buy eight wheels, not just one pack.

Wheels come in different widths, and different skaters have different preferences. The more narrow you go, the more agility you gain, but the more power you lose. There is definitely a tradeoff.

There are also different types of hubs—aluminum and nylon. Aluminum hubs don't flex, and nylon hubs do. The wheels roll differently, and which one is better really depends on your preference. There are smaller-diameter wheels, which can be a bit lighter and a little easier to accelerate with, which is good for blockers. They take more energy to keep moving at high speeds, so they may not be best for skaters who jam exclusively. That said, the need for explosive movement and fast pickup speed, and the slower general pack speeds of the current sport, might make the tradeoff worthwhile. A skater's weight can also impact how grippy a wheel feels, or what kind of hubs work best for her.

When you first get new wheels, they are often very slippery, and it can take a few practices to break them in. I tend to scuff mine up with sandpaper or by skating outside on pavement for ten or fifteen minutes, which speeds up the break-in process.

If you're skating outside, you should get a separate set of outdoor wheels. They are typically much softer and grippier (with a durometer in the 70s to mid-80s rather than the high 80s to 90s), which makes it easier to skate over sticks, rocks, and uneven pavement. If you skate outside on your indoor wheels, it'll wear them out too fast and might ruin the surface for skating indoors. A lot of people will buy an extra set of bearings and keep them installed in their outdoor wheels to make it easy to switch between indoor and outdoor wheels quickly.

Bearings

These are the small metal pieces that help your wheels spin. They are rated with a number system called ABEC (which describes the tolerances of a ball bearing). Bearings come in ABEC 1, 3, 5, 7, and 9, ranked from fast to fastest. Bones China REDS and Bones Swiss are great bearings; they are not rated but are likely faster. The best value for your money is the Bones REDS bearings. Many people use them, from beginners to the most advanced skaters. You can upgrade to better bearings when you're really comfortable with your skills. Swiss bearings are great, but there isn't much of a reason to get ceramic bearings for derby, since we don't skate fast enough for it to make a difference.

Plates

A plate is a metal or nylon part that is screwed into the bottom of a skate boot and attaches to the trucks, which attach to the wheels. For the most part, you get what you pay for—more expensive skate parts are lighter and more responsive. But the plates that most rookie packages include will be fine for most skaters' needs for the first year or two while they get the basics of the sport under their belts. The primary differences between nylon and aluminum plates are responsiveness and price. There is flex in nylon plates, so some of the power you transmit through your foot into the boot, then into the plate, will be lost. With aluminum plates there is much less flex, so you get more power compared to nylon plates. However, aluminum plates can be heavier than nylon ones, which can make it harder to pick up your feet. To get a lightweight aluminum plate, you have to pay more money, which is why most skaters start out with a nylon plate.

Trucks

These are the metal parts attached to your plates that your wheels and axles attach to, which allow you to shift your weight and turn on your skates. The looseness or tightness of your trucks determines how easy it is to turn your skates. Before you skate for the first time, check the tightness of your trucks, as pre-assembled packaged skates are usually shipped with very tight trucks, which can make it harder to do crossovers or use your edges. If you have never adjusted the trucks of the skates you are currently using, ask someone for help, or get a skate tool or wrench and slowly, slowly loosen the trucks by twisting to the left until there's a little bit of play in the trucks and you can tilt the skate side to side a little bit. Adjusting your trucks properly makes a huge difference to the mechanics of basic skills.

Toe stops

The way the game is played now, skaters spend a lot of time on their toe stops—digging in, running on them, and pushing off them. It's important to have a good set of toe stops that are grippy and big enough for you to balance on. The stock toe stops that come with many rookie packages are totally insufficient for how we use them.

A few good brands to check out are Gumball, Roll Line, and Moonwalker. Gumballs have different stem lengths, so depending on how close you like your toe stops to be to the ground, you can pick short or long. You can adjust either one to be closer to or farther from the ground.

Bushings

These are the cushions that are located in your trucks. When you lean side to side, they compress a bit, almost like a spring, which helps you push off, do crossovers, and use your edges. They come in different types of urethane. The higher-quality urethanes are more responsive and take some time to get used to if you've only ever skated with the bushings that come stock with most trucks. Bushings also come in different ranges of hardness. If you prefer loose trucks, you may want to try a soft bushing, which can be produce a similar effect without you having to loosen your trucks so much that they are almost falling off of your plate.

Skate maintenance

Over time, parts of your skates will wear out or need to be adjusted. You should make sure to have a set of skate tools so you can change your wheels, adjust your toe stops, and adjust your trucks. The same tool doesn't work for those three tasks, unfortunately, so you should make sure you have the right tools for your plates and trucks.

Some people oil their bearings or clean them on a regular basis. There are YouTube videos that show you how to do that. It's not something I've ever done—I typically just replace my bearings when I buy new wheels, about once a year.

Some skaters like to buy skate guards or toe caps to protect the toes of their skates. Especially if you practice outside, the fronts of your skates can take a lot of abuse, so that's one way to preserve the life of your skates. (Sometimes people will duct tape the toes of their skates, but the toe caps are pretty cheap, and once they're threaded through your laces, you forget they're even there.)

Laces do sometimes break, so it's good to have an extra set on hand. You should also consider keeping an extra set of toe stops around when yours start to wear down, especially if you have a bout coming up.

Pads

To play derby, you'll be required to have knee pads, elbow pads, and wrist guards. I highly recommend putting a big chunk of your equipment budget into a good set of knee pads. If you decide to learn the sport, you'll be practicing falling and dragging one knee on the ground a lot, not to mention wiping out in drills or getting knocked down. It's all part of the learning process. But it's important to protect your knees from all that impact.

Try to find a good set of knee pads that are meant for roller derby or vert skateboarding, and make sure they fit well and don't shift around when you move. They'll stretch a bit over time, so too tight is better than too loose, as long as you can still bend your leg. If your knee pads move around or are a bit too big, or you just want more padding between your knees and the ground, consider getting a set of knee gaskets as well. I describe these in more detail in the Optional Gear section below.

Elbow pads and wrist guards should have hard plastic caps or inserts in them. They're a bit less likely to slip around than knee pads, but it's still important to make sure they fit well. Some people duct-tape their wrist guards if the Velcro doesn't stay fastened during scrimmages and bouts.

Helmets

Helmets are another crucial piece of gear. It's important to get a multi-impact helmet (such as one meant for skateboarding), rather than a single-impact helmet with rigid padding (such as a bike helmet), which is only meant to take a single impact and might weaken or crack in response to a hard hit or a bad fall. Before skating, you should inspect your helmet and make sure it doesn't have any cracks or other visible damage.

Your helmet should fit well, which means you'll be able to fit only two fingers snugly between the strap and your chin while it's fastened, and the helmet shouldn't wiggle around on your head. The right size will skim the top of your eyebrows when you put it on, and probably feel a little snug. If it tilts to one side or the other when you move around, it's too big. This is a common problem, and it's totally unsafe! This might start to happen with a helmet that used to fit, because the helmet liner is worn out. That means it's time to replace your helmet. For some helmets, you can just buy a new liner, which can save some money.

Some players choose to wear hockey helmets, which can offer more protection, especially if you add a face shield. These tend to be much more expensive than skateboarding helmets, but they can last for years. I talk more about face shields in the Optional Gear section below.

I am not an expert on helmets and concussions, but even with a good helmet, concussions are a possibility in this sport. I highly encourage you to do your own research on helmets, safety certifications, and concussions.

Mouth Guards

There are a lot of mouth guards on the market. You probably won't need one for just learning to skate, but when you want to get into playing derby, it's a critical (and required) piece of equipment.

Most sports stores sell mouth guards, and some of them are as cheap as two or three dollars, but you get what you pay for. There are some brands of mouth guard that are way better and more comfortable than others, but they cost much more, so using a two-dollar mouth guard from the local sports store is fine until you decide that roller derby is something you want to stick with.

As you get more serious about the sport, you might want to upgrade to a more expensive model, or even a custom one. These will likely be less bulky and make it easier to breathe, drink water, and talk with the mouth guard in—all important for roller derby!

The SISU brand has a moldable, small mouth guard that you can pick up at sports and derby shops. Gladiator will make you a custom mouth guard based on a mold you create of your own mouth. These better mouth guards can be expensive (around $20 to $50 or even more for a custom one, though Gladiator will sell replacements for less money once you've created the custom mold). However, having a comfortable mouth guard you can talk through can make a big difference to your game.

Make sure that you mold your mouth guard before trying to use it (unless it's a custom one). It usually takes five to ten minutes and requires some very hot water. If you don't mold it in advance, you'll be very sad and uncomfortable at your first derby practice!

Optional Gear

In addition to the required gear, some skaters choose to wear additional gear, such as hip pads, tailbone protectors, or padded pants. Though not required, they can help prevent pain or injury.

Padded shorts

When you're first starting out, you'll definitely fall a lot, and you don't usually have a lot of control over how you're falling. Some skaters like to wear padded shorts to cushion their falls and cut down on bruising. There are many different types of padded shorts, some of which have a very thin layer of padding, and others with an inch of foam sewn into them in the areas that are especially sensitive and where you're likely to land when you fall. These can help prevent pain and bruises, but some are quite bulky and might stand out underneath a uniform.

Other fall protection

If you don't want to wear a whole set of padded shorts but do want to protect a specific area, you might consider a tailbone protector or a set of Waxel pads. Tailbone protectors are padded foam inserts that you can slip into a pair of Spandex pants so that they sit over your tailbone and help cushion a backward fall. I've seen these slip around a lot or even fall out, so your mileage may vary. The best thing to do is to learn how to fall *forward* as soon as possible!

I have very pointy hip bones, and after suffering an excruciatingly painful bone bruise, I started wearing Waxel pads, which are thin foam inserts that you tuck into Spandex over your hips. They were originally designed to help protect figure skaters when they practice jumps. These pads move around a little bit, but not too much, and they can prevent the agony that comes when two bony people hit each other in the hips. They're not too expensive, and they come in several thicknesses and sizes.

Shoulder protection

Some people choose to wear shoulder braces if they've suffered a shoulder injury. I've never seen anyone wear shoulder pads, and in order to be legal, they'd have to be soft, not hard-shelled, since a hard-shelled shoulder pad (like a football pad) would hurt other skaters.

Shin guards

Some skaters find themselves getting kicked in the shins a lot, especially when they're first learning to skate in a pack. You can get quite a lump when you take a wheel or truck to the shin! If you have that problem, you can wear a pair of shin guards to protect yourself. I haven't found a lot of derby-specific sets, but if you look at soccer gear, you should be able to find a set that either straps around your shins with Velcro or slips inside knee socks.

Knee gaskets

As I mentioned above, if your knee pads don't quite fit or you want some added protection for your knees, you can get a set of knee gaskets. There are different types of gaskets, but they're usually tight neoprene sheaths with some form of gel or padding around the kneecap. Wearing knee gaskets has made a big difference over my long derby career, both cushioning my knees and preventing my pads from slipping during awkward falls. I wish I had worn them from the very beginning! But if you're looking to save money when you're starting off, you can skip the gaskets until you're sure you want to play.

Chest protection

Some women opt to wear a hard-shelled bra (sometimes called a turtleshell bra) to protect their chests, especially since there is a lot of chest-to-chest contact in the game these days. Originally designed for female boxers, you can also buy them at some derby shops.

Face shields

Some helmets, such as hockey helmets, have optional face shields attached. Skaters without hockey helmets who are concerned about breaking their noses sometimes opt to wear fitted plastic face shields, which are legal. Some of them are clear, which can make it easier to see through them. Helmets with cage-like face masks (either metal or clear plastic) are not allowed under the WFTDA ruleset, as other skaters might get their fingers caught and broken.

Skate goggles

It's generally a pretty bad idea to wear glasses while playing roller derby. They can get knocked off or damaged, and they don't offer great peripheral vision. Most skaters who need vision correction wear contact lenses, but some don't like contacts or can't wear them. You can get prescription goggles that are meant for sports. They are held in place tightly with an adjustable strap and are less likely to get knocked around or damaged than a pair of glasses.

Cups

Male derby players might choose to wear a cup to protect their vulnerable bits from a stray hit or a weird fall. There are many options available for hockey players and football players. This is a subject that's outside my area of expertise, but a local sports equipment shop should be able to help you out.

Where to Find Equipment

This might all seem like a lot to handle, but don't worry! There are many fine derby-oriented skate shops with very knowledgeable employees. Many are even owned by skaters or former skaters who can give you advice and steer you in the right direction. It's best to go in person if you can, since it helps a lot to try on gear, figure out how different pieces of gear fit on your body, and see what is comfortable. However, that's not an option for many skaters, as skate shops dedicated to roller derby are few and far between. Some skateboard shops stock pads and helmets that work for roller derby, so you can look for those if you don't have a local roller derby skate shop.

The next best thing is to try on the gear your friends or teammates have. Ask them what they like and why, and see if the size they have fits you. Some teammates might even be willing to let you try out their wheels on a day they aren't at practice.

You can also call or email skater-owned roller derby skate shops. Most of them are great at talking to skaters about what equipment they'll need and will ship it anywhere in the world. Some skate shops even have discounted rookie packages that include good basic gear and skates for someone just getting into the sport who doesn't want to spend too much. I've included several excellent skate shops in the back in the Additional Resources section.

Now Put It On!

When people are learning to skate and skating outside, they don't always wear all the pads that a derby player wears, but I recommend that, at the very least, you wear knee pads, wrist guards, and a helmet. People just learning to roller skate fall down a *lot*, and a bad unprotected fall on your hands or your knees can injure you very seriously. Helmets are a good idea in case you fall backward and bonk your head—your brain is very important. If you go to a local roller rink, you'll probably see people skating without any of that protective gear, but that can be really unsafe.

Skills Nights & Rec Leagues

Once you have your gear and a pair of skates, spend as much time on them as you can! That's the only way to build the skills and muscles you need to feel comfortable and confident on skates.

Many established leagues will host skills nights, recreational leagues, or boot camps, where experienced skaters and coaches from the league will teach skating and derby skills. These events typically cost money to attend, but it can be totally worthwhile to learn good habits from experienced coaches right off the bat, instead of struggling to teach yourself how to skate based on what feels right and what you can find online. When you learn skating skills from more experienced people, they can give you specific pointers if you are struggling with a skill.

I've heard from many skaters that they met some of their best derby friends in these types of classes. It can be really helpful to have friends and cheerleaders to support you during the learning and tryout process. Plus, you can meet skating buddies who will skate with you outside or at the local roller rink on non-class days. Skating is more fun with a friend!

Beating the Fear of Falling

One of the first things a new skater must confront is a fear of falling and getting hurt. Some lucky skaters are fearless by nature, and others have already overcome their natural fear by playing other aggressive sports. But what about everyone else?

Your body and brain have a very understandable desire to protect themselves from injury. So the first thing you'll need to do is show yourself that falling doesn't mean getting injured—even if it might hurt a bit.

Step one in that process is to make sure you have good pads. It's not enough to haul out the terrible Walmart pads you used that summer you learned to Rollerblade at age twelve. Those won't cut it in a sport that's as physical and high-impact as roller derby. Earlier in this chapter, I describe how to find a good set of knee pads. If you haven't done it yet, go back and read that! Got it? Good.

Once you're well protected, you should practice falling properly. This will make it less likely that you'll injure yourself in a fall, and make you feel more in control. Most fresh meat programs spend a lot of time teaching new skaters how to fall properly before getting into advanced skills or contact.

If you're learning on your own, the first step would be mastering the "controlled lowering" technique for knee falls, or touching one knee to the floor in a controlled way, then getting back up and continuing on your way. You can practice it in sneakers first. Take a step forward, then gently touch your knee to the ground until you're balanced on one foot and one knee. Hold that position for a second, then stand up without using your hands. Keeping your core tight by squeezing your abs will make it easier to stand back up. Doing this will help create the move in your muscle memory, as well as strengthen your legs and core so it will be easier when you try it on skates. You can wear knee pads or gaskets for this if you want.

After you feel comfortable with that, try it on skates while stopped. This would be a good time to wear all your pads! On skates, it will be more challenging to stay balanced and keep from rolling, but keeping your core tight will help. When you're doing that like a pro, try doing it again from a rolling start.

Make sure you're sliding and tapping your knee gently, not slamming your knee down on the ground—you've only got two of those!

Getting good pads and learning how to fall safely are two of the most critical steps to prevent injury in roller derby. If you can tell your brain that, you're well on your way to becoming the fierce, fearless skater that you want to be! Once you feel good about knee falls, you should practice falling again and again until it doesn't faze you.

Newer skaters who are still working on their balance have a tendency to stand straight up when they start feeling unsteady on their skates, which throws their weight back and can make their wheels shoot out from under them, leading to that dreaded coccyx injury—the tailbone break. You should always stay low in a good derby stance, which looks a bit like you're sitting in an invisible chair (or squatting over a public toilet!): knees bent, shoulders pulled back and back straight, with your nose above your knees above your toes, all lined up vertically. It feels awkward at first, but with some practice, it will begin to feel normal.

If you start to feel unsteady, sink into your stance instead of standing up and flailing your arms. If you get in the habit of sinking into your stance and getting lower when you're off balance, it'll bring you back into balance—or, worst-case scenario, you'll end up falling forward instead of backward.

There are a few other things to think about if you're still feeling nervous about falling. Thinking about how you're going to get back up is an advanced move that can help take the fear out of falling. If you're already planning your next move, your brain won't have time to freak out or dwell on the fear.

I also find that adrenaline can make me more fearless. Try skating a few hard laps or listening to an awesome pump-up song as you put your pads on.

Finally, work on overcoming the fear with a positive phrase or mantra. If you dwell on your fear, it might end up getting bigger and more unmanageable. If you tell yourself instead that you can fall and everything will be fine, again and again, you'll start to believe it. I talk about this more in Chapter 12.

Derby-specific Skills

Once you feel good on your skates, you can start working on some derby-specific skills. These skills will take you to the next level and help prepare you to stop and start quickly, skate in a pack near other people, and take and recover from hits.

The more you can build up your agility and footwork, the better you'll be at roller derby. Even Bonnie Thunders practices her basic skills every single week. These skills are the building blocks for the whole sport.

A few of the skills you should work on:

- Stops
- Crossovers
- Balancing on one foot
- Knee taps
- 180-degree turns
- Backward skating

The Women's Flat Track Derby Association (WFTDA), one of the primary governing bodies of modern roller derby, has a list of skills that are required before a skater can compete in a WFTDA-sanctioned bout. Many leagues use this list of skills as a test that new skaters must pass before they can play in a scrimmage. If you want to make sure you're working on the right skills, you can use this as a checklist. These required skills are updated on occasion, but the basics don't change too much. You can find a list of these skills and descriptions of what they mean on WFTDA's website at http://wftda.com/resources/wftda-minimum-skill-requirements.pdf.

Teaching Yourself New Skills

It would be nearly impossible for this book to explain to new skaters how to execute derby skills, so I'm not going to try to tackle that. There are many ways to gain familiarity with derby skills, such as boot camps or basic skills nights at local derby leagues, or even watching videos online and imitating what you see. There are a number of great skaters and coaches who create useful videos to teach derby skills. You might want to check out the following:

Sarah Hipel

Sarah is a skater for Texas Rollergirls and Team Canada. She is also the powerhouse behind Faster Skates, a derby company providing coaching and skate gear, such as wheels. Sarah produces many videos breaking down specific skills, which she links to through the Faster blog: http://www.fasterskates.com.

Kamikaze Kitten

Though she has now retired, Kamikaze Kitten of London Rollergirls and Team England is an incredible skater and teacher. She's also notable for her experimental approach to derby and her willingness to try something crazy for its own sake in the hopes that it might be useful to her in derby at some point. You can find her videos here: http://vimeo.com/user26765885.

San Diego Derby Dolls

One of the banked-track leagues based in California, the San Diego Derby Dolls have created many great videos that break down basic skills. Many of the skills, such as turn around toe stops, plow stops, and power slides, can be used on either a banked or a flat track. SDDD has created a whole playlist of original instructional videos: www.youtube.com/user/sandiegoderbydolls.

This should get you started, but there are many more great resources online that you can likely find with a little digging. (Note: these URLs are all accurate as of this writing, but there's no guarantee that they will stay live.)

There is also a lot more information about how to get good at roller derby in Chapters 11 and 12.

Cross-training

If you haven't played a sport recently, and you're not much of a gym buff, you might think about doing some basic exercises to strengthen your muscles and build up your endurance. This will help you with every aspect of derby, from skating with a good derby stance to picking up speed, and even stopping.

Even spending ten minutes a day doing a mini fitness routine can make an impact over time. After a few weeks, you'll start to notice that things that felt impossible before have started to feel easy.

Skating long distances or jogging outside or on a treadmill can help build up your endurance, which you'll appreciate during two-hour derby practices!

Chapter 14 talks more about good exercises to do to start building up your derby muscles.

Taking the Next Step

Once you've been skating for a while and you feel comfortable on your skates, you might think about the next step: trying out for a league. Contact the local roller derby league to find out what their tryout process is, and then flip to the next chapter for some more advice!

Rose City High Rollers, photo by Jules Doyle

CHAPTER 5

TRYING OUT FOR A LEAGUE

EVERY ROLLER DERBY LEAGUE HAS A different way of recruiting and training new skaters. Some leagues have a formal tryout once a year or every few months, while others accept anyone who's interested all year round. Some leagues have special fresh meat practices for new skaters, and others just carve out a corner of the track to do basic drills with rookies while the veteran skaters scrimmage or do endurance drills on the track. Some leagues have open skates at the local roller rink, or skills nights or rec leagues led by current skaters. These can be a great way to get comfortable on your skates.

Some leagues will have fresh meat information on their websites or Facebook pages, but many derby websites are very bare-bones or infrequently updated. If you'd like to learn more, your best bet is to email your local league's coaching contact (or the general information email address if there isn't one listed for coaching.)

The more comfortable you are on your skates before tryouts, the better! Even if there isn't a formal way for you to learn from the local derby league, there are many things you can do on your own to improve as a skater and derby player, which I describe in Chapter 4.

How to Prepare for Tryouts

You've been practicing your skating skills for weeks, or even months, and now tryouts are coming up fast! How do you get ready?

Spend as much time on skates as you can between now and tryouts. Don't go crazy and make yourself too sore or neglect your job or other responsibilities, but if you can, try to skate at least a few times a week leading up to tryouts, especially the week of tryouts. If you feel comfortable and natural on your skates, it will make everything feel easier, and you'll look much more confident. If you feel rusty, it will be an uphill battle.

Work on polishing one or two basic skills, such as your plow stop, 180-degree turns, or one-knee taps. It will definitely boost your confidence if you have a few skills you know you can totally nail.

The week of tryouts, make sure to get plenty of sleep so you feel fresh and well rested. Drink *lots* of water. This will help you be hydrated at tryouts. (If your pee is so light it's almost clear, that's a sign that you're drinking enough.)

Try to eat well, too. Give yourself good fuel for the tryouts. That said, you shouldn't make any drastic changes to the way you normally eat. This is not the week to go on a crazy diet or try a cleanse. The day of tryouts, eat a light meal at least an hour or two beforehand. I like to snack on dried fruits and walnuts or cashews an hour before I skate. They give me energy and make me feel full, but they don't make me feel sluggish or queasy on the track, like a heavier meal or greasy foods would. There's more information about hydration and nutrition in Chapter 14.

What to Wear

Even though the image of a derby girl sometimes brings to mind fishnets, tutus, or booty shorts, you should probably leave those at home during tryouts. Wear something comfortable that you can move in, such as leggings, yoga pants, bike shorts, or compression shorts. If you prefer not to wear anything too form-fitting, soccer shorts or basketball shorts should work fine, too.

Some leagues have loaner gear available, but with others, you'll need to bring your own skates and pads. Make sure you communicate with the coaches in advance so you know what they can provide and what you will need to have already.

The safety gear you absolutely need to have includes wrist guards with a hard plastic insert, elbow pads, knee pads with hard plastic caps, a helmet that fits well, and a mouth guard. No matter what, you'll need your own mouth guard, which you should mold to fit your mouth before you arrive at your first practice! If you bring a brand-new mouth guard in its package to tryouts, it won't fit, and you'll be very sad.

What to Bring

Obviously, you should bring your skates and equipment, but there are a few more things you should bring with you to tryouts. Make sure to have a water bottle, and think about picking up a sports drink as well, in case you feel like you need a quick hit of sugar. You might want to bring a towel or a bandana in case you get sweaty. If you want to warm up by jogging, bring a pair of sneakers, and definitely bring a sweatshirt or track jacket to stay warm while you're waiting for your turn. You might also want to bring a change of clothes for afterward. Bring skate tools if you have them, in case your toe stops or wheels need to be adjusted.

You'll probably need some form of identification, such as a driver's license. Some leagues charge a token fee for tryouts to cover the cost of the space, so you might need cash or a check.

Finally, bring a good attitude!

What to Expect

Every league's tryouts are different, so make sure to read the website and any emails the coaches send out. You can ask the league's coaches if you have any specific questions.

You should be prepared to wait around a lot. If there are many skaters trying out, you might be separated into smaller groups so the coaches can observe everyone. You might be given a number or be asked to put your name on your helmet with tape so the coaches can identify you.

Typically, tryouts will involve one or more coaches leading the group through sets of basic skills and other drills that might resemble a basic derby practice. Skills might include the ones I listed in Chapter 4 and others from the WFTDA minimum skills list. You might be asked to skate in a paceline: skaters line up in a single-file line about an arm's length from each other, then weave through from the back to the front, or do some other skating formation. Skaters might also be asked to skate close to one another in a pack. Sometimes tryouts might include skating as many laps as possible around the whole track in two minutes. They might even involve some contact drills.

If there are many skaters trying out, your tryout might be short, so make sure you give it 100 percent the whole time! Even if you're tired, keep trying to do the drill exactly the way it was described. Derby coaches love to see potential skaters working hard and pushing past pain and exhaustion, which are traits that serve derby players well.

There might be a round of callbacks after the initial tryouts. These provide coaches with a chance to observe a smaller group of skilled skaters more closely. The coaches might ask you to try some higher-level skills or introduce something you've never tried before to see how you learn. They are also likely observing how you work with others and paying more attention to skaters' attitudes than they were at the first tryout. They will probably let you know what to expect from callbacks at your initial tryouts, or when they call you back. Just give it your all and stay positive, even if it gets hard.

Transfers

Every league has a different transfer policy, including when skaters can transfer, what makes them eligible to transfer, how the process works, and whether or not the transferring skater can skate for a home or travel team that season. If you're contemplating a move, make sure to get in touch with the coaching committee for the league in your new city well in advance.

So You Made the League! Now What?

First, congratulations! Your hard work has paid off, and you've reached your goal. Give yourself some time to enjoy this feeling.

From this point on, different leagues work in different ways, so it's really important to make sure you pay attention to what the coaches tell you. Check your email regularly, as many leagues communicate a lot of critical and time-sensitive information that way. Your new league will most likely have requirements for what it takes to be an active skater—from minimum practice attendance requirements to league committee work. If you fail to meet these, there can be serious consequences, from missing a bout to not being placed on a team to being expelled from the league. Leagues take these rules seriously, so you should, too, if you want to remain a member!

Now that you're part of a league, the next chapter will tell you more about what to expect.

Screaming MEME, photo by Sean Hale

CHAPTER 6

FRESH MEAT

EVERY LEAGUE APPROACHES THE "FRESH MEAT" period differently. Some leagues call new skaters something different (such as freshies or skater tots). No matter what it's called, it's an intensive training period to get new skaters' skills up to par so they can safely scrimmage and bout with the rest of the league. Some leagues have a dedicated time period with a whole group of incoming fresh meat, while others have rolling admission all year long and require new skaters to spend a certain number of practices or hours learning basic skills before joining the larger pool. Most leagues use a skills test to determine when skaters are ready to scrimmage. Check in with your coaches to find out what the policies are for your league if you're unclear about this. Most leagues work hard to make new skaters feel at home and welcome.

No Pain, No Gain

When you first join roller derby, everything is exciting—and everything hurts. Even if you're already in good shape, the things derby demands of your body will leave you achy, exclaiming, "I didn't know I even *had* a muscle here!" It's totally normal for your lower back and abdomen (AKA your core) to be very sore till you build up strength there. That goes double for your legs.

But ratcheting up your workout routine has a lot of upsides, too. For one, it's a great bonding experience. Some of my fondest memories from my first season involve stuffing my face at a diner with my fresh meat buddies after practice, marveling over how hard it was to do a plank for a minute, and trying to convince the waitress to bring us a bag of ice for a bad bump.

You'll be astonished by how quickly this new routine starts to feel normal, and how fast your body starts handling the new demands you're placing on it like they're no big deal. Of course, any coach worth her salt will increase the difficulty at practice as you become more capable.

The fresh meat period can feel very intense and frustrating, and sometimes even lonely. It might seem like everyone else easily masters skills that you struggle with. You might feel like everyone is judging you or laughing at you when you fall down.

I promise, they aren't! Learning new skills is hard, and everyone struggles with some derby skills. Even your coaches were learning these skills just a few years ago, and they still have skills and strategies that they are working to master. Almost no one who's playing in adult derby leagues today grew up playing roller derby. I bet every vet in your league can tell you about the skills she struggled to learn—or still struggles with.

Getting better at anything requires you to constantly push beyond the limits of your comfort zone, which can feel awkward, scary, or even humiliating. But the only way to get better at skating is to try something, fail, and learn from that. Failure can teach you so much as a skater—and a person! When I'm coaching, I love to see skaters falling down, because it means they are trying hard. Often, the skaters who fall the most end up improving the fastest, because they are embracing the learning process and taking risks.

Even eight years into my derby career, when we're learning new skills I try to give 100 percent and commit to trying with all my might. I see it as a good sign when I fall—it means I'm out of my comfort zone. And ultimately, being good at derby isn't about *never* falling. It's about how fast you get back up.

Welcome to the Pack

When you first start playing, you might feel totally overwhelmed, with nine other skaters zipping around in close proximity to you when you skate in a pack and a dozen things to be thinking about at all times. It's OK! We've all been there. If you feel rattled, take a deep breath and see what your track leader is telling you to do. If all else fails, get with a teammate who is experienced or has good instincts. From there, you can make and execute a plan.

One Thing at a Time

When I first started playing roller derby, a veteran skater gave me some great advice: each jam, focus on doing one good thing. It really helped!

Trying to do everything right all the time is going to drive you crazy, so try to set a goal of one thing you want to accomplish in a jam—whether it's getting with a partner, remembering to switch to offense when your jammer is coming around, or sprinting back to the pack after getting knocked down. Having a small, achievable goal will make your mission in each jam more clear and help you remember what to do when you feel a little out of control on the track. Over time, all of your small goals will add up, and you'll find that you have developed a lot of skills in the pack. I talk more about setting goals in Chapter 12.

Making Friends

It's natural to feel shy when you first join a league. Especially if you've been watching the vets skate for years, it can be intimidating to show up and suddenly be expected to partner with the awesome superstars you've admired from afar.

But every skater has been where you are now. Even the brightest stars in the derby world are real, normal people—and their pads do stink!

The fresh meat period can be a great time to make friends, especially with other meat, because everyone's on equal footing (figuratively, if not literally). It can feel like summer camp or freshman year of high school. Derby is intense and provokes strong emotions and incredible passion, so it's a crucible that can form very tight, lasting friendships. Then again, not everyone plays derby to make friends. Some people just want to skate, and that's fine. Just be nice and give those skaters space, and maybe they'll eventually come around.

Derby Names

One of the most fun and flamboyant parts of modern roller derby, something that sets it apart from the original, is the names. A roller derby name is the moniker a skater chooses for herself when she begins playing the sport. In some leagues, skaters must wait until they finish the fresh meat period or till they are drafted onto teams to get their derby names.

Derby names are generally fun, funny, or fierce. There's a lot of room for skaters to express their personalities or interests in their names. The standard formula for a derby name is a first-and-last-name combination, frequently with a pun or a reference to pop culture, speed, or toughness. However, not all names fit this formula. Some are a single word. Some names are just fun to say.

Not all skaters choose to use derby names, and some skaters have chosen to skate under their real names even if they used to have derby names. For example, the skater formerly known as Francey Pants now skates under her given name, Francine Rangeon.

Some skaters choose to use their real names on certain occasions. Many skaters who typically use derby names use their real names when competing at the World Cup, for example.

Then there are the lucky ducks who were given names at birth that are so awesome that they sound like derby names, such as Charm City's Susy Pow and Gotham's Roxy Dallas.

How to pick a good name

So how do you pick a good one? Think about some derby names you love. What do you like about them? Is there anything in common among them? Do you have any hobbies or interests with specialized language? Are there any celebrities or well-known people you admire that you'd like to riff on? Or are there any words you really love?

Many people ask friends and family for help, and it becomes a fun game for people to brainstorm possible names. But whatever you do, make sure you pick a name that *you* love. Just like a tattoo, your derby name will be sticking with you—if not forever, at least for a good long time.

Say it a lot. Live with it for a while, and see if it's still fun a week or two later. Think about how it might be shortened, and keep in mind that you don't always get a say in the matter. Most derby names get shortened to one or two syllables so teammates can get your attention quickly on the track. (I knew a skater who chose the name Jocelyn D'Jewels, which was shortened to "Balls.")

It's totally fine to skate by your real name, too. Some leagues prefer it, while other skaters and leagues are very in favor of derby names.

Adult skater names tend to be registered with a database called Two Evils[21] to prevent duplication, though in recent years, the explosion of roller derby seems to have overwhelmed the process, and it has become hard to find a name that's completely original. Some skaters have started using Derby Roll Call instead. The JRDA also has its own names registry for junior skaters.[22]

Awesome derby names

Good names can be very subjective, but here are some derby names I've heard over the years that I think are great.

Pop culture

belle RIGHT hooks
Stevie Kicks
Olivia Shootin' John

Skaty Perry
Joy Collision

Punny names
Demanda Riot
Shenita Stretcher
Anne Phetamean
Juke Boxx
Hoosier Mama
PENALTYna
Claire D. Way

Fun to say
Bork Bork Bork
Bob Loblaw
Gogo Baibai
Fisti Cuffs
Jalapeño Business

Tough names
Devoida Mercy
Layla Smackdown
Lois Slain

Nerdy names
Lois Carmen Dominator
Polly Gone
Harlot Brontë
Anne Persand
Stone Cold Jane Austen

Junior names
Lollie Pop-Ya
ElectraCUTE You

Luna Shovegood
Addi Tude
Underage Rage
Hello Hitty

Manager names
Ballistic Whistle
The Dispatcher

Official names
Buster Cheatin (He's better known for being a manager, but he started as a ref.)
Collin DeShotz
Loren Order
Colin M. Fairly
Hewlett Smackard

Numbers

Skaters must also pick a number for themselves, which gives them another area for creativity. A skater's number will sometimes relate to her name. For example, my derby name is Em Dash, and my number is #— (which is a punctuation mark called an em dash). However, when I play interleague games, I have to use a different number because of WFTDA's regulations about numbers.

Each ruleset will have its own regulations about numbers, so check with your leaguemates to find out the rules before getting your heart set on a number. It's best to make sure that you don't have the same number as anyone in your league, even if you're on different home teams, in case you end up playing on a travel team together.

You might consider picking a one- or two-digit number if possible. The number I skate under in WFTDA play is four digits, which is kind of a hassle. It's more expensive to print on uniforms, it takes longer to draw on my arms with Sharpies when I forget my armbands (and then redraw when I inevitably sweat it off halfway through the game), and it feels like the longest number in the world when I'm standing in the penalty box, waiting for the penalty timer to get through "Eight two one two, done!" when they could just be saying "Four, done!" and then I could be sprinting back to the track.

Scrimmages

A scrimmage is any informal instance of playing roller derby. It might be shorter than a regulation bout or have more or fewer skaters or refs than official regulations dictate. It might be as casual as your own team splitting in half and putting on different-colored pinnies, or as organized as a team from another league traveling to play your team in a full-length game with refs and stats being tracked.

Gotham has one scrimmage practice each week. The four home teams trade off playing each other in shortened forty-minute scrimmages. We use these scrimmages as opportunities to test our skills and strategies against other teams, train players in their positions, and let skaters try out new roles. Managers can also learn skills, such as how to deal with penalties, when to call a timeout or an official review, how to gauge the team's morale, and many others. Scrimmages are also a good opportunity to build trust and rapport among teammates.

Sometimes our home teams will invite teams from nearby leagues to play us in more formal scrimmages during the team's practice time. We wear our uniforms and treat these matchups like they are bouts, but they don't affect our standings in WFTDA's rankings, and there are no spectators, so it feels like there is less pressure than on bout day.

These scrimmages can be a great way to get a sense of how we're doing as a team and what our strengths and weaknesses are. They also give each of our skaters a chance to test herself and see where her game could use improvement.

How to prepare for scrimmage

Even though they don't count toward rankings, you should take scrimmages seriously as a chance to play the sport you love, try new things, and learn about your team and yourself.

Make sure you eat well and drink a lot of water on scrimmage days. Think about bringing your water bottle to your desk at work to remind you to hydrate. You might want to eat the way you'd eat on bout day. If you don't have a bout routine set up yet, check out the section on nutrition in Chapter 14 for some ideas about how to fuel your body for your best performance. I try not to eat heavy or greasy lunches on scrimmage days, because they slow me down and can even make me feel queasy if I'm jamming a lot. I also make sure to eat a healthy snack on my way to practice so I don't power down in the middle of a jam.

Plan ahead so you have everything you need at scrimmage. Nothing takes you out of your game like scrambling to find a pair of socks or trying to borrow someone's water bottle when you're supposed to be warming up or connecting with your team. If you're as forgetful as I am, you might want to create a checklist of everything you need, and review it before you leave home so when you get to practice, you can focus on playing well, knowing that you aren't overlooking anything. Scrimmages often happen on weekdays, so it can be easy to forget about them in the flow of your workday, or you might show up at scrimmage with your brain still stuck on something that happened at school or your job.

It can be very helpful to set a goal for each scrimmage. Getting into the habit of thinking of your goal on your way to scrimmage can help you transition your focus to derby. Setting a goal can also help you get the most value out of your scrimmages. Even if your team has a tough night, or you let the jammer by you on the inside line, if you've made progress toward your goal, you can feel like you did a good job. There's more information about setting goals in Chapter 12.

You should also take a second before each scrimmage to mentally review your team's strategy, so you are working well with your teammates and everyone is on the same page.

Scrimmages are great opportunities to test out skills and strategies you've been working on in practice in a low-pressure environment. For example, if you've been working on apex jumps and you think you see a chance to try one in a scrimmage, go for it! If you end up falling down or going to the box, at least you've learned something. And if you pull it off, then you can feel more confident about trying one in a game.

The same goes for trying different positions. If you're a solid blocker but a reluctant jammer, try volunteering to jam a bit in scrimmage. Playing different positions will give you a different perspective on the game and might teach you things that will make you better at your primary position. And you might even discover that you like it more and you're better at it than you expected!

Bout Day

After working hard for months off on and off the track, bouts give you a chance to show off what you've learned.

Many skaters' families, friends, and coworkers attend bouts, along with hundreds of other fans, so it can feel like there is a lot of additional pressure, especially if the bout impacts the competitive standing of your team or league. Many skaters feel nervous on the day of the bout, and sometimes even the week leading up to it. That's totally normal. The first time I bouted, I was so nervous that I had to pee seven times between arriving at the venue and taking the track with my team! I promise, it gets better.

Remember, this is what you've been practicing for! Plus, roller derby is a team sport, so no bout or jam relies just on you.

It can be very helpful to create a ritual for bout day, which can help make sure you get everything done and dispel any nerves. On the day of a bout, I tend to eat a big brunch, then putter around a bit, gathering my pads and uniform and cleaning my wheels and bearings. I bring a light meal to the venue to eat about two hours before the bout starts, and also some dried fruits and nuts to snack on. I try to eat the same food at the same times every bout day, to I make sure I have enough fuel to skate well but am not sluggish or queasy when I take the track.

You might consider creating a bout day packing list, to make sure you have everything you'll need to skate. It's also good to bring extras of anything (within reason) that might break, or that a teammate might forget, such as laces, toe stops, athletic or duct tape, a skate tool, a bandana, a pair of socks, and leggings. If you need any knee or ankle braces, special foot-care materials, or anything else like that, make sure to bring it. And don't forget your mouth guard!

Boutfits

Some skaters wear elaborate "boutfits" and makeup, while others prefer to dress more simply. This is a chance to express yourself, so you can go wild. As long as you feel comfortable and your uniform is within regulations, there is a lot of leeway to create the look and persona you want. Some skaters even paint their faces! I don't personally go in for elaborate face paint or outfits, but I do make sure to put on some makeup. There are often photographers at bouts, and the flashes and gymnasium lights can really wash out your features, so my bout makeup has more in common with stage makeup than with the bit of eye shadow and lip balm I tend to wear in my day-to-day life.

What to expect

Even though you've been training for this for weeks, months, or sometimes years, bout day is always something special and different. Suddenly, there are announcers and jeerleaders and mascots, along with hundreds of fans yelling and cheering. There might be elaborate lighting, halftime shows, and other elements that make the night into a spectacle. In spite of how athletic the sport has gotten, there is still a fun, campy vibe at many derby bouts that is different from the businesslike and straightforward practices most of us are used to.

Typically, teams will have time to warm up, either simultaneously or taking turns. After that the teams and skaters will be introduced by the announcers, often skating out to a special intro song they have chosen. Your team might have time for one final pep talk or cheer, and then you'll take the track and the bout will begin.

Things might feel faster than you expect, and it will almost definitely be louder than you're accustomed to, depending on the venue, the sound system, and the number of fans. Try to stay calm, take deep breaths, and check in with your teammates or managers if you feel overwhelmed.

Make sure to take some time to enjoy the whole experience. On bout nights you're a mini-celebrity, with hundreds of people cheering for you! How cool is that? Just don't let it go to your head or distract you from what you should be doing.

Good luck!

Jonathan R, photo by Manish Gosalia

CHAPTER 7

RULES & STRATEGY

TO THE UNINITIATED, ROLLER DERBY SEEMS like an intensely physical sport—and it is! It makes serious demands on skaters' bodies. But if you're only focused on the hitting and sprinting, it is easy to overlook what an intensely *mental* sport it is.

Great skaters aren't great just because they're fast and strong; they're great because they also know where they need to be, and what they need to be doing there, and can predict what will happen next. This requires them to have a strong understanding of both the rules and strategy of the sport.

Rulesets

There are several different types of roller derby being played, each with its own governing body and set of rules. What's more, because the modern version of the sport is so young, the rules tend to change a bit each year. For that reason I won't talk about the rules in detail, because by the time you read this, they will probably be different.

General Rules

Roller derby is a full-contact sport played on quad roller skates on an oval track. Each team fields four blockers and a jammer (the point scorer) at one time. On the whistle, the jammers from both teams try to get past the other team's blockers without fouling them (committing an illegal action). Whichever jammer passes the opposing blockers legally and gets out of the pack first becomes the lead jammer, which earns her the right to end a jam by tapping her hands on her hips repeatedly. Otherwise, a jam goes for a set period of time (two minutes in most rulesets). On her second and all subsequent passes, a jammer scores one point for each opponent she passes legally.

If a skater commits a penalty, she is sent to the penalty box to serve for a designated amount of time (thirty seconds in most current rulesets). A jammer can still score points on a penalized opponent when she passes the other blockers on the opposing team. A jammer can also be sent to the penalty box, in which case her team cannot score until she returns to the track.

Bouts are made up of many jams that last for two minutes (or one, under some rulesets). Typically bouts are sixty minutes of play time separated into two halves (or three 20-minute periods).

Different Rulesets

Every derby ruleset follows the same general pattern described above. There are a number of different organizations that govern the modern sport of roller derby. Some of these are affiliated with others, while others are independent and compete for membership. Some skaters play under multiple rulesets, depending on which teams they're on, such as a skater who skates both flat track and banked track. Some teams play in both WFTDA and USARS tournaments. Here are a few of the different sets of rules that govern different types of derby.

Flat Track

The majority of modern roller derby is played on a flat surface. This surprises people who are familiar with derby from the 1960s and '70s, or from the movie *Whip It*. But it makes a lot of sense—if you play flat track derby, you can skate in any parking lot or school gym, while banked (slanted) tracks are expensive to buy and hard to move and set up. Flat track derby has made roller derby much cheaper and more accessible and is probably partly responsible for how quickly modern derby has spread.

WFTDA

The most prominent ruleset in modern roller derby is the one created by the Women's Flat Track Derby Association (WFTDA).[23] As I describe in Chapter 2, the Women's Flat Track Derby Association was the first governing body for the modern sport of roller derby. WFTDA is a 501(c)(3) not-for-profit that is run by skaters and its member leagues, who vote on the rules and regulations that govern the sport. WFTDA has 308 member leagues and 100 apprentice leagues. In addition, many leagues that are not part of the WFTDA play by their ruleset as well.

MRDA

The Men's Roller Derby Association (MRDA) uses a gender-neutral version of the WFTDA ruleset but has its own competitive structure, which includes interleague bouts, invitational tournaments, and a championship each year.[24] It currently has fifty-eight member leagues around the world.

JRDA

The Junior Roller Derby Association (JRDA) is the flat track governing body[25] for junior skaters. They use the WFTDA ruleset as a base but have their own addendum to make the sport safer for kids to play. They also have a strict rule about unsportsmanlike conduct. The JRDA runs a number of regional tournaments, a championship, a junior World Cup, and Juniorcon.

USARS

USA Roller Sports (USARS) is recognized by the United States Olympic Committee (USOC) as the US National Governing Body of Roller Sports such as roller figure skating, roller hockey, roller speed skating, and roller derby. It is also a 501(c)(3) not-for-profit organization.

USARS established its first ruleset[26] for roller derby in 2012, with a goal of emulating the original rules of roller derby. Membership is fluid over time, but according to a USARS representative, they had several hundred member leagues in 2014. They allow their members to play under any ruleset, though their tournaments are played by the official USARS ruleset.

USARS accepts players of all ages. Its adult program accepts skaters as young as fourteen years old. Unlike WFTDA, it also accepts mixed-sex and men's teams as members.

Banked Track

As I mentioned earlier, banked track derby is what many people envision when they think of the sport. It's frequently what is shown on TV even today, partly because there is a highly organized and visible banked track league in Los Angeles—the LA Derby Dolls—where a lot of filming takes place. The Doll Factory, the space they skated in through 2014, has appeared in shows such as *The Bachelor*, *Bunheads*, *Weeds*, and others.

Banked tracks can be a bit scary to skate on at first, and it's a little unsettling the first time you step onto them, as your feet are literally at different levels.

As you get more comfortable on the banked track and start to pick up speed, you will notice that some parts of the track help you gain speed, while other parts are much harder to skate on. A talented banked track skater will know just how to use the track to her advantage. The speed of skating on a banked track is very appealing to a lot of players.

Some players play only banked track roller derby, or only flat track, but other skaters skate on both types. There's a bit of an adjustment, but the two versions of the sport are quite similar, with slight variations in the rules.

RDCL

The Roller Derby Coalition of Leagues is a group of five banked track leagues that teamed up to promote and support the sport of women's banked track roller derby in 2011. The RDCL has its own ruleset[27] and oversees and supports the Battle of the Bank tournament, an annual invitational tournament for banked track leagues.

MADE

Modern Athletic Derby Endeavor's (MADE) stated mission is "to protect and promote our athletes while providing our spectators with an organized and entertaining experience." MADE's focus on fans has led it to create a concise ruleset that currently fits on just four pages. According to the organization, MADE's rules[28] "are designed to keep the game flowing, scores close, and are easy for skaters, refs and fans to understand. They are also fun and challenging to play." MADE is open to all leagues, including women's, men's, and mixed. It also accepts both flat track and banked track leagues.

Penalties

When you first watch roller derby, the penalties can be a little baffling. There are a few different types of actions that are penalized: ones that are dangerous, such as tripping other players or hitting them in the head; ones that give you an unfair advantage over other skaters, such as cutting (going out of bounds and coming back in in front of a player who hit you out or who was in front of you before); and actions that break the basic principles of the sport, such as skating out of bounds to avoid a hit or leaving the pack to continue blocking a jammer all the way around the track. There are also rules about sportsmanship, which prohibit things like helmet throwing and insubordination to the officials.

When a skater commits a penalty, the ref blows a whistle, calls her color and number, and sends her to the penalty box, where she serves a penalty by sitting out some portion of a jam, usually thirty or sixty seconds, depending on the ruleset. Under some rulesets, penalties can span multiple jams if the time hasn't been served in the first jam.

Each ruleset has its own set of penalties, so it's important to carefully read the rules you'll be playing under and ask a coach or a ref for clarification if you don't understand what something means.

Positions

If you look only at the number of distinct positions, roller derby might seem like a simple sport. Unlike other sports, there are only three positions—jammer, blocker, and pivot—with a total of five players from each team on the track at any one time. However, the roles that the skaters in these positions play and the way they execute strategy make it a very complex, layered sport.

Jammer

The jammer is the point scorer. She wears a helmet cover (often called a "panty") with a star on it so you can tell which one she is. It's her job to fight her way past all of the opposing players, then sprint around the track and do it again. Jammers tend to be fast and agile, with good endurance and mental toughness—though every skater has her own take on the position and her own skills that help her excel.

Blocker

Each team has four blockers on the track at a time. (The pivot is technically a blocker but has other responsibilities as well.) The blockers from both teams line up in front of the jammers, between the jammer line and the pivot line, in a group called the pack. It's their job to prevent the opposing jammer from passing them and escaping from the pack.

There are many different formations that blockers might start in, and many different plays they might execute, depending on the team's strategy. Some teams prefer to have one or two blockers play offense for their team's jammer when she's in the pack, while others prefer to have all the blockers on defense for as long as the opposing jammer is still trapped in the pack. On some teams positions are very fluid, but on others they can be more fixed and predetermined.

Pivot

The pivot is a special type of blocker. Each team has only one pivot on the track at a time. She's indicated by the striped helmet cover she wears, which gives her two special powers. If she chooses to line up touching the pivot line, all the other non-pivot blockers must line up with their hips behind hers, or else they'll get a penalty. The second is that she can receive a star pass: if the jammer hands her the jammer panty, she can become the new jammer. This can add an element of excitement and unpredictability to a jam.

Many teams play a strategy where the pivot calls the plays on the track and acts like the quarterback or track leader for the blockers. Other teams give the pivot stripe to the blocker who's best suited to become the jammer in the case of a star pass, and choose a different blocker to be the track leader.

Track Leader

Whether or not this is the same player as the pivot, the track leader has a taxing and important job. It's her responsibility to make sure everyone is on the same page, executing plays and adjusting if the first strategy doesn't work or the situation on the track changes. It can be hard to hear the manager from the track, so it's critical that one player can make calls on the fly. The track leader should be decisive and have a deep understanding of the team's strategy. She should also have a loud voice and be able to communicate quickly and calmly to her teammates. She should be focused, disciplined, and not be inclined to go off by herself and make crazy hits.

Strategy

Roller derby is complicated and constantly evolving. Each ruleset has its own nuances. Since the modern sport is still so young, those rulesets are updated, altered, and clarified at least once a year. Because of this, it doesn't make a lot of sense to get too specific about strategy in this book. However, Chapter 12 includes information about resources to learn more about rules and strategy.

There is a lot of fluidity in the roles blockers play at any given time. A blocker can find herself in a wall with her teammates, blocking the opposing jammer, then be called to do offense for her jammer, then rejoin the wall—all in rapid succession.

Some teams have many strategies and plays in their arsenal and will execute the one their manager or track leader chooses. Other teams are more flexible about strategy and plays evolve more naturally. Some teams have strong leadership that calls plays for everyone; on others, skaters are more empowered to do what they think makes sense. As long as everyone is in agreement about what the team's approach is, either one can be good.

Defense

Jammers can be fast and wily, so it's much easier to block them with a partner or a few other people than to try to block one-on-one. For this reason, the basic formation of defensive strategy is the wall, which is made when two or more skaters work together in close proximity to trap and slow down a jammer. Sometimes a wall will be four skaters next to each other covering the whole track from side to side, and sometimes there are more elaborate formations with supports from the front or back. It's important for the blockers in a wall to communicate with each other and work together to stay in front of the jammer.

Offense

The jammer has a hard job, facing off against three or four blockers from the opposing team and trying to sneak through a crack in their wall or push the wall forward till the wall goes out of play (which happens when the wall is more than twenty feet from the pack). It can be much easier for her to get through if one or more of her blockers plays offense for her. There are many different ways to play offense, but the basic goal is to introduce confusion or chaos into the opposing team's defensive formation or to physically create an opening or a hole in their wall for the jammer to skate through.

Jam starts

Some teams play all defense right off the line and let their jammer fight against the other wall while they keep the opposing jammer locked down. Others prefer to have one or more blockers play offense, trying to disrupt the other team's wall to make holes for their jammer. Either way is fine, as long as your team is on the same page about which strategy you're playing.

Offense/defense switching

Roller derby is an unusual sport for many reasons, but one of the primary ones is that teams play offense and defense at the same time. While both jammers are in the pack, blockers must decide whether to play offense or defense. Once one of the jammers escapes from the pack, the blockers can focus on just one job for about ten seconds before that jammer returns for another scoring pass. This can be a really tricky thing to get right. It requires good awareness and fast reaction times. Otherwise, you might find yourself playing offense for your jammer and still making holes when the other team's jammer hits the pack, zipping through and picking up easy points as your team doesn't even try to block her. That happens to everyone sooner or later, but it always feels bad to have a jammer whiz by you without even attempting to block her. Teams at every level practice this a lot to get the timing and execution right.

Lead jammer

Whichever jammer manages to fight her way through the pack and pass all the opposing blockers legally first becomes the lead jammer. The jammer ref will indicate this by blowing two short blasts on her whistle and pointing to the jammer who is lead. The lead jammer is the only one who can end the jam before two minutes elapses, by repeatedly tapping her hands on her hips.

Why would she do this? If the other jammer gets out of the pack behind her, the lead jammer might sprint through the pack for a scoring pass, then call off the jam before the other jammer can score, ending the jam with a 4–0 score in her favor.

There are some times that it makes sense to keep running the jam longer. For example, if a jammer believes that her blockers can catch the other jammer and hold her on the second pass, she might choose to go for a second scoring pass, opening up the possibility of a 9–4 jam, or even a 14–4 jam if the other jammer is really stuck. A jammer will also frequently keep a jam running longer to burn time when she has one or two blockers in the box, or close to the end of a game when her team is in the lead.

Typically, the bench manager will tell the jammer whether or not to call off a jam, so it's important that the jammer look to the manager on occasion. When I'm jamming, I make sure to look at my manager when I'm safely out of the pack on my speed lap, then I check to see where the other jammer is. When I'm approaching the pack, I check in with my manager again and then look one more time to see where the other jammer is before I enter the pack to score. I usually also glance at the box to see whether it makes sense to keep the jam going longer if I can.

Watching Footage

There are way more nuances and advanced strategies than I could ever begin to include in this book, and more are invented every day. I'd recommend watching as much footage as possible, by yourself or with teammates, to see how other people play the game. There are also many online resources and blogs where people talk about strategies. I talk more about this in Chapter 12.

The sport and its rules are constantly changing and advancing, so studying strategy is important for skaters at every level of the sport.

Photo by Manish Gosalia

CHAPTER 8

DERBY CULTURE

ROLLER DERBY IS AN EXCEPTIONALLY OPEN, welcoming, accepting community. All you need to become part of it is enthusiasm for the game. Most derby people are very generous with their knowledge and experience. Because the sport is so young, and we've reinvented it from the ground up, modern derby has a strong culture of teaching others—both on and off the track.

The roller derby world is a very tight-knit community, and although derby has grown to a worldwide phenomenon, if you repeatedly attend the same events such as the East Coast Derby Extravaganza or the WFTDA Playoffs, you'll see many of the same people year after year. Big derby events like those can feel a bit like family reunions.

Because derby people tend to travel so much to bouts, tournaments, and other events, the sport can have a six-degrees-of-separation vibe, though typically it's only one or two degrees of separation in the derby world. Derby people often stay with other local derby folks when they travel for a bout or tournament, or they may crowd two or four to a hotel room to save money.

The Roller Derby Network

People in the derby world use social media, such as Facebook, Twitter, Google+, and Instagram, to stay in touch and share articles, photos, videos, and stories with one another. Because most people use derby names, it can be a little tricky to find your favorite derby players online. However, even on Facebook, many derby people add their derby names as a middle name, or they'll have a separate fan page under their derby name. On Twitter and Instagram, you can follow hashtags such as #rollerderby or #Talk2WFTDA, which is especially active during tournament season.

Derby Fashion

There's a very distinct look that people associate with the modern sport of roller derby. It derives primarily from the punk/rockabilly roots of the sport's rebirth in Austin in 2001 and tends to include fishnet stockings, knee socks, tiny booty shorts, colorful leggings, tattoos, campy makeup or full face paint, and maybe even tutus or corsets.

Some of these things, like the leggings and knee socks, are fairly practical and have persisted as the sport has gotten more athletic. And the tattoos are real—many skaters do have tattoos. Some even have a derby tattoo (or many derby tattoos). However, not all skaters have tattoos, and you're not more of a real derby player if you do have them, or less of one if you don't.

Roller Derby Stereotypes

There are many stereotypes about roller derby players: that they're huge and terrifying, that they're covered in tattoos and piercings, that they wear fishnets and listen to punk rock, that derby girls don't date men (or that derby guys do), that everyone who plays works as a bartender, or likes violence, or gets paid to play.

Derby players come in all shapes and sizes, and we have a huge range of different jobs and backgrounds. Some skaters listen to punk rock, but probably just as many listen to country music or play the classical viola. Derby people have all different sexual orientations, and the sport as a whole is very welcoming to all of them.

The one completely incorrect perception is that skaters are paid to play. With just a few rare exceptions, nobody is making any money by playing roller derby.

Being a Good Teammate

Having good teammates can be one of the greatest joys of the sport. The bond among teammates can be incredibly intense—you are literally putting your bodies on the line for each other, and spending many hours each week working together, pushing each other, and learning how you all move and even think so you can play as a cohesive unit on the track.

Everyone has a different idea of what makes a good teammate, but there are some character traits most people would agree on.

Drive

Teams get better when each skater on the team plays to the best of her abilities, both in bouts and in practice. Skating hard every time you hit the track will not only make you better but make everyone else on your team better, since they play with you and block against you. Your strength will make them improve their game play.

Reliability

It's critical that players can rely on their teammates. In a bout you need to know that if you can't get to that jammer, your teammate can stop her. Outside of a bout it's important that if you say you're going to come to practice, you actually come to practice. Or if you say you can give your teammate a ride to the bout, you have to show up on time to give her that ride.

Everyone has lives outside of derby that make us flaky on occasion, but it's important for that to be the exception, not the rule. If a skater is habitually flaky, nobody will be able to trust her, and nobody will want her on their team.

Self-control

It's great to have passion for the sport; that's one of the things that makes a good player. And things frequently get heated on the track—because a player has fouled you, or you've had a bad jam, or the score is tight, or your team is down. Players with good self-control can shake off negativity and refocus on the task at hand. Players without it often return to the bench angry, infecting their teammates with their bad moods, which can have a negative impact on the whole game. Learning how to reset in these types of situations will make you a better teammate.

Team Culture

I've been lucky to find an incredible home team that has shaped my whole derby career. Manhattan Mayhem's cheer, which we yell before scrimmages and bouts, is "Mayhem for life"—a joke based on our team's prison theme, but also an earnest sentiment we tearfully invoke at the end of each season when we part ways with retirees. The team has gone camping together, traveled to New Orleans to play together, even gotten matching tattoos. It feels like the best aspects of a college fraternity or sorority.

Many skaters aren't as lucky as I have been. The culture of a team can be negative or even nonexistent. On some teams, skaters bicker or gossip about one another. They compete for playing time instead of supporting each other and helping each other grow. That is a bummer, but fortunately there are many ways to work toward a better team culture.

Like any culture, it's not something you can design or declare. Team culture is built slowly over time and consists of hundreds of individual interactions as well as what the captains and managers say at practice and over email. Each team member contributes to building it, but it takes only one or two bad apples to poison it. Here are a few ways to build a positive team culture:

- Go out for post-practice dinners or drinks with teammates.

- Host parties to watch roller derby footage—either your own scrimmages or bouts, ones on WFTDA.tv, or other streaming footage online.

- Dedicate a night to going out to distribute flyers for the league together. This has the added benefit of promoting the league as well as creating a bonding opportunity.

- Create expectations that are reasonable and aspirational. At the beginning of the season, have the team vote on what the team's policies and goals are so everyone buys into them from the start.

- Work hard together. Facing adversity can bond you together like nothing else. Try playing tough teams from the local area, or do a challenge like a 5K or a mud run, or even set up your own obstacle course on the track one day.

- Support each other deliberately. My team has a program called Cellmates, in which teammates are grouped into cells of three. Cellmates are all meant to look out for each other, help each other when we struggle with skills, offer advice, motivate each other, and cheer each other's successes.

- Celebrate the achievements of your teammates. My team captains pick an MVP for every scrimmage and announce afterward who it is and why she was chosen. This helps create a culture of looking for what our teammates are doing well and calling attention to it.

Dealing with Derby Drama

Derby is an intense experience. Leagues tend to be close-knit organizations of fifty to a hundred people (or more!) who see each other at least a few times a week; work together on committees; elect and lead each other; and hang out with, travel with, and sometimes even date each other. On top of that, we teach and learn from each other, scrimmage with each other, hit each other, and battle each other in home team bouts. Those many interactions can create a lot of strong, mixed emotions. It's no wonder things sometimes get heated.

Generally, in roller derby, we have a policy of leaving it all on the track, which means that what happens in a bout or scrimmage stays there, and you don't let it affect your personal relationships with other skaters, officials, and league members. If someone high blocks you, it's safe to assume it was an accident. (Though if you high block someone, an apology goes a long way!) Now, that's easier said than done, but if you can, it will make derby a better place for you.

It can sometimes be harder to deal with negative emotions off the track. In any big group of people you interact with, there will be some folks you don't see eye to eye with. Some people will not be your favorites, and that's OK! There is plenty of space for all of you in the league and the sport.

If you can, take the old grade-school advice: "If you don't have anything nice to say, don't say anything at all." It's always a bad idea to gossip or trash-talk, even if it's tempting. Derby leagues are small, and word will get back to the skater you've been talking about, which can lead to hurt feelings and league drama. Nobody likes that.

Bullying

If you have a problem with someone, or someone says something nasty about you, there are a few options for how to deal with it. One is to just ignore it. If you can brush it off, do. Talk is cheap, and if you don't feed it, it's likely to die down next week.

But if you feel like you can't get past something someone says or does, or if a person or group is habitually bullying you, that's not acceptable, and you should speak up.

If you feel comfortable, talk to the skater (or skaters) directly. Tell them how it made you feel, and ask them to stop. That might seem naïve, but the skater might not have meant something the way it came out, or maybe she was just blowing off steam or being a jerk on a bad day. You might find you have more in common than you thought and come out the other side with a stronger relationship.

Another option is to talk to a league rep, coach, or some other league member you trust. Gotham has several elected league representatives who work to mediate conflicts among league members. Many other leagues have someone in a similar role. Most leagues have policies about how members should treat each other, and they take these policies seriously.

Generally, derby people are wonderful and supportive, so with any luck, you'll have a great social experience. Just don't be afraid to speak up for yourself (or your leaguemate) in cases that warrant it.

Dating in Derby

It is very easy to fall for another skater or league member. It's completely understandable—you're both excited about the same awesome sport, experiencing similar things, and spending a lot of time together. You might admire each other's skills on the track, or end up working on the same committee, or help run an event together. And with as much time as a lot of people put into roller derby, it can be hard to carve out enough time to even meet someone outside the sport, let alone date them.

But in spite of all these very understandable factors that make dating a derby person seem attractive, it can sometimes be a very bad idea. Just as it's generally considered unwise to date a coworker, many of the same pitfalls are present in the derby scenario as well. If you hit the skids or break up, you'll still be forced to interact constantly and work together, even if you're hurt or angry or temporarily hate your ex. That can make playing and working for the league very difficult and stressful, when derby is meant to be an enjoyable hobby.

Even if all goes well, it still means that your partner is around all the time. You might find derby issues cause conflict within your relationship. You might also find it difficult to play against your significant other if you're on opposite teams. You might disagree with him or her if you have different perspectives on committee work or league business.

Ultimately, everyone has to make their own decisions about whether the benefits of dating someone in the small, close-knit derby world are worth risking the problems that can arise.

Derby Wives

The derby zine *Hellarad* defines a derby wife as a "skater's best friend in the entire world of derby,"[29] but that doesn't really do the concept justice. Although there isn't anything sexual about the relationship between derby wives, the feelings can be powerful enough to almost feel romantic.

Frequently, skaters who start playing derby around the same time or who are on the same team will form a really fast, tight bond. If there's one skater who consistently has your back, cheers you up when you're down, calls you out when you're in the wrong, texts you when the rosters come out or the day after a bout, and always hangs out with you after practice, you might find yourself wanting to take your relationship to the next level.

Skaters will propose to each other, sometimes with a real ring of some sort, or even just a Ring Pop. Sometimes two skaters will even stage an elaborate derby wedding. The pool at East Coast Derby Extravaganza is a favorite location for derby weddings, which are often public affairs including other teammates and even an officiant. RollerCon has a big mass-wedding ceremony where skaters can marry their derby wives. (I even saw some skaters in white wearing veils.)

Winning the Afterparty

Skaters might be rivals on the track, refs might send skaters to the box, and officials must stay neutral and unbiased during a bout. However, after the bout is over, skaters from the competing teams often hug each other right after the fourth whistle has been blown, then everyone heads off to the afterparty to celebrate a game well played and get to know each other better. Sometimes people shower and dress up, but others choose to wear their game jerseys out to the party. To each her own, but I'm way too sweaty for that to work for me!

The afterparty is a beloved derby tradition, and it can get pretty wild. There is frequently dancing, antics such as human pyramids, pranks, and sometimes even a derby wedding. Teams sometimes compete to see which one can "win" the afterparty, which usually involves having the most fun, carousing the most wildly, or closing down the bar at the end of the night or in the wee hours of the morning. There is sometimes as much pride on the line around which team wins the afterparty as there is for which team wins the bout!

Not everyone in the derby community chooses to drink alcohol, and some folks don't attend the afterparties at all, but most people show up for at least a little while. It's nice to have a chance to connect as people with your helmets off.

The morning after a bout, you tend to wake up sore and tired, frequently with bruises and traces of your Sharpied number on your arms. You might be inexplicably covered in glitter or discover among your sweaty gear a tiny party hat that you definitely hadn't been wearing at the beginning of the night. Some teams meet for brunch the day after a bout as a team bonding activity, while others just go right back to work with a tough practice.

Photo Evidence

One of my favorite post-bout activities is finding the bout photos online in the next few days. Derby photographers frequently capture incredible moments on the track, and it's cool to see what that sweet hit looked like to everyone else. These photos will often be posted on Flickr or Facebook, but if you can't find them and you know that there were photographers at the bout, ask a vet where to look.

Roller derby isn't all fun and games, planks and push-ups. It also takes a lot of work off the track to make everything run smoothly. To learn more about the business of roller derby, just turn the page.

Loren Mutch, photo by Tyler Shaw

CHAPTER 9

MAKING YOUR LEAGUE RUN

THE SKATING PART OF ROLLER DERBY might seem hard enough, but because of the DIY nature of the modern sport, in most leagues, every member is also responsible for volunteering her time, energy, and skills to make the league and its events run smoothly. This is pretty much standard across all types of leagues under all the different governing bodies, though the specific requirements will vary a lot from league to league.

It would be impossible for me to list every task leagues must complete, but this is a broad-strokes look at what it takes to keep an amateur sports league going.

Coaching

Because most of today's adult skaters didn't grow up playing roller derby, there's a strong culture of skaters teaching each other, innovating, and growing together. Most coaches are current or former roller derby players or refs, though sometimes leagues will also have coaches from other sports, such as speed skating or hockey.

Roller derby coaches are responsible for helping skaters learn skills, evaluating and training new skaters, creating fitness programs to help skaters build strength, and other jobs relating to skaters' proficiency at roller derby.

In some leagues, the coaches are also tasked with difficult jobs such as selecting travel team rosters, establishing rules for drafting skaters to teams, and creating and enforcing policies around attendance and safety.

Being a coach requires maturity, patience, and good communication skills. It can be an incredibly rewarding job for a skilled skater who enjoys teaching others.

Bout Production

To actually compete, leagues must find a suitable venue large enough to house a track and seat fans, organize ticket sales, spread the word about the event, recruit announcers and DJs, and take care of all the tasks it takes to put on a bout. These include laying the sport court (or at least taping down the track if the floor is an acceptable skating surface), running the ticket table, selling merchandise and concessions, answering fan questions, and keeping the environment safe and fair for skaters and officials. A lot of moving pieces are required to put on a bout, and it's critical that you have a good team in charge of organizing everything and making sure it gets done.

The bout production team must be very organized and thorough, tough enough to deal with venues and enforce contracts and crack the whip on the skaters and volunteers who are working the bout, and flexible enough to change plans on the fly if something goes wrong.

Events

Derby players love to have a good time, and they frequently host events such as parties and fundraisers, and participate in community events. It's important to have a team managing all the elements of events, which can include finding a space, soliciting sponsors, providing food and beverages, working with the creative and marketing teams to get the word out, and staffing the events.

Someone who enjoys parties and is also responsible enough to handle money would be a great fit for the events team.

Publicity & Marketing

Once you've planned some bouts and events, you'll need to let people know that they're happening! This is where PR and marketing come in. Every league approaches this differently—some have a single communications team that covers publicity, marketing, and social media, while others split the different functions into separate committees.

Publicity is sharing a story or message via news and media outlets. It might involve writing pitch letters or press releases, reaching out to publications, and networking with writers, editors, and producers. It requires a good sense of how to tell a story and how to match your message to an audience that might be interested in it.

Marketing involves crafting a message and making it visible in places where it might resonate with your intended audience. One major difference between marketing and publicity is that marketing typically involves you creating content and buying ads, or getting information out via your own channels, such as social media and newsletters, while publicity is getting someone else to tell your story for you. You might have more control over marketing, but good publicity can get your league in front of a new audience in a meaningful and intriguing way.

Both of these are professional skills that are in high demand. Developing these skills in roller derby can help you get raises or promotions at work, or even help you discover a new career path.

Web

Leagues must create and maintain their own web presence, so there is typically at least one person, if not an entire team, that is dedicated to creating and running the league's website.

You'll need at least one person with some web development skills, though there are many tools and content management systems that make it easier for people who aren't tech-savvy to keep up a website. The web team might work with the creative team to produce art and other visual elements for the website, and with the communications team to create features and informational copy for the site. This is also a professional skill that can help you in your career.

Creative

Someone has to design all the ads, flyers, posters, merch, web banners, and everything else that draws people's attention to the league. A good graphic designer will find her skills much in demand in roller derby. Some leagues have a dedicated creative committee, while others will just beg anyone with drawing skills or a copy of Photoshop to help out. If you're a creative person and have graphic design skills, this might be the committee for you.

Merchandise

One major source of revenue for many leagues is the sale of merchandise such as tee shirts, tote bags, and league programs. Someone needs to design, create, and sell this merch.

There's a lot of room for creativity in the creation of merch, but it's also important that the people involved can keep track of money, fill online orders if you choose to sell merch online, and keep up your stock levels.

Sponsorship

Another way leagues make money is through sponsorships from businesses and other organizations. The sponsorship team must reach out to these businesses, sell them on the benefits of partnering with a roller derby league, negotiate an agreement, and make sure the league holds up its end of the bargain. If the sponsorship team is good at their job, it can be very lucrative for the league and help support its operations.

Finance

Money is a big deal in roller derby. Renting bouting venues and practice spaces and paying for insurance can be very expensive. There are a lot of different streams of revenue and costs, and all of this must be tracked to make sure that there's at least as much money coming in as there is going out. The finance team also works with the other teams to set and enforce budgets, collect skater dues, and reimburse skaters for travel costs and other expenses (based on the league's policies).

If you have someone with bookkeeping experience, that's great! It's not required, though—having someone who's very organized and responsible keep the league's books is also fine.

Advisory Board

Every league has some sort of committee governing it, setting priorities, creating and enforcing rules, and generally guiding the league. There are different requirements for different league structures. The advisory board might be made up of the heads of other committees. Not-for-profits also have boards that must comply with 501(c)(3) regulations.

A good advisory board is responsible, thoughtful, fair, and transparent. It carries a lot of responsibility, but it can be very rewarding to help lead the league.

League Reps or Mediators

Though roller derby is full of wonderful people, there are so many decisions being made and interactions happening that there are sometimes serious differences of opinion or friction. Add in the physical intensity of the sport, and there are definitely some situations that need a little outside help to resolve. Many leagues have a few designated people who take on a mediator role. They work with league members who are having some sort of dispute and help them reach a satisfactory resolution. They might also represent the league's interests to league leadership, count votes, or have other official jobs.

It's a great role for someone with good people skills who is also mature, calm, thoughtful, and fair.

Officials

Officials are a necessary part of any roller derby league; the game can't be played without them. Official jobs are not committee roles to be filled by anyone in the league who is interested, though sometimes a skater for one league will ref for another league. But no description of what it takes to run a roller derby league would be complete without mentioning the refs and officials who keep the sport safe by enforcing the rules, and who run the games by counting points, tracking fouls, and timing each jam.

WFTDA Reps

If a league is a member of the Women's Flat Track Derby Association, it will be required to have several league representatives who do the work to keep the WFTDA running, influence policy, and vote on the league's behalf. These people need to be responsible, thoughtful, and good communicators. If a league doesn't stay active by doing work and voting at least a certain percentage of the time, it can be barred from competing in WFTDA tournaments.

It might seem like all of this has nothing to do with skating around and hitting people, but all of these jobs are necessary to make a league run. Without good people filling these roles, the league will fold. So the work you do for your league is as important as what you do on the track.

In many leagues, the same people can always be relied upon to shoulder the majority of the work and pick up the slack, while others can never be found when there's work to be done. People do notice which skaters are which, though.

Doing the work of keeping a league going can be really satisfying and rewarding, and give you the opportunity to learn new skills and work with people who aren't on your home team.

When I asked Suzy Hotrod, "What makes a great skater?" part of her answer focused on meeting responsibilities and off-the-track work. "They check their email, meet their committee work deadlines, show up on time, and don't take forever to pay teammates back when a shared purchase is made. I feel like this 'great skater' definition is clearly coming from someone who has been a team captain for many years."

Bonnie Thunders & Scald Eagle, photo by Juan Paden

CHAPTER 10

LEVELS OF COMPETITION

THERE ARE MANY DIFFERENT LEVELS OF competition in roller derby, from casual scrimmages to international All-Star teams representing their countries at the World Cup, and plenty of levels in between. Depending on your skill level and how much time and effort you want to put into the sport, there are many options open to you.

Every league does things a little differently, so I'll describe the levels of competition in general terms. You should talk to your local league to see how it's organized and what specific policies are in place around each level.

For many leagues, the first level of skating is as a part of a recreational league or basic training program. Depending on the league, this can be very casual—drop-in sessions that beginning skaters can pay for one at a time, or a more formal program. At many leagues this program doesn't require any previous skating experience.

Many people are happy at the rec level, putting on skates, learning skating skills, and making friends with some other great people.

If you want to get more serious about skating, you can try out for the league. Different leagues vary wildly in how they are structured and what their tryout policies are, so it makes sense to check with the coaches at your local league to find out more.

Home Team Competition

Most leagues have a number of home teams—teams that compete against each other locally. Frequently, the season will end with a home team championship, in which two teams will compete for a local title. Some leagues have trophies with unique names, such as Windy City's Ivy King trophy, TXRD's Ann Calvello Cup, or Gotham's Golden Skate.

Many home teams have specific themes, with names and uniforms that play up the theme. For example, one of Gotham's home teams is the Brooklyn Bombshells, whose skaters wear blue uniforms with nautical embellishments. Teams frequently develop their own cultures, and teammates often hang out together outside practice, developing inside jokes, rituals, and even dance moves. Some teams are closer than others, and this varies a lot from league to league, team to team, and even year to year.

Home team competition can be more or less serious depending on the league and its culture. Some leagues see it as a venue for developing skaters' skills and prioritizing equal playing time. In others the competition is very serious, and there's a lot of pride on the line at home team bouts.

Travel Teams

If you want to compete at a higher level or have more opportunities to play than you will just skating for your home team, most leagues have at least one traveling team (or All-Star team) composed of members from the home teams in the league. These teams frequently require skaters to go through a separate tryout process and have additional or more rigorous practice requirements. Frequently, these teams are much more oriented toward winning than the home teams, and they don't prioritize nurturing skaters or equal playing time.

These teams typically play tough competition from other leagues. Some of them compete in tournaments, playoffs, even championships. The stakes can feel very high, and the skill level of competition can be significantly higher than on home teams. Some people thrive on these teams with greater intensity and the added excitement of travel and tournaments. Others feel that competing for a roster spot and playing time, along with the increased requirements, is not workable for them. Skaters also typically pay for some or all of their travel costs, which can be another factor in whether or not a skater chooses to play on a travel team.

World Cup

Blood & Thunder Magazine hosts the World Cup, an international competition that takes place every few years. It features the best skaters from around the world, who try out for teams representing their home countries, then converge on one city to compete with each other for the coveted title of the best national team in the world.

The first roller derby World Cup occurred in December 2011 and featured seventeen teams. The second took place in December 2014 and featured thirty teams from all around the world, including Team Japan, Team South Africa, and Team West Indies.

There is also a World Cup for juniors run by the Junior Roller Derby Association.[30] In 2014 the first-ever Men's Roller Derby World Cup took place.[31] There is another one planned for 2016, which will be governed by skaters who make up the Men's Roller Derby World Cup board of directors.

It's a huge challenge for teams with skaters from across a country to get together and practice so that teammates can become familiar with one another and learn the same strategies. Each team has a different approach to solving this problem. Team USA tends to meet up the Monday following the WFTDA Championship, which means that skaters who were competing against each other viciously just the day before suddenly become teammates.

Polly Gone, who skated for Team USA in 2014, says, "The opportunity to play on Team USA has exponentially enhanced my opportunity to teach and be taught by my teammates."

State All-Star Teams

In the last few years, a series of events called State Wars has sprung up.[32] The goal of these competitions is to create opportunities for skaters to play in high-level bouts outside their home leagues and pull from the talent of derby players all over each state. According to the State Wars website, "You no longer have to be on a top 10 WFTDA, MRDA or JRDA team to compete in a national tournament, or be forced to compete against the league that is the next town over from you. Now you have the opportunity to become stronger and play together for your home state. ... Each state will pool talent from across their entire state to face off against other states for cash, prizes and state pride." This can be an interesting way to push yourself to grow as a skater and compete with and against a new pool of skaters.

Mash-up Teams

The derby world offers frequent opportunities to play with skaters from other leagues, even outside of state All-Star teams and the World Cup. Some of these are at events like RollerCon or the East Coast Derby Extravaganza (ECDX).

Some mash-up teams are formal and have similar rosters over multiple years, such as Team Awesome or Team SeXY. Other mash-up teams pull from membership in a wider organization, such as the Vagine Regime, a queer derby organization, which describes its aim "to build an international community of queer derby folk. Through a commitment to inclusive solidarity we hope to create networking opportunities, cultivate acceptance, and foster derby love matches. We endeavor to dominate challenge scrimmages with our traveling Team Vagine, inspire awesome cheerleaders, and throw brilliant parties for all to attend."[33]

On the informal end of the spectrum, some leagues regularly host drop-in scrimmages open to anyone who can play derby. They usually just split the people who show up into two teams, trying to make sure that each team has a few jammers.

As you can see, there are so many different ways to participate in the sport. Some people pick just one, while others mix and match, and still others strive to do all of them. It's all about what you want out of the sport, what feels comfortable and meaningful and fun to you, and the time and resources you have. Many skaters move between levels as their interest, skills, and priorities change.

Finding the Right Level

In roller derby, there is frequently a lot of pressure to compete at the highest level possible. This can be great, since it makes people push themselves to get better and play at the edge of their comfort zones, which leads to fast improvement.

It's important to evaluate what your goals are and what your priorities are, in life and in derby. Make sure you're being realistic about what kind of time and effort you're willing to put into the sport and what it will take to get where you want to go. For example, if you join a top-forty WFTDA league as a brand-new skater, it's great to set a goal of being on the All-Star team. Just expect to spend a couple of years working your butt off, attending as many practices as you can, cross-training, attending boot camps, and soaking up all the derby knowledge you can. On the flip side, if you know you can skate only twice a week for two hours at a time and can't afford to spend a lot of money on the sport, you probably shouldn't join the traveling B-team. And if you don't want the sport to take over your whole life, you'll have to carefully weigh the costs against the benefits of being on each kind of team.

Judge Knot has the following advice for other refs: "First and foremost, participate at the level you are comfortable with. Find what interests you in this sport, and pursue it. You don't need to officiate Champs in your first year (or two, or three). Want to have a fun thing to do a few times a week? Go for it. Want to pursue certification? Go for it. Want to learn the rules? Have at it. But there is no rush. Take the time to learn, and don't measure yourself against other officials. Do this for you." That same sentiment holds true for skaters as well.

Traveling for Derby

Many people think that traveling for derby and playing against skaters they aren't familiar with is one of the most fun parts of the sport. It can be a great bonding experience for your team, and a fun challenge. It can also be stressful, frustrating, and even a little scary.

What to expect

Because much of roller derby travel is self-funded, many skaters like to travel on the cheap. Sometimes that means staying with skaters from the host league, while other times it means piling four or five skaters into an inexpensive hotel room. Derby trips frequently involve boisterous carpools with music, joking, and lots of snacks. (Derby skaters never stop eating!)

When picking roommates, think about skaters who have similar habits. If you're an early-to-bed type, try not to room with the biggest party animal on the team. Pick people you like who are also respectful of other people's space, time, and belongings. It sucks to be in a room with someone who throws her stuff everywhere, or always shows up late when it's time to leave for the bout venue, or drinks your game-day Gatorade without asking! Playing against a new team can be stressful enough without a thoughtless roommate getting on your nerves.

What to pack

Obviously, you need to pack all your skating gear (including your armbands or a Sharpie for your numbers!), but that's not all. Packing for derby is an art!

Bring tools and a backup of small things you might need, like toe stops and laces. Bring the uniforms you'll wear for the bout, and a few options for pants, especially for a tournament weekend. Bring first aid items such as ibuprofen and Band-Aids, along with braces or any special foot-care items you might need.

Also bring a water bottle, energy gel or chews, or sports drinks if your favorite one isn't universally available. Bring lots of snacks that don't need to be refrigerated. When you're on the road for derby, it can be hard to find a certain type of food, and you will find yourself eating at odd times. It's up to you to take care of yourself, keep yourself fed, and get yourself ready to bring your A game to the track.

Bring sneakers and a sweatshirt—sometimes venues are cold, and you'll want to keep your muscles warm. Bring recovery drinks and food, especially for a tournament.

Bring makeup if you wear it, and an awesome outfit for the afterparty!

Other things to consider

Make sure you've written down where you're staying and where the venue is, just in case your phone battery dies at an awkward moment.

Not to sound like your mom, but always leave plenty of time when you travel. Figure out how long it will take you to get to the venue, and make sure you arrive by call-time! Be respectful of your carpool and your roommates, and don't make them wait for you!

Enjoy yourself

Traveling for roller derby can be incredibly fun. You have the chance to see places you might not otherwise have seen and to hang out with some cool people. If you do some research in advance and budget your time well, the trip can feel like a mini-vacation. Consider hitting some of the highlights of the city, such as a famous landmark, museum, or tourist attraction. You have to eat anyway, so why not sample the best of the local cuisine?

Even if you're not into museums or sightseeing, going thrift shopping or visiting a local farmer's market with your teammates can be a fun way to bond and take your mind off the bout.

Miss Tea Maven, photo by David Dyte

CHAPTER 11

HOW TO IMPROVE

ONE OF THE GREATEST—AND HARDEST—ELEMENTS OF the sport of roller derby is that pretty much everyone who plays is constantly pushing themselves to improve. It's such a young sport that we're all learning or inventing new skills and strategies each year, so skaters must continue to work hard or they'll find themselves falling behind their teammates and skaters in other leagues.

What Makes a Great Player?

There are many factors that make a derby player great, and one great player doesn't necessarily play the same way another one does. I asked some of the best players in the sport what makes a great roller derby skater, and here are a few of the responses I got.

"A love of gliding. When the experience of soaring brings joy."

— Polly Gone

"A great skater transforms roller skating and playing roller derby into a beautiful art."

— Jonathan R

"A great *derby* skater is well rounded in all areas. They have all types of skating skills, they're strong physically and mentally, they can recognize their weakness, and they help build up the derby around them."

— *Wild Cherri*

"A great skater is a person who loves to progress, is never scared of working hard, and is never 100 percent satisfied with the level she's at."

— *Swede Hurt*

"To be a great skater I think you need to actually enjoy skating. However, you don't necessarily have to be a great skater to be a great derby player."

— *Kamikaze Kitten*

"A great derby player is somebody who has the mental game, has the physical game, and has the ability to put all those things together and be a good team player. Someone who tries hard. It's really hard to teach someone how to try harder. Some people are naturally gifted. Other people, through perseverance and trying really hard, get to the same success level."

— *OMG WTF*

"Prodigious skill does not a complete athlete make. I firmly believe that one's mental game requires just as much practice as one's physical skills—particularly one's ability to work with others. Putting the team's needs first, their ability to foster trust and respect with their team and leaguemates, on and off the track, and one's ability to cope with hardship, are essential.

"When coaching, I often talk about the 'meat 'n' potatoes' skills that every roller derby skater should constantly be working on. In my opinion, crisp stops are key for any type of player. If you can't control your speed and lateral movement in this game, it'll be really hard to advance. Great skaters have great plow stops, half plows, hockey stops, and turn around toe stops."

— *Scald Eagle*

"A great skater is a good skater that worked extremely hard to become great. A great skater falls and gets up faster than everyone else. That's a physical thing but it says a lot about the skater mentally.

Great skaters value technical skate skills practices in addition to just scrimmage practice. They may or may not like off-skates workouts, but they respect training the body as an athlete and stay focused and work hard off skates. They speak up or ask questions of authority when it's actually important, and more importantly, they listen. When they have bad days they cope with it personally and don't let it affect their team."

— *Suzy Hotrod*

How to Be a Great Blocker

In addition to being a great skater, there are some other skills that will make you a great blocker. Strength, agility, teamwork, and being able to predict what will happen next—and then get to where you need to go to make a play—are all important.

"Blockers need to be able to stop their forward and lateral movement as quick as possible. Be ready for any quick transitions, and know your extremes. For example, how hard can you lean back into someone and hit the brakes before you fall over or clockwise block them."

— *Wild Cherri*

"A great blocker needs to be able to read the game and have great track awareness."

— *Swede Hurt*

"Physically, quick footwork is super important; understanding mechanical body movements and how people move when they're in skates.

"Great blockers also have the ability to communicate in any way, whether it be verbal or nonverbal. It's super important to be aware and be very cognizant of everything going on around you at all times, whether you're on the track and actively blocking somebody or whether you're on the bench. Everything that's on the bench comes onto the track, so it's super important to be aware of your teammates and their feelings. You're going to know how to communicate with that teammate on the track if you see how they're reacting to a certain situation off the track."

— *OMG WTF*

How to Be a Great Jammer

Jamming is one of the most challenging positions in the game. Jammers must be fearless, tireless, and incredibly mentally strong to pit themselves against a wall of four opponents.

Jammers have to be able to read the pack, see how people are moving, and predict what the pack will look like in a few seconds so they can react to an opportunity that doesn't exist yet. They should be able to work with their teammates or go it alone, switching back and forth in an instant. Jammers must also be bold—ready and willing to burst through a hole the second it starts to open up. Jammers also need to be able to shake off a bad jam and return to the track with a clean slate and a calm head.

> "Jammers need to have quick feet in all directions. Not only the feet but also the body reactions. Moving the hips, dipping the shoulders, spinning and maintaining your center of balance."
>
> — *Wild Cherri*

> "Jammers have to be physically strong, have precise footwork, explosive movements and be focused in their mind. It's the strangest combination of power and evasion—the mark of a great jammer is identifying when to use that power and when to evade the hits. A jammer's training is predominantly about moving forwards, whereas blockers are primarily concerned with preventing forward movement. Keeping that key concept at the core of your drill and skill development can really help you to be efficient at training."
>
> — *Kamikaze Kitten*

> "Fearlessness and determination are crucial skills for jammers. It has to be in your heart. Much of jamming is an instinctual thing. You need to immediately respond to out-of-control situations with fast survival instincts to get yourself quickly out of crazy

situations where everyone is trying to kill you! I compare jamming to getting out of a house that is on fire. You need to get the hell out of there! It doesn't have to be pretty, it just has to be faster than everyone else. The best jammers get up the fastest—and yes, the best jammers fall all the time.

"While I do think a lot of jamming is about instinct, the best way to program yourself to not be thinking about jamming is to be prepared and execute what you have repeatedly practiced. For jammers, footwork and agility are crucial, on both toe stops and edges. Practice speed control with edges for plow and hockey stops. Work these individual skills into fakeouts and juking, and add in speed increases for that quick explosion to make those passes. Practice using your footwork with powerful pushing that uses all the power of your body through your legs.

"Finally, stay focused. Mental composure is crucial to jamming. Let your survival instincts and your practiced skills carry you. When in survival mode, there's no time for anger or frustration. If you've practiced all your skills, they will work their way into those crazy situations that are out of your control."

— *Suzy Hotrod*

"Tenacity and determination are two of the most important things that you need to have. Jamming is certainly a physically challenging position because of the really strong, stopped, multiplayer walls. You have to have strength and you need to have determination because you're also the one everyone wants to stop, wants to beat up.

"If you're training at practice, you are going to end up getting hit and hit and hit and hit a million times over. Everyone's gunning for you, and they aren't going to go lightly on you. So there's that mentally taxing part of it, when you're training as a jammer, and you're feeling like your teammates are just beating up on you all practice long. You have to be able to push through that—they're just challenging you so you can be better."

— *Bonnie Thunders*

Play to Your Strengths

In many sports there's an ideal body type that many athletes tend to fit into. Roller derby is unusual in that any body type can have serious advantages and disadvantages. Strength, speed, agility, a low center of gravity, and the ability to take up a lot of space are all valuable traits that are not usually all seen together in one type of body.

I asked a few of the top skaters to describe the upsides and downsides of their body types and how they handle them.

> "I'm pretty short, and I was quite concerned coming into this season that there wasn't room for small jammers in the scrum style of roller derby. However, weight lifting has done a lot to bring up my confidence—if I can squat 90 kg (200 lbs), then there aren't that many skaters that I'll face that are more than that, and regardless, it's not like I have to throw them over my shoulder and carry them through the pack. It was also a big eye-opener to realize that I needed to lift blockers upwards rather than just outmuscle a four-wall completely. Already being lower to the ground meant this was a useful technique to have."
>
> — *Kamikaze Kitten*

> "If I had a dollar for every time someone told me to get lower, I'd be really rich right now. I think sometimes being a taller woman, it's hard to actually claim all that space on the track that we can take up, since we've been told since we were young that we are big, and taking up space is not really something you are encouraged to do as a woman. I think sometimes I could use my size even more, and I am working on learning how!"
>
> — *Swede Hurt*

> "I'm super tall compared to most jammers and have had to learn to initiate my contact with different portions of my body to avoid back blocks and other penalties. On the other hand, because I'm so large I can certainly use my weight to dominate my opponents on the track."
>
> — *Scald Eagle*

> "I have a naturally strong build. I play roller derby very aggressively, and being strong helps me throw myself around and not just

bounce off. I sometimes take the path of most resistance, and I wonder if I should be taking a smarter route. People always ask me how I get the body I have, as if there was a magic answer. I try to be patient, positive, and encourage people to be the best *them* they can be and not look at me and compare me to anything."

— *Suzy Hotrod*

"My body type—around average height and weight—has not given me significant challenges nor benefits. My studying of how people of all different body types skate has allowed me to overcome my opponents."

— *Jonathan R*

"I'm small (not big and tall in a sport that favors big and tall). I'm quick as the dickens. I'm smart. I'm a good communicator. And I'm still trying to figure this out."

— *Polly Gone*

"I'm smaller than a lot of people who I play against. In the past, small used to be synonymous with 'in shape' and also with agile and quick. That's not the case, especially as athletes evolve and the sport evolves. And as the walls become more about partnerships and people working together, that small size has become a slight disadvantage, and it's important to work on your strength and your ability to pack a lot of punch behind whatever small frame you have.

"But one advantage is that people underestimate your strength as a small skater. I think that helps small jammers, because they are underestimated by opponents thinking they're just small and not going to be able to drive forward or get through these giant clumps of people."

— *Bonnie Thunders*

"I'm considered to be a smaller skater, even though I don't feel like I'm as small as people think. I think it's super important to figure out what works for you and look at skaters [of a] similar size who are where you want to be, and see what's working for them. I learned that I don't need to be hitting people as a blocker; that's not the most important thing to do. I figured out where I could fit, and where my actual strengths are: in being communicative and leading.

"Find someone that's your size, and figure out their blocking style, and see—can you make that work for you? And once you find out which style you should be doing, make your strengths work for you. Be able to observe and use your skills to your advantage.

"All too often you see skaters want to just mimic the best team—'I want my strategy to be the strategy of the #1 team'—but they don't have the same players that team has. You have to make your team the best team it can be with what you have. It's the same thing for individuals. You can't make yourself be bigger if you're not big. Same thing with being small. And it's OK. That's what's neat. You can totally be a kick-ass skater and be any size."

— OMG WTF

How to Build Your Skills

There are as many ways to improve at roller derby as there are skaters, but here are a few strategies that have worked for me and many of the other skaters I've met.

Skate, skate, skate!

When you're trying to improve at derby, nothing helps more than being on your skates constantly. Go to every practice you can attend. Try different types of skating. OMG WTF suggests:

> Go to the roller rink. Look at different styles of skating. There are a lot of things that people do in different genres of skating that can really pertain to you. They don't need to be a derby skater for them to be awesome. When it comes down to it, any skating is going to make you better. Be resourceful with what you have around you and who you have around you. Bonnie Thunders doesn't have to be the person. Look at Joe Schmo from the roller rink who has a really sick hockey stop on his rhythm boots, and he nails it every time. All of these movements—we didn't make them up. We're taking

them—so why not go to the root? We're totally stealing things from other sports and other genres of skating. There's so many different things we can learn from so many different sports.

Skate around outside on the weekends. The faster you feel comfortable on your skates, the faster you'll be able to build up derby-related skating skills. Polly Gone suggests, "Learn to skate well before getting too excited about all the other wonderful things coming down the pipe. Develop the nuances of acceleration (the second definition: changing your speed and direction), then begin to engage the complexities of the sport."

It's OK to fall

When a coach demonstrates a new skill, pay attention to what she says, watch her demonstrate it, then give it your all when it's your turn to do it. There's a reasonable chance that you'll fall down, and that's OK! You've got pads on, so you won't get physically hurt. When I'm coaching a practice and leading a new drill, I see falling as a sign that skaters are trying hard and really giving the skill everything they have. Skaters who never fall are skating too safe—they aren't pushing the edges of their comfort zones, so they'll never know the full extent of what they're capable of.

Remember to play

Try to approach each practice with a sense of play. When you're first starting out, nobody's judging you for not being perfect—nobody *expects* you to be perfect. People expect rookies to try each new skill with their best efforts, and to get better over time. Swede Hurt advises, "You have to have fun while progressing, or you will lose sight of why you do it." If you can approach each new skill as a game to have fun with instead of something that you must master ASAP, you'll have a much easier time and enjoy yourself a lot more.

Fail better

If you've tried a skill and flubbed it big-time, falling again and again, now it's time to engage your brain. At what point are you struggling? Pay attention to the position of your body. Now watch someone who's awesome at the skill, or watch the coach demonstrate the skill again. What is she doing differently? Look at the position of her body—what are her feet doing? Her hips? Her shoulders and head? Where is her weight? How does she move her weight from the beginning to the end of the skill?

Try the skill again, and try to add in what you've learned. Try it ten times in a row. When it works better, what are you doing differently? When it works less well, can you feel what's causing it?

Over time, using this process will help you refine the skill till you can nail it every time. And breaking a skill down to its base components will help you really understand it, so you can improve even more by refining each of the mechanics, instead of just muddling through without understanding why it sometimes works and sometimes doesn't.

Be a mimic

Find a skater whose style you like, or whose body type is similar to yours, and watch how she skates. Pattern your skating after hers. Try pacing her when your league skates laps—cross over when and how she crosses over. Watch how she stops. Can you stop like that? How is your stop different from hers?

Paying attention to one person can minimize some of the overwhelmed feeling you get when you see a whole league of veteran skaters skating really well, and lets you focus on the specifics of how she skates so you can emulate her technique.

Find a mentor

If there's a skater or coach who's totally awesome at a skill you're struggling with, you shouldn't hesitate to ask her for help. Everyone has had help along the way, so people are generally very willing to give another skater some pointers. She might ask you to demonstrate the skill—if so, try not to get nervous, just give it your best shot. She is looking to diagnose where your problem might be, so seeing *how* you're struggling with the skill can make it easier for her to help you. It's often easier to see how someone else can improve a skill than to feel it for yourself.

Whatever advice she gives you, try it out a few times, even if it seems crazy or liable to make you fall down. Even if the advice doesn't help you out right away, remember to thank her and be gracious about receiving it. She'll be more likely to help you out again in the future if she feels like you actually took the advice she gave you.

Wild Cherri says:

> Everyone wants to help you to grow and become the best you can be. It can be overwhelming at times. Ask questions; soak everything up like a sponge. People have different ways of teaching skills, so take a little something from everyone, and practice over and over.

Celebrate your accomplishments

Roller derby is very, very hard, and there is a lot going on. But as you practice, you'll nail some skills and have some shining moments. As Scald Eagle says, "Means are as important as ends, and skaters should enjoy practice and the mini-victories that happen along the way." Holding on to those victories will help fuel you to keep working hard and achieve more success in the future.

Be patient

Swede Hurt advises, "Things take time, so you have to be patient. The first few months you will probably develop really fast, but at one point, the development will become slower."

Why Am I Not Improving? (AKA The Plateau)

When you first start playing derby, it seems like every practice brings major breakthroughs—from getting lower to learning how to cross over properly to the first time you take a hit and stay on your feet. So even though it all feels like the hardest thing you've ever done, it seems worth it because you can see and feel yourself getting better.

But after a while, you might find yourself working your butt off but feeling stuck. You just can't nail that hockey stop, and your thighs are bruised with the evidence of your attempts. Every time you think you're sitting on the jammer, she pulls some tricky move and skips away—or worse, you go to hit her and whiff horribly, sailing past her. Naturally, you'll get frustrated, because it seems like you're putting everything you can into this. You might even wonder if this is *it*—have you maxed out? What if you can't get any better than this? Is it all worthwhile?

Take a deep breath. This is totally normal. You've hit a plateau. It happens to skaters at every level of the sport. Sometimes, annoyingly enough, it happens when you're working your hardest and feel like you should be seeing the greatest return on your efforts.

But improvement in derby is not linear or predictable, unfortunately. And after the initial stages, once you've learned the basics, skills can be really hard, and that's frustrating. It especially sucks if you're comparing yourself to other skaters. *She skipped practice on Monday—how is she picking up that skill so fast?*

Stop comparing yourself to other skaters—that way lies madness. Everyone comes to the sport with a different body, background, and learning style. If you do see a friend who's totally killing it at a new skill, ask her for tips! She might explain things in a different way than the coach does, which might help things click for you.

Beating the Plateau

Feeling like you've hit a plateau is no fun, but here are a few ways to get past it.

Take a rest

If you're dog-tired and realize that you've been skating ten out of the last eleven days, slow your roll and give yourself a night off. See a friend, do some laundry. (If you've been skating that much, you probably need to!)

Giving your body and brain a little rest can help you come back to derby fresher, with a better attitude and more energy. And I find that my mind keeps working on a problem while I focus on other things, so sometimes when I return to something that has been difficult for me, I'll make a new connection that I wasn't seeing before.

Set goals

Try setting small goals for yourself at practice. (I talk more about setting goals in Chapter 12.) Don't set a big goal like "Get awesome at blocking," and don't set competitive, achievement-based goals like "Score at least thirty points." Instead, set small, concrete, achievable goals, such as "Get lower in the paceline," or "Stay with my partners in a wall," or "Take a breath and reset if I'm knocked out of bounds," or "Keep my arms tucked against my body when going for a hit."

When you're working toward a small, focused goal, it's easier to notice success and improvement than if you're thinking about your overall performance. You're not going to improve your entire game every time you step on the track, but if you make a little progress on a small but important skill each time you skate, pretty soon that will add up to a lot!

Mix it up

Many skaters suggest coming at the problem from a new angle or changing up what you're doing. "Sometimes a change is as good as a rest. Do something different, change your patterns, and look at yourself as a whole athlete," Kamikaze Kitten recommends.

Ask for help

Another thing you can do is ask a coach or a veteran skater you admire for tips and advice. You probably *are* improving, but it's hard to see your own improvement. A coach or vet might even offer to watch you for a few practices and give you suggestions. She will be able to see your progress much more clearly than you can.

Smile

Finally, focus on having fun! Improvement will come with time. If you're having fun at practice, you'll stop noticing the plateau and feeling stressed about it. When you're least expecting it, you'll probably rocket forward, and one day soon, you'll totally nail a skill that you remember struggling with just a few weeks ago.

Throughout your time playing derby, you will constantly be building new skills and refining old ones, which keeps the sport exciting and challenging. And as if that weren't enough, you will also constantly be working on your mental game so you know how best to use all the physical skills you've developed. The next chapter talks more about the mental game.

Justine TimberSkate, photo by TJ Chase

CHAPTER 12

THE MENTAL GAME

ROLLER DERBY IS A SPORT THAT requires awareness, timing, split-second decision-making, and fantastic teamwork. At any given time, there might be several useful things you can be doing, and those can change in a second. It's as important to train your brain as it is to build muscle.

So, how do you train your brain to play roller derby?

Learn the Rules

The rules of roller derby can be complicated and have significant strategic implications. Many new players get sloppy penalties because they aren't quite sure what the rules are, or what they mean.

Start by reading them. A bunch. Commit a few weeks to really knowing the letter of the derby law. If that feels overwhelming, just read one section at a time. Print them and mark them up with questions, comments, thoughts, or even funny doodles. Try to see the rules in action at scrimmages, or while watching footage online.

If you have questions about what a rule means, or if you see a call you don't understand, ask a vet for clarification—or, better yet, ask an official! Most refs and NSOs are happy to explain the finer points of derby to skaters who approach them politely. Just try to wait until the end of practice, so you don't interrupt a scrimmage or drill, and thank them afterward.

Learn the Strategy

Your team will probably have a set of go-to strategies for various situations, so make sure you learn them and understand *why* you're supposed to do a certain thing in a given situation. If you're allowed to, stay and watch your league's high-level team practices. All-Star teams are more likely to spend time talking about and working on refining strategy than the coaches at the general skills practices.

Watch Footage

One of the best ways to learn about the sport and its strategy is to watch roller derby footage on your own or with a focused friend. The WFTDA.tv website live-streams many high-level tournaments, such as the East Coast Derby Extravaganza, playoffs, and championships. There's also a free archive of bouts going back at least a few years, so there's always something to watch!

Try to pay attention to what skaters are doing, what's working, and what isn't. Do the teams you're watching use your team's strategy? Is it effective? What does the other team do to counter that? If the teams do things that don't make sense to you, write down the time in the bout and your question, and ask a coach what's going on.

It might help to pause and replay something a few times—you might notice something new in subsequent viewings. Check out what other skaters are doing on the track, and try to figure out why they're doing it.

Also be sure watch the skaters in different positions. It's easy to focus on the jammer and forget about watching the blockers, but even if you only play as a jammer, watching blockers and how they play will help you. You'll learn what to watch out for, how to tell that a blocker is about to hit the jammer, and what kinds of mistakes blockers can make that let the jammer sneak through a wall.

If there are skaters who are built like you, or who play your position, you can single them out to watch when they're on the track. Different body types can have different strengths and challenges in derby, so it is great to find a really good skater whose body is similar to yours to draw inspiration from.

Roller Derby Junkies[34] is a blog that includes brief clips of derby footage and a note about what the skaters are doing well (or poorly). It can be a great way to learn about derby in small, manageable chunks, even when you don't have time to watch a whole bout.

Watch derby in person, too, if you can. It's much easier to see what's happening at a live bout than on a tiny screen. You can pick out one skater who skates like you (or skates like you want to skate!) and watch what she does and how she moves on the track.

Set Goals

I recommend to skaters at every level that they set a goal for each practice and scrimmage. Before you take the track, think of something you've been struggling with or a piece of feedback your coach has given you, and set one or two goals for yourself for the practice. When I know I'll be jamming and blocking in a scrimmage, I set one goal for each position.

How do you set a good goal? Everyone has a different way of motivating herself, but I find that the best goals have a few things in common. Here are a few things to think about when setting goals.

Be focused

Saying you want to improve in roller derby is great, but that's a pretty tough thing to accomplish in a single practice. Try to drill down and think of one element of your game that can use improvement, and set a goal that is one step in that direction. A few examples:

- "Keep moving my feet when I'm stuck behind a wall."
- "Get lower."
- "Stay close to my wall and reform quickly when separated."

Be positive

I've always found that goals work best for me when I frame them in a positive way, and say what I *do* want to achieve, not what I *don't* want to do. For example: "Come in legally when hit out of bounds" instead of "Don't cut."

In the first example, you're focusing your attention on what you should do. In the second, you're trying to tell your brain what not to do. I find my brain tends to ignore the "don't" anyway, and then I'm just dwelling on something negative. Positive goals seem much more achievable and friendly, and they force you to think about how you will avoid cutting, not just the end result you want.

Push yourself out of your comfort zone

Don't stick with the same goal every practice—mix it up! Especially when you're new to derby, focusing on something specific for a whole practice will really get it into your head (and your muscles). Also, aim high, and set ambitious goals, not safe goals. Try a new skill or something that scares you. You don't have to be perfect at it when practice is over, but focusing on a dozen skills a month, one at a time, will give you a wide breadth of ability. You can continue to work on refining those skills in related drills.

Share with a friend

It can be helpful to get in the habit of telling your goal to someone such as a friend, a vet on your team, or your derby wife. This forces you to state what you're working on very clearly. It can also give you another set of eyes on your progress. Your buddy might notice a way that you can improve the skill—or catch you doing a great job and celebrate with you!

Build Your Mental Toughness

Roller derby is a hard sport—it taxes your endurance, and taking hits and falling can be physically painful. It's also incredibly frustrating—skaters who are strong and fast and talented are directly opposing you, physically and mentally. To be a good derby player, you'll have to develop mental toughness.

What is that? Mental toughness is a fairly common concept in sports psychology. It's generally defined as a mental state that allows you to perform at the top of your game, even in situations of difficulty or stress. Roller derby is one of the most difficult and stressful situations that most skaters intentionally put ourselves in day after day, so mental toughness is a very important attribute.

Being mentally tough can help you overcome doubt, stay focused on what's important, perform well under pressure, and bounce back after a bad jam or a penalty. If you're jamming and get stuck behind a tight, hard-hitting wall for a long time, or you're blocking and get trapped as a goat by the other team, your body might tell you that the smart move is to give up. It will start to feel like you have no energy left and can't even pick up your feet, let alone blast through a wall.

At this point your brain has two choices: agree with your body and give up, or get tough and tell your body that it's wrong—that you can keep skating. You'll find that your body is pretty suggestible and has vast reserves of energy that you can draw on—if only you believe you can. It's a bit like the scene in *Peter Pan* where Tinkerbell is dying, but believing hard enough brings her back to life.

In derby, belief and outlook are a huge part of success or failure. That might seem unlikely, but I've found it to be true. For example, if you're jamming and you see a tiny hole open up between two blockers, if you don't believe you can actually make it through, you might approach it in a tentative way. If you know with all your heart that you can make it, you'll sprint your butt off and power your way through before the blockers can close that hole up again. So many situations in derby are like that.

So how do you get mentally tough? Everyone starts at a different level, but it's definitely something you can build. The same way that you build a muscle by working on a movement or skill, you can increase your mental toughness. Here are a few techniques that I've seen work for people over the years.

Mantras

The word *mantra* comes from Hinduism and Buddhism. According to Deepak Chopra, the word "has two parts: *man*, which is the root of the Sanskrit word for mind; and *tra*, which is the root of the word "instrument." A mantra is therefore an instrument of the mind, a powerful sound or vibration that you can use to enter a deep state of meditation."[35] The concept has been broadened in our culture to refer to a significant word or phrase that one repeats frequently, which some people believe has spiritual or psychological power.

You can use mantras in roller derby to change your thought patterns, replacing negativity and fear with positivity and calm.

When I first started playing with Gotham in 2008, I learned that my team wanted me to jam in my first bout, when we'd be facing off against the Queens of Pain—the team that included Suzy Hotrod, Donna Matrix, and many other legendary skaters. I was so nervous that I was feeling a little queasy every time I thought about it, even a few weeks before the bout.

Finally, I asked myself what skills I'd need to be able to face off against Suzy and win. I decided that I'd need to be fast, agile, and fearless. So I started to tell myself that I already was. Every time I thought about the bout and started to get nervous, I'd repeat those words. I'd repeat them in my head when I took the line at practice. I'd say them out loud before I went to bed.

The day of the bout, I was nervous, but not quite as much as I expected to be. And when my manager handed me the star and I started to skate toward the jammer line, I saw Suzy waiting there, just like in all my roller derby nightmares.

So I went back to my mantra: "I'm fast, agile, and fearless." I took a breath and lined up. "I'm fast, agile, and fearless."

Repeating those words centered me and gave me confidence. And while I'd love to tell you that I blasted through the pack and picked up lead jammer easily, I'm pretty sure that what actually happened was that I struggled in the pack while Suzy scored at least one pass on me. But that's OK. What's important is that I was in the right space, mentally, to give the jam my all.

Self-Talk

If you don't go in for Eastern religions, a similar concept called "self-talk" exists in psychology, especially sports psychology.[36]

Antonis Hatzigeorgiadis, an expert in self-talk and the psychology of sports performance, believes that self-talk can definitely have a positive role in sports. He advocates choosing phrases that are short, precise, and consistent for your self-talk—so a few concrete specific words that you repeat are more helpful than long eloquent sentences.

Addressing yourself in the second person (you) can also be more beneficial than thinking in the first person (I), according to research published in the *Journal of Personality and Social Psychology* in 2014. Ethan Kross, a psychologist at the University of Michigan, suggests that using one's own name can be even more powerful and leads people to address themselves with positivity and encouragement, like a supportive friend.[37] (Somewhat unsurprisingly, the literature I've read on the subject does not actually address whether it's better to use your real name or your derby name, so try experimenting with both.)

Visualizing

Many athletes and coaches in different sports advocate using visualization to train your brain and prepare for competition. Visualization refers to the practice of mentally rehearsing your sport or individual performance. It can help build awareness and confidence, and set intentions in your mind or solidify your reactions to a competitive situation before you ever take the track.

It's helpful to find somewhere quiet and take deep breaths while you do your visualization. Everyone has a different way of doing it, but I like to imagine a situation I'll face on the track, such as lining up at the jammer line or building a wall with my teammates. I imagine the whistle blowing, then envision what I will do, what the other team's blockers will do, and how I will react. I let the jam play out, imagining the details and actions I will take to fight my way through the wall and get lead, or to work with my teammates to hold the opposing jammer back. If I do this right before a bout, I feel very centered, calm, purposeful, and capable before I take the track.

Visualization can also help you build mental toughness, since you can face a stressful situation in your head and figure out how to handle it, then rehearse it till it feels like no big deal when you actually encounter that scenario on the track.

Mental Skills for Bout Day

Your mental state can really influence your performance on the track, so it's great to think about the state of your brain and not just your body leading up to a bout. Being in a good place mentally can be as critical as being physically strong and agile. You can practice the techniques and approaches below during scrimmages, and then they'll feel like second nature when you're playing in a bout.

Be flexible

If you're too fixated on a single idea, a setback will seem catastrophic. But if you can stay calm and evaluate each new situation as it comes and adapt your plans accordingly, you'll be in much better shape. Whether there's an injury to an important member of your team's lineup before (or during) a critical bout, or you're asked to play a different position than you expected, or you face a tough wall that won't budge when you try your go-to moves, you can't control external circumstances. You can control only how you react to them.[38]

Focus on what you can control

If you go into a game thinking that the outcome rests on you, that's a lot of pressure—too much for most normal humans. Instead, think about what's actually under your control—playing clean, resetting between jams, and pushing yourself to play your best.

Breathe

It's hard to overestimate the positive impact of taking a deep breath. Breathing deeply releases endorphins, relaxes your muscles, and lets you take in more oxygen, which is helpful for an endurance athlete!

Draw air in slowly through your nose (count to ten if you have to!), then slowly breathe out through your mouth. Try it a few times. Empty your mind, and just focus on your breathing. This can help you relax and lets you reset yourself so you can plan your next move or the next jam.

Remain calm

There's no situation that's improved by freaking out. A clear head will always serve you better than a head that's clouded by intense emotion. Rage and frustration are enemies that will take your attention away from what's important, and likely send you to the box.

If you feel yourself getting angry or frustrated, try to reset with deep breathing or by reciting your mantra, or however else you like to reset.

Stay in the present

As a roller derby athlete, it's important to learn how to let go of the last jam, or even the last pass. If you get mired down in thinking about what you should have done, your confidence might be rattled, and you definitely won't be focused enough on the present, so you might compound the original mistake or bad jam. Try to see the past as valuable training,[39] but don't let it rattle you or dictate your future performance.

Make your own luck

Sometimes in sports, people will watch a great play and say it was a lucky catch, or a lucky hit, but this ignores the most important part of the play—that the athlete was in the right place and was physically and mentally able to make the play happen. Sports, including roller derby, are full of opportunities to make great plays.

To make your own luck, you must train as hard as possible and prepare yourself to take advantage of the opportunities that present themselves—such as holes that open up, or the jammer who unwisely tries to take your outside in the turn. Part of that training is mental, so you recognize the situations as they start to happen; and part is physical, so you can get where you need to go and physically execute the play when you have the chance.

Dealing with Disappointment

Roller derby is a tough, competitive sport, and every skater will sometimes be disappointed: whether it's not making the All-Star team, not being rostered, not feeling like you got enough playing time in a bout, losing a championship, or even feeling like you didn't play your best, there are many good reasons that a skater might feel bummed. Disappointment is a horrible emotion—it combines the frustration of working hard but not meeting your goal with sadness, self-doubt, and maybe even a bit of envy. That said, every single player feels it sometimes. Dealing with disappointment with a brave face, and continuing to work hard, is one of the most challenging parts of roller derby.

When you feel disappointed, here are a few questions to ask yourself:

- Why am I disappointed?
- Is that valid?
- Can I fix this?
- How can I grow?

In a sport as tough as roller derby, there will naturally be setbacks, but these can help push you to the next level by inspiring you to work harder, or to examine what you're doing and recalibrate your approach to be more effective.

If you find that you're consistently disappointed in the same way or by the same type of thing, make a plan to fix it. Revisit some of the sections of this chapter and Chapter 11, and think about what you'll need to do to reach your goal.

Putting It All Together

The skills and techniques I've described in this chapter and Chapter 11 can help you start to build up your physical and mental game. However, this is only the very beginning. As you advance in the sport, you'll figure out what kind of player you are, what positions you like and excel in, and what works best for you. Look to the players around you and the ones you admire to see what is possible in the sport—and dream big!

Jamie Williams & Cassie "Raven" Beck, photo by Manish Gosalia

CHAPTER 13

INJURIES

ROLLER DERBY HURTS. AT SOME POINT, as you learn to play the sport, you're going to take a hard hit or fall badly. I'm warning you now. It happens to everyone; it's just a matter of when, and how much it hurts.

Does It Just Hurt, or Is It Injured?

Right after it happens, you might feel like you're going to die. You aren't going to die, I promise. Try to take deep, slow breaths through your nose and exhale through your mouth. This will help you calm down enough to assess whether something is really wrong or you're just surprised or in pain. If you believe you are not seriously injured, make your way off the track as soon as possible. Teammates, refs, and medics (if it's a bout) will be on hand to help you. Try sitting in a chair or on the floor, taking your helmet off, drinking some water. Keep taking those deep breaths.

When a jam gets called off because you go down and don't get back up right away, it can be very scary and also quite embarrassing. Don't worry about it—it happens to everyone. Your teammates just want to make sure you're OK.

There is a tradition in roller derby of skaters and refs taking a knee while a skater is down, as a sign of concern and respect. When the skater gets back up, everyone always claps and cheers to show their support and relief.

Getting Back on the Horse

Sometimes after a bad fall or a hard hit, you can feel scared or tentative about returning to play. This is natural, but it definitely won't help your derby career. Try to remind yourself how tough you are—you took a hit or fall like that, and you're still standing! That's something to be proud of.

Think about the mental toughness section in Chapter 12. This is a great place to work on developing those skills. Learning to shake off pain and get back on the track is a big part of becoming a great derby player.

In some cases, you might not be sure how hurt you are. Adrenaline can make it very difficult to tell how serious a potential injury is. If you're not sure whether you're injured, play it safe and sit out for a while, breathing deeply and taking sips of water until you feel like you're in touch with your body again.

If you suspect that you're injured, definitely don't return to skating, even if you feel like your team needs you. Your health is way more important than one bout or scrimmage. You should always feel empowered to tell your coaches and captains if you are hurt and can't play.

I asked Papa Doc, a fixture in the derby community, for some advice about diagnosing and dealing with common injuries you might see in roller derby.

• •

DIAGNOSING INJURIES

Papa Doc

Many times skaters are practicing without a medically trained person on hand. Although it is difficult to cover all the possible injuries or medical events that can occur in a contact sport, I will attempt to give you some general rules to help you when you have an injured or sick skater and no medical person is on site. The advice here cannot cover all possible situations and is intended to give guidance on how to proceed after an injury. However, this information is not the final answer or treatment for any person's specific injury. *If you have questions about a specific injury or condition, you should consult a medical professional.*

Bumps & Bruises

Deep, large, or rapidly-swelling bruises should be iced right away, followed by a compression dressing (if the area permits) to reduce bleeding and swelling into the tissues. The compression dressing should be worn for twenty-four to forty-eight hours, except for bathing. You should ice the injury every two to four hours for several days to keep bleeding and swelling down. This can be done by partially unwrapping the compression and rewrapping it over the ice.

If you have an abrasion or a cut, you should cover it with a clean cloth or gauze and apply pressure until the bleeding stops. After that, clean the cut as soon as possible. Hot soapy water is the best, but antiseptic sprays are useful if clean water is not available. Once the wound is cleaned, including removing any dirt or debris, you should cover it with a clean dressing or Band-Aid. If dirt or debris can't easily be cleaned out, clean and dress the wound and see a doctor.

If you can't stop the bleeding or if the wound is more than a half inch long or deeper than a quarter inch, you will likely need stitches, so you should see a doctor within six hours. After six hours, the wound usually can't be sutured, because of the risk of infection. Be sure you have received a tetanus booster in the past five to ten years.

Too Sick to Skate?

Some general rules of thumb apply for deciding whether to skate when you are ill. If you have a fever, severe cough, shortness of breath, chest pain, uncontrolled vomiting and/or diarrhea, muscle aches, or fatigue, skating is a bad idea. If you can't drink or eat enough to keep your hydration and strength up, don't skate.

If you can't skate but want to stay around to observe, remember to protect your fellow skaters by covering coughs and sneezes, washing your hands, and not sharing drinks, whistles, or equipment.

Rashes are most likely contagious if they are crusting or blistering or have open sores, so stay away from your teammates until treated. Reddened eyes with thick yellow drainage and discomfort rather than itching are likely to be contagious (i.e., pinkeye) until treated for one or two days.

Allergic reactions can be very serious. If you have hives and/or itching skin with general symptoms such as breathing difficulty, problems swallowing, faintness, nausea, and vomiting, you should see a doctor urgently or call 911. If you have hives without generalized symptoms, you can likely take an oral antihistamine for relief.

First Aid

Because injuries do happen during practice, every league should make sure to have at least a small first aid kit on hand at every practice, scrimmage, and bout. This should include sterile gauze pads, tape, Ace-type wrap, Band-Aids, nasal plugs, and cleaning materials for wounds. Leagues should also have a source of ice and bags, or a supply of disposable ice packs, along with a wrapping material (Classic wrap®, Ace-type), since many injuries will need icing as part of the first aid treatment to relieve pain and reduce swelling.

Concussions

Concussions are a common injury in contact sports. Individual events of concussion can range from a mild head injury all the way to emergency situations.

As we currently understand a concussion, the injury is a change (probably chemical) in brain function induced by acceleration-deceleration and shearing forces on the soft brain inside the hard skull, rotational forces being more damaging than straight linear force. Actual structural changes are not demonstrated by imaging (CT, MRI) in the case of a concussion. Repeated concussions, or a single severe concussion, have the potential to induce long-term changes in the brain function.

On the good side, most who suffer one or more concussions will not have long-term effects, though some will. Unfortunately, at this point in time, we do not have a 100 percent way of predicting which skater will have long-term consequences from concussions, although amnesia for events before the injury suggests a more serious concussion. We are left with the options of careful monitoring of the skater and ensuring that brain healing has time to take place.

Diagnosis

If an event occurs during which a skater's head is violently shaken, the skater might have a concussion. The event does not have to involve a direct head blow; in fact, most concussions don't result from direct blows. The symptoms, which occur in various combinations and severity, are: headache, "pressure in the head," neck pain, nausea, vomiting, dizziness, blurred vision, amnesia for events before or after the injury, balance problems, sensitivity to light and/or noise, feeling "slowed down," feeling as if "in a fog," "not feeling right," difficulty concentrating, difficulty remembering, feeling fatigued, confusion, drowsiness or trouble falling asleep, more emotionality than normal, irritability, and nervousness.

The victim of a concussion will demonstrate difficulty in balance, concentration, mental function, and behavior. Note: a loss of consciousness is not actually a common symptom, resulting in under-reporting of concussions. Please, if you suffer the symptoms or signs above, report them to your medical team.

If there is a loss of consciousness, evaluation in an emergency room (ER) is needed. If there is no loss of consciousness, the severity and number of symptoms will determine whether the skater will need to go to the ER. *All* skaters with symptoms and signs of a concussion must be evaluated by the team medical personnel and be excluded from play that day.

There is a useful free evaluation form (SCAT2) which can be used to evaluate a potentially concussed skater.[40]

Treatment

First, because more serious brain injuries (such as bleeds into the brain) can start out with symptoms similar to a concussion but not show up right away, the injured person should be monitored by someone for twenty-four to forty-eight hours. It may be necessary to waken them every two to three hours during the night to ensure their sleep is normal sleep, not unconsciousness.

Nausea or vomiting may occur after a concussion, so the injured skater should have a bland, mainly liquid diet for twenty-four to forty-eight hours. Because of possible problems with concentration, confusion, and mental slowness, the injured person should not drive or operate dangerous equipment for twenty-four to forty-eight hours. Prevention of another brain injury until the brain heals the first one chemically is critical.

Rest is the only actual treatment for concussion. This includes both physical and mental rest. The harder part is resting the brain, but it is the most important part of recovery. This involves not using the brain for anything other than basic life functions until the symptoms subside. Initially, for a day or two, a quiet, dimly-lit environment is beneficial. Reading, tasks requiring mental effort and concentration, watching TV, and the like should be avoided till the symptoms subside.

Ideally, this involves time off work. Physical rest is also needed. If the symptoms subside but re-occur on resuming mental and normal physical activity, rest must be resumed. Pain treatment for the head or neck pain may be needed. Rest and ice bags will often be sufficient. If not, acetaminophen (Tylenol is one brand) is all right. Aspirin and NSAIDS (ibuprofen, naprosyn, and the like) must be avoided because they promote bleeding.

Although bleeding is not a result of a concussion, the concern is that a more serious injury involving bleeding may present with concussion symptoms initially. Sedative and narcotic medicines must be avoided because they mask important symptoms or cause symptoms that mimic head injury, such as dizziness, lethargy, or nausea. If the skater is on regular medications (prescription or over-the-counter) for another, unrelated medical condition, a doctor must be consulted as to whether the medicine is OK to continue. Alcohol and hard drugs should absolutely be avoided.

Return to Play

Because each concussion is so individualized, the return to play (RTP) must be individualized for the skater. Blanket rules don't work well. In general, the milder the concussion, the sooner RTP can happen. The timeframe may be a week to as long as several weeks. But it must be under the supervision of the skater's physician. The key determinant is that the symptoms and signs must have resolved completely *and* must not start up with the resumption of normal, non-sport activities.

Once that is true, gradual return to sport-related but non-contact activities may be instituted. If the skater remains symptom-free, the skater can gradually return to contact sport activities. There are instances where the skater will be well, return to contact sport activities but have a relapse of symptoms some days or weeks later even without a new head trauma. This is known as a post-concussion syndrome and requires further medical evaluation with a neurologist.

Prevention

It is obvious that complete prevention of concussion in contact sports is not possible. But the use of a well-fitted, well-made helmet and mouth guard helps reduce the likelihood. This is also the reasoning behind prohibiting hits above the shoulders and using the head to block. There is evidence that increasing the neck strength may reduce the forces generated in falls by reducing the violent shaking of the head. This is still being investigated, but strong, flexible neck muscles are helpful in reducing neck injuries in any case.

Preventing the long-term consequences of repeated concussions requires that skaters be honest in reporting symptoms in the first place and follow medical advice carefully. This will give the best chance for the brain to "heal" and allow the best chance for the skater to return to derby safely and soon.

When to See a Doctor

In our league, we recommend that all injuries be seen by our medical staff. For those without a medical staff onsite, here are a few guidelines. In general, an injury that results in a skater's inability to use that body part or a reluctance to use the part due to pain should be evaluated by medical personnel. Some injuries, such as a small cut, an abrasion, or a simple bloody nose obviously need only first aid care. Some injuries would obviously need an M.D. to manage: laceration, uncontrolled bleeding, unconsciousness, heat stroke, an open fracture (bone sticking through the skin), eye injuries, head and neck injuries, or an injury for which no one onsite knows what to do. If in doubt, err on the side of caution.

Dealing with an Injury

As Papa Doc says, there are times that you'll need to seek medical care for an injury. It's a huge bummer to get hurt, but it's something every player goes through, and how you handle it can dictate how quickly and completely you recover, and how fast you get back up to speed after you're back on skates. Here are the steps to take when you're dealing with one of the worst parts of roller derby: being injured.

Stay cool

When the doctor announces that you have a serious injury, you might feel like a truck just hit you, or like your world has just been shattered, but try to save the five stages of grief for later. It's important to get as much information from your doctor as you can about your injury: what kind of injury it is, what your treatment options are, what to avoid doing, and what the recovery timeline is. If there might be surgery involved, this goes double. If you're overwhelmed with emotion, you won't be able to think of the right questions or focus on what the doctor is telling you, which will make it harder for you to get better. If the injury is serious enough to possibly warrant surgery, it might help to have a friend or loved one accompany you to the doctor so they can ask questions and take notes for you, or just be a shoulder to lean on.

Mourn ... for a while

Once you're out of the doctor's office, call your mom or your partner or your derby wife. Six weeks off skates?! With playoffs coming up?! You're allowed to wallow ... for a little bit.

Tell the team

Your captains, managers, and teammates are probably worried about you, and will be even more concerned if you just drop off the face of the earth. Tell them what's up, and let them know what you need. Most derby people want to help their fallen comrades, but they don't always know how. Do you need someone to drive you to a doctor's appointment, bring you groceries, or just come over to your apartment to goof off and watch silly DVDs with you to take your mind off your injury? You should ask your teammates. They might not always be able to, but someone might be wondering how she can help, and she'll feel good about doing something nice for you. You'll return the favor when you're healthy and she's the injured one.

Make a plan

Maybe this one's just me, but I feel better when I know what the next steps are. Come up with the timeline for your recovery, and figure out what you need to do (and what you *can* do) to stay in shape while you're off skates. That way, you won't feel like you're broken forever, and you'll have an end in sight! However, every injury is different, so don't adhere rigidly to your plan if you aren't healthy enough to do it, and make sure your doctor approves of the plan.

Take care of yourself

Do your physical therapy. Do not sit around eating Twinkies and drinking beer on the nights you would have spent skating. Once you get back on skates, you'll really appreciate all the work you put into staying in shape and getting your injured part back to top fighting form. That said, don't overdo it and injure yourself even worse in an effort to stay in shape. Your first priority is recovery.

Stay involved

Even if you can't skate (or even do off-skates drills), try to stay involved with your team and your league. Keep doing work for your committee—or you could even volunteer for more responsibility than you could take on when you were skating six to ten hours a week. Go to your team practices and scrimmages, and consider running lineups or helping your manager. If you aren't mobile enough to get to practice, watch some derby footage to develop your derby brain while your body heals.

Celebrate

Once the doctor clears you to get back on skates, it's great to celebrate a bit. But you're only through the first stage of this process. What comes next is just as important as what you've already done.

Don't push too hard

If the doctor says you can get back on skates, great! But that doesn't mean you should do three hours of full-contact practice and a hundred squat jumps your first night back from a knee injury. Start slow, and give yourself permission to do that. See how it feels to do squats off skates before you put your skates on. See how it feels to gently touch your knees to the floor before you start doing knee falls. The last thing you need is to reinjure your carefully healed injury by doing too much too fast.

Derby will still be there in a few weeks, and you'll be better in the long run if you're strong and healthy. Most leagues have policies about when skaters can return to doing contact and bouting after an injury, so you might need to go through a period of skating without contact before you can scrimmage again. That will also help you to build your muscles and endurance back up before you attempt to do the crazy apex jumps and other advanced moves you could do before you hurt yourself.

Stay strong

Are there areas of your body that are weak? Work to strengthen them with a program of off-skates exercises. Chapter 14 includes many exercises to strengthen various muscles. You can also consult a trainer or physical therapist who can design a program for you. Building strength and flexibility is the best way to prevent injuries from happening in the first place. And you know more than anyone how much injuries suck!

Helping Injured Teammates

It's a bummer to be injured, but it can also be incredibly isolating. Being in pain and having impaired mobility can make it hard for an injured skater to make it out to practice or other team events. Your injured teammate already feels bad, but if it seems like her team doesn't care about her or has forgotten about her, that can make an already bad situation truly crappy.

Make sure to reach out to your teammate to find out what she needs. If she has a serious injury, such as a broken leg or torn ACL, she might need help getting to doctors' appointments, getting groceries, or even getting around her apartment for the first few days.

If you can't help out with any of those things, your teammate might still appreciate a visit, or even regular emails and texts. It's really important to stay in touch with her and make sure she knows you haven't forgotten about her.

Caring for your injured teammates is good for team cohesion and morale, and it'll help motivate your teammate to care for herself and get back on the track as fast as she can.

Obviously, injuries are a big problem in roller derby, but there are ways to reduce the risk of hurting yourself. The next chapter covers topics such as building fitness and increasing your flexibility, two things that can help keep you healthy.

Polly Gone, Bonnie Thunders & Lucille Brawl, photo by Jules Doyle

CHAPTER 14

DIET & EXERCISE

DERBY PLAYERS SPEND A TON OF time skating and building skills and muscles, so obviously it makes sense to get as much out of the work you put in as you can. As you develop your roller derby training regimen, you'll start to notice that choices you make about what and when you eat make a big impact on how you feel when you're on the track, and how effective you are. You might also notice veterans talking about cross-training, and reaping big rewards from the strength and flexibility it helps them build.

So, how can you take your game to the next level? The first step is learning more. As I'm not an expert on fitness or health, I've called in several experts to provide more information in this chapter. I must stress that this is for informational purposes only, and before committing to a diet or exercise routine, you should consult a medical professional about your particular situation.

First up, a subject close to many of our hearts: food! When I first started playing roller derby, I was amazed at how ravenous I was all the time. I've consulted Lilith NoFair about how to channel that hunger and make good food choices to build up a healthy body.

• •

NUTRITION FOR ROLLER DERBY

Lilith NoFair

There is an absolutely staggering amount of information out there when it comes to food. Too often, we get inundated with fad diets, quick fixes, and crazy schemes, and miss the nutritional building blocks that are the foundation of a solid strength base. Sports nutrition is complex, but that doesn't mean you can't keep it simple when it comes to devising a nutrition plan that works for you. Here are the (very) basics when it comes to eating like an athlete.

Understanding Your Food

To eat like an athlete you should understand your food. Know your macronutrients: protein, carbohydrates, and fats. These are the categories used to classify the majority of the food that goes into your body. How you break down the ratios depends on what your body type is, your level of activity, and your goals.

Protein

Protein is critical for your metabolic activities, for maintaining and improving your body composition (building and repairing your muscles), promoting immune function, and helping you to feel full after eating.

Traditional food guides say the average sedentary adult should eat 0.8 grams of protein per day per kilogram of body mass to avoid protein deficiency. But we're not sedentary adults, are we? We're athletes and our protein requirements are higher.

Basically, you can start at 0.8g/kg (0.36g/lb) and go all the way up to 1.4–2g/kg (0.64–0.9g/lb), depending on your goals and level of activity. A portion of protein is usually 20–30g for women (20–30g is about the size of your palm). Since men generally have more muscle and less fat than women, the number of calories burned at rest (basal metabolic rate) is higher, so you should double the intake if you're male. For example, a 150-pound, reasonably athletic female skater should consume 95–135g of protein per day.

Here are some foods that are high in protein and won't break the bank:

- Can of tuna: 40g/can
- Whole eggs: 7g/egg
- Whey powder: 26–30g/scoop
- Ground beef or turkey: 25–100g serving
- Milk: 30g/liter
- Chicken breast: 25g/100g serving
- Cottage cheese: 12g/100g serving
- Hempseed (for the vegans): 10g/2-tbsp serving

Carbohydrates

Carbs are a major source of energy within the body—they are stored as glycogen in the muscle tissues and liver and are converted to glucose when your body needs energy. When the intensity of your activity demands more glucose than is available in the bloodstream, glycogen stores are used as an energy source. Without enough glucose in your system, your body will start breaking down protein into glucose, and then the protein can't serve its primary role in muscle growth and repair. Your brain also needs glucose—when it's lacking, your focus, performance, and mood suffer.

There are three types of carbohydrate:

1. **Monosaccharides**: the simplest carbs, such as fructose, which is found naturally in honey, fruits, berries, and many root vegetables and is produced commercially from sugar cane, sugar beets, and corn. They cause the fastest (and shortest-lived) spike in energy.

2. **Oligosaccharides**: short chains of monosaccharides, like sucrose (table sugar), lactose (milk sugar). Again, energy is quickly produced, but it lasts only a short time.

3. **Polysaccharides**: long chains of monosaccharides, including starches and fibers such as rice, wheat, maize, corn, and potatoes. These carbs take longer to digest, creating a slower increase in blood glucose and insulin levels.

As an athlete, you also want to make sure that your glycogen stores exist before and after athletic activity. Even in short bouts of high-intensity activity (like derby), carbs can enhance performance. Eating carbs before exercise and games preserves your liver and muscle glycogen and helps to prevent protein breakdown. After vigorous activity, you are more insulin-sensitive, and your muscle glucose uptake is enhanced, so eating starchy carbs after exercise is generally a good idea.

Look to whole carbs and fruit to replenish glycogen stores post-exertion, especially if you'll need to be at your peak athletic performance the next day, like on tournament weekends. Here are some healthy, whole, unprocessed carbs:

- Plain full-flake or steel-cut oats
- Plain amaranth
- Plain quinoa
- Plain millet
- Plain barley
- Plain wild rice

Fats

Dietary fat doesn't make you fat. That's a major misconception. We actually need healthy fats in our diet for our systems to function properly. Fats help our bodies to support the growth of body tissues (including those that protect our brains and nervous systems), aid in hormone production, and help our immune systems. Many of us don't get enough healthy fats in our daily intake, so load up—but keep in mind that fats are more calorically dense (9 cal/g) than protein and carbs (4 cal/g), so your portions of fats should be smaller.

There are three types of dietary fats. You should try to eat all three in roughly even amounts.

- **Saturated fats** generally come from animal products and are solid at room temperature. These include butter, lard, cheese, and milk, and also coconut and palm oil.

- **Monounsaturated fats** come from seeds and seed oils (hemp, flax, and chia seeds are great places to start), nuts and nut oils, olives and olive oil, and avocados and avocado oil.

- **Polyunsaturated fats** are broken into two categories; you should aim for an even mix of both in your diet.

  - **Omega-6s** abound in the vegetable-based oils we use for cooking, and in factory-farmed animals that are fed corn and soy diets.

  - **Omega-3s** are found in marine oils, such as fish and krill oils.

Eating Like an Athlete

Once you understand why you're eating what you're eating, you can eat like an athlete. Eating like an athlete means not falling prey to those fad diets. It means having a clear sense of your goals. Fat loss and athletic performance are different goals. Most of the diets out there are focused on fat loss, since it's the most popular reason that people go on a diet. Eating for fat loss often involves cutting calories. It almost certainly involves being mindful of your dietary choices and choosing foods that are more nutritionally dense than they are calorically dense. Eating like an athlete often involves increasing caloric intake, or at least shifting intake to foods that will give you the right fuel at the right time. This doesn't mean that fat loss and performance improvement can't (and don't) sometimes happen simultaneously, but chasing both will likely deny you the results you're seeking in both areas. Choose the result you're after, and then make your plan.

How Much Should You Eat?

Let's say you're a derby skater who practices two to three times a week, and cross-trains three additional days. If you're aiming to maintain your body composition, you'll need to eat roughly twelve to eighteen times your body weight in pounds in calories per day. If you're looking to gain weight, you'll want to eat sixteen to twenty-two times your body weight in calories.

That means that if you're a 150-pound skater and you want to stay that way, you're looking at 1,800–2,700 calories per day. That's a far cry from all of the 1,200-calorie diets you see advertising a ten-pound weight loss in ten days!

How should you divide up those calories? Forty percent carbohydrates, thirty percent protein, and thirty percent fat tends to be a good starting point for most people. That said, your optimum nutrient breakdown depends on your personal metabolism. If you have an extremely fast metabolism, you'll need more quick-burning fuel; therefore, you could tolerate a higher percentage of carbs (with a lower percentage of fat). If your metabolism is slower than normal, raise your percentage of fats and lower your carbs.

Our theoretical 150-pound, medium-build athletic skater would want to eat roughly 720–1,080 calories (180–270g) from carbohydrates, 540–810 calories (135–202g) from protein, and 540–810 calories from fat (60–90g) daily. Don't get bogged down in the numbers, though—just track what you eat, how it makes you feel, and whether it is improving your performance.

Tracking your food often helps to identify foods that you tolerate better than others, and might alert you to micronutrients (vitamins and minerals) that are missing in your diet.

Putting It Together

On days that aren't game day

> **Plan ahead.** You know which days you have practice. Make a meal plan with your family, so you're not left scrambling when things get crazy. This might mean cooking extra portions and

putting them aside or freezing them so you can eat healthfully even when you're too busy to cook.

Make your prep easy. When you grocery shop, tack on an extra hour to cut up veggies and pre-cook proteins. That way it's not a chore, and you have lots of smart snacks ready for those late nights after practice.

Try to listen to your body rather than your habits. We all have habits we've developed over the years when it comes to food. Some are great, some not so great. When evaluating what and when to eat, be mindful and listen to the cues that your body supplies. Most of all, remember that eating is natural, and we all need to do it, so save yourself any guilt and shame that you tie to food—it's just not worth your energy.

During practice & cross-training

Before you train, you should have food in your system that will keep you energized, help you perform, maintain your hydration, and encourage recovery.

Take a mixed approach. Eat a protein source to help reduce the markers of muscle damage, eat a carb source to enhance short-term high-intensity performance, eat a fat source to slow digestion, and make sure to include your veggies.

Eat a normal mixed meal two to three hours before training. Make sure it contains lean protein, fruits and/or veggies, high-quality carbohydrates, and healthy fats. Drink water.

Have a smaller meal in the hour before training. The closer to your training session the meal is, the less time you have to digest, so a shake with protein, fruits and veggies, and healthy fats is often a good choice. Include one scoop of protein, one handful of veggies, one or two handfuls of carbs (usually berries), one thumb-size portion of fats (nuts, nut butter, or oil), and liquid to mix (usually water).

Research your sports supplements. Some supplement companies are more scrupulous than others, so make sure you know the difference. If you need guidance, seek out a professional who can give you a hand. Examine.com has an incredible database of supplement information, and is a great place to start your research.

Remember your post-training nutrition! Your nutritional focus after training should be rehydration and refueling. To maximize recovery, eat inside a two-hour window after training. Eat a high-protein meal or shake (20–60g of protein, depending on your sex and goals), and you'll be good to go!

Training nutrition mirrors itself, so treat your recovery meal much like you did your prep meal. Eat lean protein, high-quality carbs, fruits and veggies, and healthy fats in the two-hour window before training, and then again in the two-hour window following training. If your pre-training meal was small (or you were training on an empty stomach), make sure to eat sooner after training. If your pre-training meal was regular-sized, you don't need to rush (but try to stay inside that two-hour window if possible).

On game days

Game days are like heightened training days. Generally the advice above will apply on a game day, too. There are added psychological factors at work on game day, and you may have to tweak things slightly, but try to keep your basics in mind.

Supply your body with energy. Make sure that your nervous system is stimulated for performance and that you have a constant supply of blood glucose. Some folks prefer to snack or eat several light meals, to provide a steady supply of calories and nutrients. Eat foods that are familiar and make you feel good and ready for action before the game, and foods that encourage recovery after you've played. Make it easy on yourself, and pack a cooler in advance to take to the arena.

DRINK ALL THE WATER. Hydrate before, during, and after your game(s). On game days, I carry my water bottle with me all day. Use sports drinks if it's really hot, or if you have to compete more than once in eight hours. During the game, your focus should be hydration, then immediate fuel if necessary (like protein bars or liquid nutrition).

Plan ahead for travel. You know which days you have away games, and where those games are going to be played. Do your research! Prepare your food in advance, or look online at your restaurant options before you travel. That way, you've got any dietary concerns covered, and you can avoid the postgame junk-gorge that seems to happen from time to time on the road.

Most importantly, do what you've practiced. Develop a routine that coincides with your pregame ritual—have one for home and one for travel. That way you don't have to think about it on game day. You already know what you're going to do; you just have to go and do it—just like you will on the track.

Eating well doesn't need to be complicated or time-consuming. Just like anything else, it's a process, and there's no one right way to do things. Find what works for you, make it a habit, and enjoy every bite!

• •

Drinking right is as important as eating right in this sport, and I'm not talking about going to the bar for the afterparty. Papa Doc has shared more of his wisdom around the subject of hydration.

• •

HYDRATION

Papa Doc

The adult human body is about seventy percent water, a bit more in women. The vital cellular processes that keep us alive and healthy depend on being hydrated to function properly. For example, the muscles work by transporting electrolytes and calcium in and out of the muscle cells to contract well. Without adequate hydration, your muscles don't perform at maximum level and are more prone to cramping. The transport of heat, nutrients, oxygen, carbon dioxide, minerals, and hormones depends on the flow of blood to all areas of the body. Adequate hydration of the body and circulation is important for all you do, including skating.

Hydration is achieved by balancing the fluid loss from the body and the fluid gain to the body. Fluid loss occurs from the normal processes of urination, breathing, and sweating, or abnormal losses such as vomiting, diarrhea, severe bleeding, fever, excessive sweating, and excessive urination from caffeine intake or diabetes. The normal losses from sweating and respiration are increased by hot environments and heavy muscular activity. To participate in a demanding sport such as derby, you have to balance the losses with an adequate gain of fluid.

Prehydration is a must for successful competition, because you want to start ahead of the game, not behind. You can prehydrate by drinking twenty-four ounces of fluids two to three hours before exercise, and another eight ounces right before your workout. The type of fluid does make a difference and should be noncaffeinated, nonalcoholic, noncarbonated fluids that supply water at first and, later, water and electrolytes. Water alone is an appropriate choice for the prehydration and the first hour or two of exercise.

Although prehydration is essential, your fluid intake must be maintained during exercise. As noted, for the first hour or two, water alone is sufficient. After that, electrolyte-containing, low-sugar fluids such as noncaffeinated sports drinks and coconut water are good choices. During moderate to heavy exercise, about 3/4 to one quart of fluids per hour, consumed in frequent small amounts (usually eight ounces every twenty minutes) is needed in temperatures over 78°F. At lower temperatures, you may need only ½–¾ quart per hour.

The maximum water intake recommended is twelve quarts a day. Underhydrating is usually more of a problem than overhydrating, although with really excessive water intake, you can induce a serious condition that is called "water intoxication" (basically, internal drowning of your cells in excess water).

The most important electrolytes to supply are sodium (salt) and potassium. Salt is obtained through adding salt to foods and eating salty foods when exercising. When not exercising regularly, a lower-salt diet is preferred. Salt tablets are not usually recommended.

Potassium can be obtained through a variety of fruits, vegetables, and nuts (e.g., almonds, bananas, cantaloupes, coconut water, and tomatoes). Sports drinks should have 15–30mEq/liter of sodium and 2–5mEq/liter of potassium. Low sugar concentrations (5 to 7 percent) are advised because of concern about excess weight gain, but also because higher levels of sugar intake can induce diarrhea.

You can "measure" your level of hydration in two simple ways. First, your urine should be pale yellow to clear. Second, weigh yourself before and after exercise. With adequate fluid intake, you should not lose more than two percent of your body weight after exercise. You should replace any weight loss over two percent by drinking about twenty-four ounces of water for each pound lost.

In situations of abnormal losses (diarrhea, vomiting, and others listed above), the important key is to treat the cause when possible. This is often something you need to consult a doctor about. At the same time, the abnormal losses must be made up ounce for ounce while continuing to supply replacement of normal losses.

• •

Now that you're properly hydrated, you're probably ready to step up your game with a fitness training program.

• •

FITNESS & TRAINING FOR ROLLER DERBY

Booty Quake of Roller Derby Athletics

Roller derby is an incredible physical and mental pursuit. Like ice hockey or American football, the sport demands a great range of physical skills and attributes; however, unlike in many other sports, there is no particular size or body type that has better success in the game. Derby athletes of all shapes and sizes have found success at the highest levels of the game, combining athleticism with strategy and teamwork.

Skaters are drawn to roller derby for a variety of reasons, and many new skaters join the community without the benefit of much sports or training experience. It is therefore important to approach physical fitness and conditioning for roller derby carefully—adjusting the level and type of training to suit your current fitness level—to avoid potential overtraining and injuries.

Elements of a Fitness Training Program

The fitness and conditioning program for any athlete, in any sport, should be designed to achieve two main goals:

1. Reduced incidence of injury;

2. Enhanced performance in competition.

Of these two, if you do nothing else, you should focus on #1. Keeping yourself healthy and on skates for your long-term enjoyment is more important than winning MVP or making the A-team.

To understand the components of a roller derby training program, we have to first examine the fundamental physical skills involved. The ten general physical skills below are adapted from the CrossFit system philosophy and applied to roller derby skills.

Cardiovascular/respiratory endurance

The ability of body systems to gather, process, and deliver oxygen.

Derby application: Maintaining speed in a paceline; practicing basic derby skills.

Stamina

The ability of body systems to process, deliver, store, and utilize energy.

Derby application: Sustaining effort and performance throughout training, a bout, or a tournament; completing the 27-in-5 test.

Strength

The ability of a muscular unit, or combination of muscular units, to apply force.

Derby application: Holding a derby stance; striding efficiently; pushing a wall of blockers forward.

Flexibility

The ability to maximize the range of motion at a given joint.

Derby application: Achieving deep crossovers, a low stance, or side stance.

Power

The ability of a muscular unit, or combination of muscular units, to apply maximum force in minimum time.

Derby application: Quickly accelerating or decelerating; moving an opponent quickly through a lean or block; using edges to booty block and slow or stop an opponent.

Speed

The ability to minimize the time cycle of a repeated movement.

Derby application: Quick skating; using fast skating or toe stops to escape a block or an opposing wall.

Coordination

The ability to combine several distinct movement patterns into a singular distinct movement.

Derby application: Using side-to-side movement and changes in speed to positionally block.

Agility

The ability to minimize transition time from one movement pattern to another.

Derby application: Juking or deeking; quickly reentering the track legally behind another skater.

Balance

The ability to control the placement of the body's center of gravity in relation to its support base.

Derby application: Staying upright when receiving hits, landing a jump on one foot.

Accuracy

The ability to control movement in a given direction or at a given intensity.

Derby application: Landing a hit on a moving opponent; executing a legal apex jump.

As you might have guessed, the elements of physical fitness build on one another, roughly in the order they are listed here. One cannot expect to have accuracy without speed and coordination; likewise, you'll need some basic strength before focusing on speed. Balance is an exception, however. Since the sport of roller derby is performed in an inherently unstable environment—on skates—balance is a fundamental skill that should be practiced from the beginning.

Training to Reduce Injuries

Derby players cannot eliminate injuries, but we can take smart, conscious steps to reduce the frequency and severity of injuries by focusing on balance, stability/proprioception, and flexibility training. Your training in this area should follow three basic principles:

- The less you fall as a result of hits and instability, the fewer chances you have for an acute injury.

- Cross-training will reduce your chances of chronic/overuse injuries.
- Flexibility training will help you on both counts!

Staying on your feet

If you can stay off the floor during scrimmaging and game play, you're likely to stay out of the emergency room, too. Perhaps an oversimplification, but a useful point of focus nonetheless. Falling during skills training can be a good thing—we need to fail sometimes when we try new things. But a fall during game play comes with higher intensity and higher risks. You can reduce falls by working on the elements of balance: core strength, particularly lateral movements and e-centric (off-axis) movements; and (in)stability training, sometimes called proprioception training.

You can also reduce your time on the floor by working on cardio fitness, strength, and stamina. If your lungs are gasping and your legs feel like jelly, you're more likely to fall down when hit. If you're feeling strong, with gas in the tank, you'll be able to draw on your strength to rebalance yourself and stay upright.

Yoga is a simple and effective starting point for balance training for derby athletes. It improves all-over strength and stamina, proprioception, and particularly core strength. Yoga provides an additional important benefit in flexibility training as well. There are many free online video resources and affordable downloads to follow along with at home, and many drop-in yoga classes in most towns and cities. Flat Mat Roller Derby even provides derby-specific online training, the basics of which are included later in this chapter. One or two moderate-intensity yoga classes per week would provide excellent benefits for most derby athletes, at any level.

I'll go into more detail below on how to improve your strength, stamina, and cardio fitness for injury prevention.

Avoiding chronic pain through cross-training

We train for roller derby, with its very specific biomechanics, for hours at a time several days a week; in doing so, we risk overtraining some muscles and undertraining others, creating significant muscular imbalances. These imbalances can have devastating trickle-down effects in some athletes, becoming the source of mysterious chronic aches and pains in other muscles that are being forced to overcompensate.

Cross-training means using alternate sports or types of exercise to train muscles and systems that may be underused in a main sport. For example, long-distance runners may cross-train by cycling. The two pursuits use different primary muscles in the lower body, thereby offsetting the overtraining and imbalances that may be caused by running alone.

Applying this concept to roller derby, we should pursue exercise opportunities that avoid duplicating the skating motion and position, in order to both avoid overtraining and promote balanced strength development. The overdeveloped muscles involved in skating are the hip abductors (several muscles that move the leg out to the side) and quadriceps (front of your thigh). Cross-training should therefore include the hip adductors (inner thigh muscles that draw the legs laterally toward each other), hamstrings (back of the thigh, responsible for bending your knee and lifting your heel), and glutes (involved in hip extension).

Once again, yoga is a great option for cross-training for roller derby, as it will work many muscles in an alternate orientation to our typical skating motion; however, it will not provide significant cardiovascular endurance training and should be supplemented.

Running, cycling, rowing, and swimming can fit the bill for derby cross-training. If you choose cycling or rowing, however, be sure to focus additional time on stretching your hip flexors. Officially called iliopsoas (ILL-y-oh-SO-az), these are muscles that connect your femur to your lumbar spine across the front of your hip bone and help bring your knee toward your chest (hip flexion). Since skaters, cyclists, and rowers all spend a lot of time in hip flexion (knees toward chest), the hip flexors can become shortened, leading to a host of related side effects, from back pain to weakness.

Using flexibility to bounce

Despite our best efforts to train for balance and stability, falling in derby is inevitable. So how do we make the best of a fall? Imagine dropping two items from six feet up: a tennis ball and an apple. Of course, the ball is resilient, made to bounce. The apple is more brittle. It will drop with a thud, becoming bruised or cracked.

When you fall, then, would you rather fall with a thud or a boing? Though we're oversimplifying here, it's clear that having more resilience will benefit you. Working on improving your range of motion in all joints will protect you in the case of an awkward fall and will also allow you to build strength and power from a wider range of motion.

Performing dynamic stretching movements before practice and competition will warm up your muscles and allow you to safely achieve your full available range of motion (your current best flexibility). Dynamic stretches involve easy movements of your muscles and joints through their range of motion. Examples include neck rolling, arm circles, leg swings, etc. Don't overlook upper body and neck movements, as they are critical in blocking, receiving hits, and withstanding falls.

Spending time after practice, or on your own, doing static stretches (held for at least thirty seconds each) will increase your available range of motion. And finally, improving flexibility (particularly in your hips and legs) will help to counteract some of the muscle imbalances discussed above.

Training to Improve Performance

As you move from being a derby hopeful to competing in the sport, you should also scale up your fitness and cross-training to provide the support and injury prevention that you need at each level.

Minimum skills

If you are newer to sports, roller derby, and fitness training in general, or you've come back from a long hiatus, then your focus should be on the basic elements of injury prevention discussed above—basic levels of cardiovascular endurance, stamina, strength, and flexibility, plus balance. These are like the WFTDA minimum skills for skating, and they correlate to the first few elements on our list of the ten general physical skills (plus balance). They are the building blocks needed to safely perform at a minimum level. These basics support the development of skill, strategy, and game play. Improving these aspects of your fitness will improve your basic skating performance at the same time as it helps to protect you from injuries.

Scrimmage-ready

Once you have passed your minimum skills (read: established a basic foundation of fitness), you are ready to work on skill development, scrimmaging, and game play. To improve your fitness to support these elements of on-skates training, you can improve your cardio, balance, strength, and stamina by increasing the intensity or frequency of training in these areas.

Adding weights to your strength training, or increasing the volume and intensity of bodyweight exercises, such as squats and push-ups, will improve your strength and stamina. You can add time or distance to your cardio training (running or cycling, for example), or you can try interval training—alternating high-intensity periods with low-intensity or rest periods.

Becoming a competitor

Continuing our skills analogy, once you've graduated to being a bouting skater, it will be time for you to start truly training for performance. At this point, you'll want to focus on the bottom half of the skills list—power, speed, coordination, agility, and accuracy.

Your training should become more explosive. You'll use plyometric movements (explosive jumps) to train your fast-twitch muscle fibers, producing improvements in power, speed, and agility. High-intensity interval training (HIIT) should be a focus of your off-skates training. These workouts usually use bodyweight and plyometric exercises, done at high intensity, giving you the benefit of both cardio training and strength/power training simultaneously. Be sure to include upper body and core exercises in your training—roller derby is not just a sport for the legs!

You can simultaneously increase the intensity of your core and stability training by using a physio ball, wobble board, or BOSU ball to add unstable surfaces to work from.

Getting to Champs!

If your derby goal includes WFTDA charter team play, and your team is aiming to rise through the ranks into Division 1 (or stay there!), then your fitness approach must reflect the higher physical demands, skill level, and speed of the game.

Ideally, Division 1 athletes should add free weight training to an off-skates program to support greater gains in power, speed, and agility. Consider adding two sessions a week of a weight-based strength program.

Everyone—everyone!—involved in strength training has a different opinion about what your program should include. But most can agree that to develop the power needed for roller derby, you should work with weights heavy enough that you can perform only eight to ten (or twelve) reps with good form, but no more. Basic weight-room exercises like squats, bench press, deadlift, overhead press, and rows are all great places to start. Machine-based exercises are generally less effective than free weights. A strength routine needn't be complicated—the most important piece of your program should be a method of tracking your progress, whether it's an app or the good old analog pen and paper.

Concurrently with increases in your strength, you can add more intense plyometrics, agility training, and HIIT workouts to your weekly routine.

In roller derby, each athlete comes to the first practice with a unique set of abilities and learns the skills and game play at a unique rate. Likewise, each athlete has a different baseline fitness level and will progress at her own rate, dependent on genetics and effort.

Listen to your body, and progress with your off-skates training when you feel ready.

Top Ten Moves for Roller Derby Fitness

Here are some great exercises that can help you build up the muscles you need for roller derby, along with variations that can add intensity as you gain strength.

Glute Bridge

Works on: Glutes, stability, core
Variations: One leg at a time, add weight

Squat

Works on: Quads, hamstrings, glutes, core
Variations: One leg at a time, add weight, squat jumps

Push-Up

Works on: Core, full body
Variations: Narrow grip/elbows in, wide grip, raise feet on a step or ball

Plank

Works on: Core, stability
Variations: One arm, one leg, side plank

Lunge

Works on: Quads, hamstrings, glutes, stability
Variations: Walking lunges, add weight, different directions (front, back, side)

Bicycle Sit-Up

Works on: Core
Variations: Lower outstretched leg closer to the floor, wear skates

Deadlift

Works on: Full body
Variations: Romanian deadlifts, one-leg deadlifts, added weight

One-Foot Balance

Works on: Stability/proprioception, lower leg
Variations: Stand on one foot and balance with your eyes closed. (Harder than it sounds!)

TFL/Hamstring Stretch

Works on: TFL, hamstring, IT band
Variations: Lie on your back, raise one leg toward ceiling, then pull across your midline

Lunge stretch

Works on: Hip, especially hip flexor
Variations: Warrior 1 or Warrior 2 from yoga, or a deep lunge with back knee resting on the ground, upper body vertical

For more information, check out: www.rollerderbyathletics.com/top-ten-exercises.

• •

As Booty Quake mentioned, it's just as important to remain flexible as it is to build strength, and yoga is a great way to gain flexibility.

• •

STRETCHING IT ALL OUT: YOGA & STRETCHING FOR ROLLER DERBY ATHLETES

Lemony Kickit, AKA *Kat Selvocki of Flat Mat Roller Derby*

We all know how it goes; we've all been there. You see your first bout and you're hooked. You drop the cash for gear; you start learning how to skate, spending all your free time getting ready for your league's next round of tryouts. You work hard to get stronger and faster. You make the league! *Yes!* And then you devote even more of your time to derby, because you love it, and because you want to stay strong, fast, and competitive.

And somewhere in there, while you're all in, you forget about balance. With the focus on going hard and growing strong, you let flexibility slide. You forget to cool down after bouts or stretch properly after practice. There is already so much packed into your week; who has time for more?

Flexibility looks different in every body, but as athletes, we need it for mobility. We need our strong muscles to be responsive and not stiff. What good is strength when you don't have the range of motion that you need on the track?

Dynamic Stretching

Static stretching (holding stretches) before playing can actually weaken your muscles—the exact opposite of what you want to do. Yikes! Since you need the combination of strength and flexibility on the track, one of the best things that you can do to ready your muscles before practice or a bout is some dynamic stretching. Dynamic stretching means that you'll gradually increase range of motion using slow, controlled movement—avoid jerking your body around! Moves like high knees, butt kicks, and arm circles are some of the most common that you may already have experienced as part of a sport.

Because roller derby can involve a lot of quick movements in different directions, you'll want to take the time to move not only your hips and legs, but also your whole body! If you're familiar with yoga, sun salutations are a great way to do this, as they incorporate a little bit of everything. You can also try this short series of dynamic stretches, which will help derby-specific muscle groups.

Wide-legged forward fold with movement

This will warm up your hips, inner and outer thighs, and quadriceps for skating. Stand with your feet about three feet apart, with toes pointing forward, parallel to each other. With your hands on your hips and elbows pointing behind you, fold forward and then reach your hands toward the floor (whether or not they touch the ground). On an exhale, bend your right knee and move your hips and torso toward your right. Inhale to straighten your right leg and come back to center, and on your next exhale, bend your left knee and shift toward your left. Repeat this 10–15 times. You might start to go a little bit deeper as you progress through the repetitions, but don't force it to happen!

Handwalks

This will warm up your abdominal and back muscles, shoulders, and hamstrings. From your wide-legged forward fold, step your feet closer together, so that they're no more than hip distance apart. Plant your hands down on the floor in front of you, bending your knees if you need to. Begin to walk your hands forward until you are almost in a plank pose (shoulders stacked above wrists, one long line through your whole body from head to heels), and then with legs as straight as is possible for you, bring your feet to meet your hands. Walk your hands forward again, and repeat this 5–8 times. Be sure to keep breathing as you move!

Arm swings

This will get your neck and back ready for action, as well as provide a little relief after handwalks. After you return to a forward fold with your feet and your hands together, inhale to lift up to standing. Let your arms relax down by your sides. With feet about hip distance apart, begin to swing your arms freely from side to side—one comes in front of you while the other goes behind—and gently tap them against opposite hips as they move. Your spine will rotate back and forth as you swing your arms, and it can be a nice warm-up for your neck to turn your head in the direction of whichever arm/shoulder is moving back as you rotate back and forth. Repeat for 30–60 seconds. There are other dynamic stretches you can do, but this is a good start to get you loosened up for practice or a bout.

Yoga for Derby Athletes

Once you've finished skating, you can do this short yoga sequence with your gear on or off—but seriously, take the time to do it! Your muscles might be willing to do a little more for you if you treat them well.

Cow/cat

Start on your hands and knees, with your hips stacked above your knees and your shoulders stacked above your wrists. As you inhale, lift your head and your tailbone up and away from each other, and relax your belly toward the floor, creating a long curve with your spine. As you exhale, draw your belly button toward your spine and curl your head and tailbone toward the ground, rounding your back. Take 3–5 breaths, shifting back and forth in this way.

Leaning lunge

Starting in the Cow/Cat pose, on an inhale, step your right foot in between your hands. Wiggle your right foot forward to bring your hips forward of your left knee, and be sure to keep your right knee and your right toes pointing in the same direction! Place your right hand on your right thigh, and stretch your left arm up toward the ceiling. On your next exhale, lean toward your right. If you want to deepen this stretch, tuck your back toes (or your toestop) and lift your back knee. Take 3–5 breaths, and release your hands to the floor. Repeat on the other side.

Cow/cat to child's pose

Step back to hands and knees, and take a few more breaths, alternating between arching and rounding your back. After 2–3 breaths, sink your hips back toward your heels—knees can be together or apart—and stack your hands to make a resting place for your forehead. Rest here for 3–5 breaths, and let your head be heavy, so your neck and shoulders can relax.

Bound angle pose

Press your way up to sitting on your heels. One at a time, swing your legs around in front of you, and bring the soles of your feet (or your wheels) together, with your knees wide apart. Place your fingertips on the floor behind you. Make sure your shoulders are stacked above your hips. Inhale, and feel your chest lift forward and up as your shoulders draw back and down. Exhale, and press the soles of your feet together, and let your knees reach toward the floor. Take 2–3 more breaths here. If you want to stretch your shoulders a little bit more, interlace your hands behind your hips, and lift your fist up and away from the back of your pelvis.

Reclined pigeon & twist

Scoop your knees up with your hands to bring the soles of your feet to the floor. Hug behind your thighs and roll onto your back. Cross your right ankle over your left thigh, and flex your right foot so your toes pull back toward your right knee. Either gently press your inner right thigh away from you with your right hand, or wrap your hands around the back of your left leg to hug your legs in toward your chest. Be sure your head and shoulders can relax on the floor as you do this! Take 3–5 breaths here, and possibly rock from side to side as you do.

Release your left foot to the floor and hug your right knee in toward your chest. Straighten your left leg, and with your right knee still bent, cross your right leg over your body. Reach your right arm out on the right side of your body, and gently press your right leg toward the floor with your left hand. Inhale into the right side of your lungs, and as you exhale, keep holding your left knee where it is and try to move your right hip bone a tiiiiiiiiny bit away from your head to lengthen the right side of your waist. Take 2–3 more breaths here, and then return to your back. Repeat both poses with your left leg.

Happy baby
While lying on your back, hug both knees toward your chest, and rock from side to side a few times. Reach your arms in between your knees, and clasp your shins, your ankles, or the outer edges of your feet. Bring the soles of your feet together and let your knees come apart. First, pull your heels toward your pelvis, and then try to keep your feet together as you bring your feet away from your pelvis and toward the ceiling. You could stay in either of those variations, or reach the soles of your feet toward the ceiling and pull your knees toward your armpits. You might rock here, or you might alternately straighten your legs, moving with your breath. Take 5–7 breaths here.

Final resting pose
Give yourself a break! Release your feet to the floor, and stretch your legs out in front of you. Relax your feet apart from each other, and let your arms rest by your sides, palms facing up. Take at least a minute to slow down here. If it's hard to lie still, count up to four as you inhale, and down from four as you exhale. You've earned this moment!

That's it! It takes less than ten minutes to bring a little more balance back into your body after practice or a bout, which isn't too bad after spending a few hours getting beat up. You'll feel better for it, and it'll show on the track—and probably off it, too.

● ●

Fitness, exercise, and nutrition might not seem as fun as skating around the roller rink, but paying attention to these things can improve your game a lot. Fueling yourself properly, building strength, and staying flexible will allow you to play at the peak of your abilities. Taking care of your body will also help prevent injuries, which can help you have a long, happy derby career.

Hyper Lynx, photo by Sean Hale

CHAPTER 15

KEEP IT ROLLING

As you play roller derby over the years, you might start to notice changes—some good, some bad, and some that are just there. This chapter will discuss some of these changes and how to deal with them.

Mental Edge

The longer you play roller derby, the better you'll understand the game. You might start to develop a kind of derby ESP, where you can just look at the way a pack is moving and know what's going to happen next. It's not a superpower; it's just the combination of becoming more familiar with the sport and learning what happens in a given situation. But it can *feel* like a superpower, since it gives you a competitive edge, making it easier to get to where you need to be and make the play you need to make.

Skating for a long time also gives you longer to develop your communication skills and learn how to work with teammates. Two good players working together in a wall are going to be much harder for a jammer to get around than two great players who are by themselves, doing their own thing.

The mental edge is one way that long-term veterans are awesome, even if they aren't the fastest or the toughest players on the track.

Physical Changes

Especially if you started playing in your twenties, thirties, or forties, as you get more years under your belt, you might start to notice the effects of the physical changes of age on your body. Some of these are unavoidable, and others you'll just have to work a little harder to counteract.

In my eight years of playing the sport, I've definitely put on some weight. It makes me a little slower as a jammer, but a lot more solid and hard to move as a blocker. To make sure I keep up my endurance and stamina, I've added more cardio-oriented elements to my cross-training, such as biking and jogging.

Chronic Injuries

As you play derby longer, you're more likely to rack up serious injuries that will have lingering effects even after you're healed and back on skates. It's important to pay attention to your body and care for these injuries so that they don't worsen. Cross-training to stay strong and flexible will help a lot!

There might also be some drills that are harder for you, depending on what the injury is. For example, many skaters I know who have been playing for a long time try to minimize the number of knee falls they do in practice, especially if they've seriously injured their knees in the past. They do rolling squats when their teams practice knee falls, as a lower-impact alternative that takes their health into consideration.

Rules Changes

The rules of roller derby usually change a bit each year. These changes are meant to improve the game and fix problems that exist in the rules, but it can be annoying and frustrating to have to learn a new ruleset each year. These new rules can mean that you have to develop new skills and strategies as well.

Stress & Burnout

Everyone in derby is susceptible to stress and burnout, but it can feel like it's compounded the longer you play.

Dealing with stress

Even though derby is a great sport, it can definitely be frustrating. Trying to improve as a player; dealing with a team or league and all the challenges and personalities that go with that; stressing about playing time and injuries; learning rules and strategies; committee work; balancing derby with your job, school, and family—it's enough to drive the most level-headed skater insane! And because we care about it so much, the stresses of the sport can feel magnified and start to sap the joy from it.

So how can you handle it when derby stress gets you down?

Take a few deep breaths

Sometimes just taking a few minutes to step back, slow your heart rate, and put your derby stress into perspective can be very helpful.

Write down what's bugging you

If you feel stressed out but aren't sure why, try writing a letter to someone. Soon you'll find yourself identifying the problem, and maybe even writing out the solution. But definitely *don't* send the letter—or at least make sure to sit on it for a day or two to see if you still want to once you feel calmer.

Take a night off

It can feel like there's pressure to go to every single practice and committee meeting, and to volunteer for every bout, but if you're feeling stressed out by everything you've got going on, it's OK to take a night for yourself every now and then. Do your laundry. Cook yourself a nice meal. Hang out with your family or significant other.

Derby will still be there tomorrow, I promise, and you might come back with more energy after giving yourself some time away.

Do something nice for yourself

Take a relaxing bath or splurge and buy yourself the cute pair of booty shorts you've been eyeing. Treating yourself well can give you a quick boost that can be enough to help you put your derby stress in perspective or make it seem less important.

Burnout

If derby stress goes on long enough without relief, you might start to feel burned out. This is something all veteran skaters (and refs, and NSOs, and managers) deal with at some point. How you handle feeling burned out will have as much effect on the length of your derby career as how well you take care of your knees and other body parts.

Signs of burnout

- Irrational anger
- Lack of inspiration or joy
- Feeling like you're going through the motions
- Making excuses to skip practice
- A sinking feeling whenever you think of derby

In some cases, there is a specific issue leading to a skater feeling burned out. Perhaps you took on a lot of responsibility as a captain or committee head and the challenges are outweighing the benefits for you. Or you're doing too much in general, and other areas of your life are suffering. Maybe you feel like you're working really hard but not getting better, or that other skaters are improving faster than you no matter what you do.

Try to determine the primary cause or causes of your burnout. When you feel really fried, what is it that most often sends you into that state? If you can put your finger on what's stressing you out the most, you'll have a better idea of how to try to remedy it. Here are a few suggestions for how to combat burnout.

It's just a game

If you are frustrated by off-the-track drama or committee work, try focusing on actually playing. When you get to practice, take a few deep breaths and let all of that go. When you're on the track, try to focus on the sensation of skating, stopping, blocking with your wall, sprinting through your speed lap. If you still love that, you can probably deal with everything else.

Get a new job

If committee work is burning you out, try to identify what aspect of the work is problematic. If there are too many hours, talk to your committee head about scaling back or delegating some of your work to someone else. If you feel stressed out by the committee head's management style, you might fare better on another committee.

Delegate & communicate

If you *are* a committee head, no wonder you're burned out! If you can finish out the season, you can hand off the job next year. Try to prioritize delegating work to your committee members, or recruit a few new ones if you don't have enough people for the work. Think about having an honest conversation with your committee members, the league president, or the board of directors. You might feel like it's a hopeless situation, but nobody wants their leaguemates to be overwhelmed, and they might have a solution you didn't even think of. And remember—if you really can't continue in the role, most leagues would rather replace a committee head mid-season than lose a skater.

Suzy Hotrod recommends:

> For administrative responsibilities, which can easily burn a skater out, one thing I have really focused on is delegation and training others. When I started derby I worked heavily on a lot of large responsibilities. Instead of killing myself and flat-out

quitting the responsibilities, I trained potential new candidates for at least a season before stepping down from my lead role. My secret is being comfortable being a "passenger." Also I know that even if I have an urge to step up and take charge of something, in roller derby there is always someone who is going to step up—always.

Scale back

If you feel like you're run ragged all the time, sprinting from work to practice to committee meetings to everything else, with barely any time for laundry or friends, you might be overdoing it. It's hard to enjoy yourself if you never have a moment to yourself or a night to hang out with your friends. Write down a list of all your commitments, big and small, and take a close look at whether there's anything on the list that you can cut. Think about what stresses you out most versus what makes you happy, and don't worry too much about letting people down. If you're feeling burned out all the time, you aren't bringing your best to anything you're trying to do. It's not unusual for skaters suffering from burnout to get sick or injured—or just to succumb to apathy and start to let things slip without meaning to. Deliberately taking a step back from the commitments that stress you out most can help you bring things back into balance.

Find your level

Some of my greatest derby stress came from skating for our All-Stars team for four seasons. The team practiced way more often and way harder than other teams in our league, and I found myself skating three hours a night three or four times a week. My body was feeling pretty broken from the intensity of the practice and how little recovery time I had. I felt like I was always rushing through everything else in my life, and I was depressed by how often I had to say, "I can't, I have derby." I didn't go on dates with my partner for months at a time, because the few non-derby nights I had, I just wanted to collapse in a heap, or maybe buy some groceries or do laundry. My professional career also stalled out for a few years.

The team was also mentally challenging, since I was competing with nineteen of the best skaters in the world for a spot on the roster. I loved skating at that level and traveling for derby, but sometime during my fourth season, the benefits of being an All Star stopped outweighing all the work I was doing and the other things I was sacrificing to be on the team. So I left the team. I still miss it sometimes, but my quality of life has improved dramatically. I believe I would have retired at the end of my fifth season if I hadn't made that choice, but now I'm in my eighth season and still enjoying myself. There are lots of ways to skate against players from other leagues, and I've discovered that other teams and pickup games are super fun without requiring the same level of sacrifice.

Make time for friends

Sometimes derby feels like all work and stress and physical pain. If you find yourself in a long negative spiral, try hanging out with your team or derby friends in a completely non-derby way. Go to a concert, or host a potluck or a game night—anything that will let you step back and remember how cool derby people are. Having a fun night out, full of jokes and laughter, can help build (or rebuild) a real connection on a personal level. That camaraderie will come back to the track with you, which can help you rediscover the joy you used to feel.

Flirt with another sport

If you feel like you're not improving fast enough or you've been stuck on a plateau for a long time, try cross-training with a different sport or activity. Was there a sport you loved as a kid that you haven't played for a while? Do you love dancing? Have you always wanted to try rock climbing? Trying out another sport or activity can make you appreciate your body in a different way, build different muscles, and let you rediscover the joy of being physical without feeling the stress of a team depending on you. And if it turns out that you can't rekindle your love of roller derby enough to stick around, maybe you've just found your next hobby.

Rekindling the Passion

I asked a few great skaters who have been playing for a long time how they have sustained their love of derby over the years, and how they deal with feelings of burnout when they do arise. Here is the wisdom they shared.

"I felt pretty burned out towards the end of last season. In fact I took a couple of months off roller derby, which is the longest break I've ever had off skates. Being away from it didn't have me itching to get back, but then I heard about an open skate session at a sports hall close to my house on Friday nights. That's actually where I found my love for derby again, because I could do my favorite thing of all—playing around on skates making up tricks. It was only through doing that and feeling like I could scratch that creative itch that kept me going through 2014. Coming from a background of skateboarding, where making up and practicing tricks is all you'd do all day long, I didn't realize how much I missed it within the confines of roller derby training."

— *Kamikaze Kitten*

"I get hyper-focused and too close to specific things. When skills or drills are not perfect, to my expectations, I feel like things are not progressing and that the team or I have plateaued. For me, I have to take a step back and refocus. Remind myself of the big picture. Allow for others on leadership to take the reins and continue to drive us forward. Then I see the progress, and it gets me excited again."

— *Wild Cherri*

"Carving out a little time for hikes with my dog is great *mental* cross-training. Over-rehearsed patterns of thinking are as detrimental as uneven hips."

— *Polly Gone*

"I got a hobby outside of roller derby. I actively sought out a hobby that involved no roller skating, no people that did roller derby, nothing like that. I got into motorcycles, and I have a group of girls that I hang out with once a month or so and have something completely outside of roller derby to talk about.

"My biggest advice for not getting burned out is acknowledging that it's going to happen. No matter how awesome you think you are, it is going to happen at a certain point, and it's better to keep that additional hobby, keep those friends. It's even more important now for me to hang out with my non-derby friends and not talk about roller derby once in a while.

"Now I have a space where I can step back and appreciate what I've been doing, and now that I have that space, I want to get better."

— *OMG WTF*

Retirement

Sometimes, no matter what you do, you can't shake that burned-out feeling. You might still love playing roller derby, but not everything that comes along with it. And that's OK. It's sad, but everyone hits that point sooner or later. It's fine to admit to yourself that you don't get from it what you used to. Or you might be shifting focus to take advantage of a new opportunity in your life, which is awesome.

The next chapter offers some advice for when you think it might be time to retire.

Alex Terminateu & Frak Attack, photo by Dave Wood

CHAPTER 16

LIFE AFTER SKATING

Roller derby can be an intense, all-consuming experience. It demands a lot and takes a lot out of you, but it can also become a big part of your identity. Your league can feel like your family. It can be hard to imagine life without roller derby.

For these reasons and many more, people have a hard time leaving the sport. Roller derby is the only hobby I've ever had where stopping is called "retiring"—as if you're leaving your life's work, or being put out to pasture.

But sometimes it's time to stop. For whatever reason, you can't or don't want to keep committing the time, dealing with the stress, putting your body back together with duct tape. And that's OK. Leaving roller derby doesn't have to mean severing all ties with the derby community, or never seeing your friends again.

April Ritzenthaler, one of the original founders and She-E-Os of modern roller derby, said about finally leaving the sport for good: "I still love it, I'm still in love with it, but I have new things in my life I need space for. I still see my girlfriends all the time, and it's all good."

How to Leave

In your own time, let your team know, and tell the head of coaching or the league president—your league probably has a process for retiring. It's best if you can retire at the end of a season, but sometimes life doesn't work out that way.

If you have league responsibilities such as running a committee, or even an important job or task you always do, make sure to let people know in advance that you're planning to leave. Give them a timetable to find someone else to take over that job, and if you can, try to help with that transition and make yourself available to answer questions. If you know someone else who might be good at doing that job, you can even reach out to her about taking over. The bigger the job, the more lead time you should give, if possible.

Gotham announces retirees at their last bouts and honors them at our end-of-season party as well. There are typically some tears, and that's OK. It's a big deal, and people will understand if you're a little emotional.

Guilt

You might feel guilt about leaving your team or your league, and your skater friends might give you a hard time about it and urge you to change your mind. We still send my old team captain messages with "#takeitback" in them, and she retired in 2012 and then moved across the country.

You're making the right decision for yourself, and your teammates will respect that. Trying to heckle you into staying is probably just their way of dealing with their sadness. If it gets to be too much, you can take them aside or send them an email and let them know that you appreciate their love, but they're making it harder than it already is.

Letting Go

After you retire, you'll probably feel a lot of strong emotions: sadness, loneliness, relief. You might feel like there's a big hole in your life. But now is a great time to try new things and expand your horizons. There is probably a long list of things you always said you'd do if not for roller derby. So do them!

Here are a few ideas to get you started:

- Take a class.

- Try out a craft or a new hobby.

- Pick up a new exercise routine. You'll need it if you want to stay in shape after cutting out six to ten hours of roller derby each week!

- Reconnect with non-derby friends.

- Focus on your career.

- Travel somewhere you want to go. I bet it's super fun now that you don't have to bring thirty pounds of skates and stinky gear in your carry-on.

- Cook more.

- Read a book.

- Spend time with your family.

- Hang out with other retirees.

Diving into new pursuits will help you understand what you were giving up to participate in roller derby.

Still Missing Derby

Ultimately, if you just can't adjust to life without roller derby, you can always return to it, in one form or another. Depending on your reasons for retiring, there are also many ways to stay involved if you want to, which might be more flexible for your schedule or less hard on your body.

Manager

If you're retiring from skating or reffing, you might consider becoming a team manager. It's a position that takes advantage of your skills and knowledge but can require less time commitment. Plus, you don't have to worry about getting injured.

Non-skating Official

Being an NSO also takes advantage of your knowledge of the rules and flow of a bout but might be a bit easier on your schedule than other roles in the sport. It's another role you can do if you've had to retire for physical reasons.

Coach

Depending on how your league is set up, coaching might be something you can do occasionally or for a few weeks at a stretch when you have time, rather than committing to a full season. Coaching your league, the rec league, or junior skaters can be incredibly rewarding, and a great way to stay involved.

Announcer

A person who already knows the rules and the skaters is well on her way to becoming a good announcer, a position that might allow more flexibility if time is a problem. And while it might be tough on your voice, it's definitely easier on your knees than skating!

Volunteer

Over the years, you've developed many skills that are valuable to the league. If you want to keep a hand in, you can volunteer to work with a committee, or even just to help out on bout day to help out some of your old teammates.

World's Biggest Fan

If you don't have the time or interest to be involved in a formal way, you can still attend bouts. It's so meaningful when my old teammates come out to watch us skate, and they make the best signs. Sometimes they even wear their old uniforms for a lark!

What Now?

April Ritzenthaler said, "Every person that's left has gone on to become something...the ones who really let it break them open and become more than they were, they take that out into their neighborhoods and their communities and to their children and into their jobs, and even if they can't keep doing roller derby, that attitude's always in their soul."

The world is wide open for you now. Even if you might be sad about not being involved in roller derby anymore, the lessons you've learned and the friends you've made will last a lifetime. You're tougher, stronger, cooler, and more capable than many people out there. And not a lot that you will encounter in the future will be harder than what you have already faced.

DERBY STORIES

HOW I GOT ROLLING

Margot Atwell, AKA Em Dash

I DISCOVERED ROLLER DERBY JUST AFTER graduating from college in 2005, when my mom gave me an article about it, thinking I might want to see a bout. The billboard across the street from my dismally paid first job in New York City advertised the A&E series *Rollergirls*. I was intrigued, but I had a lot to pay attention to.

It wasn't till the summer of 2006 that I finally made it to a bout. The details are blurry, but I have a few strong lingering impressions of bright colors, campy outfits, and funny names. I'm pretty sure the irrepressible banana mascot, Bane Ana, was there. But the thing I remember most was the passion. Skaters might have been wearing tutus and swinging floggers around in the introductions, but they were deadly serious once the whistle blew.

A skater got her nose broken by another skater's elbow (which I later learned wasn't legal), but in spite of that, I was hooked. My friend and I spent the drive home brainstorming our new derby names.

Within a week or two, I had bought myself a set of cheap, terrible quad figure skates from Modell's. I discovered a local group called Sweet Action Skate Club, a group of women (and a few men) who met up after work to roller skate and then drink beer at a local bar. The skate club's name derived from our favorite local brewing company.

Several of the other skaters aspired to try out for the New York league, Gotham Girls Roller Derby. (The league hadn't yet developed its dominant reputation; Gotham lost to Providence Roller Derby that year.)

We tried to skate as much as we could, attending Ladies Night at Empire Roller Skating Rink and taking our lives in our hands skating down a steep hill at a local park.

When tryouts rolled around, we were all nervous. Knowing I couldn't do anything more about my skating skills at that point, I wore a flamboyant, short, red-and-white satin cheerleader-style skirt to make myself stand out.

Tryouts took place at my local hangout, Empire, allegedly the birthplace of roller disco. I had spent many nights there, learning to skate to R&B music, so at least I was comfortable with the setting and the floor.

The Gotham Girls had set up stations to check us in, but with so many people trying out, it was a scene of barely organized chaos. Eventually, we were given race-style numbers and safety pins, then put our gear on and met out on the track.

Several Gotham coaches would demonstrate a skill, then ask us to copy it a few times. Some (skating, stopping) were familiar to me, but others (the two-knee "Rockstar Fall," which has since fallen out of favor) were new.

I felt good about the tryouts till the very end, when they brought us to the large rink and made us skate as fast as we could for a set period of time. It could have been five minutes, or only two, but it felt like an hour. I thought I was going to die. The rink was hot, and my wheels slid around on the worn wooden floor. Even though I was supposed to be skating as fast as possible, I was tempted to linger in the narrow part of the track with a fan.

After tryouts, I waited anxiously for what felt like ages, but didn't hear back. Gotham was in the process of moving into its new home, the inconveniently located warehouse they called the Crashpad. Finally, I got an invitation to return for callbacks.

The coaches asked us to wear the same thing we had worn to tryouts, and I seriously regretted the skirt, which I had discovered was very impractical for skating in. I don't remember much except that I slipped all over the Crashpad's slick blue plastic floor, which was made of a material that they called "sport court."

A week later, the day of the Gotham-hosted screening of the modern derby documentary *Hell on Wheels*, I got an email informing me that I hadn't made it. "As a tall skater, you'll have a particular challenge with balance unless you get lower," it read. I was devastated.

It was even harder on me that two of my crew had made it. I cried a few tears but then went to the movie. I had already bought a ticket, and I wanted to congratulate my friends.

At the party after the screening, I met a Gotham skater in a cowboy hat, Ginger Snap, who was friendly and encouraging. I resolved to try out again.

In a movie, this would be where the montage starts. I skated as much as humanly possible. At first I skated at Empire, until the rink closed its doors in April 2007, after sixty-six years in operation. After that I skated outside—sometimes with Sweet Action or others I'd met at tryouts, sometimes by myself or with my boyfriend. I'd skate to brunch on the weekends or roll around on the fabulously smooth-but-grippy linoleum floors of the nearby grocery store, startling other shoppers.

That summer, skating up the West Side Highway one evening after work, another derby-obsessed friend told me that she'd heard a new league was starting in Westchester, a local suburb. We decided to check it out, even though it was about an hour and a half from my apartment in Brooklyn.

We trekked out to Westchester a few days later and met a scrappy group of about a dozen skaters of different skill levels on a cracked concrete basketball court in a park. It was one of the first meetings of the nascent Suburbia Roller Derby, so we talked about what the league would be, what the goals were, and how to recruit other players, and then skated around a bit on the badly maintained surface, ducking around the tufts of grass sprouting through the concrete. I was hooked.

I skated with Suburbia twice a week for the next few months, getting better at skating, stopping, and being in a pack with other people. I upgraded my skates and wheels to a pair of actual quad derby skates, and wondered how I had ever skated on the cheap white dance skates I had been wearing for a year.

Though I loved the other skaters on Suburbia, I couldn't handle the commute; I'd have to leave work at about five in the afternoon and wouldn't get back to Brooklyn till about midnight. When Gotham tryouts came around again, I realized I either had to make it or probably had to stop skating, since the commute was just too disruptive to my career and relationship.

This time Gotham's coaches ran a few skills nights before tryouts, so I was able to skate with other hopefuls and learn the skills that I'd need for tryouts from coaches who were already skaters in the league. My nine months of obsessive skating and four months with Suburbia had paid off—I was much more steady on my skates, and my fitness level was way better than it had been the previous year.

I befriended one of the other skaters at the skills nights, and we spent a few evenings and rainy weekend days skating around her office, which had beautiful painted concrete floors. We looped in between the cubicles, down to the kitchenette, where we used our plows and T-stops, then turned around and did it all over again. We wanted to be ready for tryouts!

This time I felt much more prepared and steady on my skates. I guess for me, the second time was the charm, and I made it! A week or so later, Gotham's 2007 end-of-year party happened, and I dressed up and volunteered to work the door with some of the other fresh meat. Standing there among my new leaguemates that night, I couldn't imagine how much my life was about to change.

THE WHEELERS:
A ROLLER DERBY MEDITATION

Nicole Matos

IN THOSE FIRST FEW DAYS OF practice, you line up, rickety. Knocking wheels, it sounds much sexier than it is—it will take weeks before you can tolerate that tripping feeling, like stepping on your own shoelace, without panic. In general, your body wants to be more in control than it is; it is always on point, eager to run a rescue mission, to overbalance, overcompensate, throw out a flailing arm. Fall on your butt a couple times—everyone does, before the drills wear into you that kneepads are there for a reason—and you'll have the fresh realization that your ass is, after all, the very bottom of your back. Those threaded segments of spinal column: a butt fall jangles them like a ziti necklace. The best kind of fall is no fall, obviously, but next best, that skimming rarity where you lower to just one knee, sliding—one quick training wheel, a rudder deployed then retracted—and hop back up without ever using your hands. More often, it's a two-knee fall, or a four-point fall—that is, wrists down too: they are named for the parts of you that touch the floor. But you imagine, darkly, that it is also for the number of points the scorekeeper will wipe away as you continue to be absolutely terrible, a hazard to yourself and others, to reinvent, again and again, the whole act of falling. This is how roller derby starts, and it is the worst at anything you have ever been.

Rarely have you touched or smelled women this much. They smell like patchouli, like mold, the soured syrup smell of limbs that have been in a cast. It is nobody's fault, it's "the pads." All that protective gear soaks up sweat in successive rings like a tree trunk, oil from hands and heads, bacteria. No matter how often you wash your pads, they still smell like that. Derby teams smell like the early stages of mummification, like zombies. But still of women, distinctly—not some crass vaginal smell (the fanboys wish), but something gendered, laden with pheromones. Every so often, in the moment you go down on someone's back (that is dangerous, a bad way to fall: the vulnerable neck exposed, those five or six inches that can't be protected) you get an unexpected whiff of clean shampoo.

"But isn't that dangerous? Won't you get injured?" And it's true, legs get fractured, shoulders smashed. There's a decent probability of you eventually becoming a little bit bionic, map pins in your thumb joint, collarbone, ankle, showing the places you have been. But those lasting injuries (you reject the word, "serious," you reject the word "permanent"), if they happen, come down still like a lightning bolt, something no more reasonable or expected than if you were hit by a bus walking along the street. There's no resignation to injury, no pre-acceptance of it. This is not practice in steeling yourself toward entropy, it is practice in thinking past it, riding above it, in tearing yourself free from it, debilitation the glorious exception, never the rule. But you've seen it, of course: the swooping stride, so lovely, raptor/rapture, crushed mid-motion by the well-timed hit. More often than not, the shared half a laugh, the mutuality of arrow and target: either way, there's something delightful in the artistry of impact, the way it sweeps you literally off your feet. But the spinning fall, and only then, laugh arrested, the sudden tremendous contracture. Something hurt, not just hurt-hurt, something shattered. The game stops for that, whistles bleat—skaters, even those on the sidelines, fall to their knees. So injury, it enters like that: an invader, something sacrilegious, foreign—an irritating side-effect, entirely beside the point, the same irrelevant relevance lead poisoning might bear to Renaissance art.

So getting hurt, that's not really part of it. But yes, to be honest, there is some activation of hurtness, something maybe less than actually getting hurt—"exertion," "engagement," "being pressed," the way a boxer presses, rallying in, in, in, over and through a volley of punches. There is certainly hurting right up to and occasionally including the fact of getting hurt: but that Venn diagram, "feeling hurt," "being hurt," "getting hurt," is much more spacious, its overlaps more forgiving and elastic, than you may have previously known. Not all pain, you'll learn, is suffering. It comes in far too many textures; how could anybody ever talk about pain—athleticized, sublimated pain, pain applied as a unit of strategy, a tactic—as if it were only one thing? Bruises alone—pain's visible ghost, its ruddy afterglow—come in so many distinct varieties. Deep squashy squid-splats are the engraving of fallen-on wheels; thin grieving armbands the lance where shoulders struck. Brown fingerholds climb your sides, never hurting—those are the work of your teammates, moving you, stopping you, clutching you close. But funny-bone tender, always, the scissoring hipbone bruises where another ilium struck yours with knockout power, crest clattering on crest.

But don't think of the bruises—too obvious, easy: again, for the fanboys—think like we do, of all the things you'll get to be! Sometimes you are the predator, and sometimes, taken unawares, or all-too-awares—a twitching hip flexion, out of the corner of your eye, predicts it, she is lunging, coming for you—the prey. And sometimes—rarely at first, but more and more often, a two-minute period of gameplay leaves plenty of chances to rinse and repeat—you are invincible. You are, improbably, the star-flashing Mario Brother that nobody seems able to touch: scampering, gamboling, while all around you the sliding tiles of other skaters are just a moment too slow. You are the pack—the beast of many backs—that evolving, protean mass that bobbles, coalesces, and breaks like mercury globules. You hunt, at a leftward-slanting lope, in step with your sisters: their hips are your protection, their hips are claws and teeth. The opposition dolphins into your stalling backs, is pinned and swiped satisfyingly out-of-bounds: a three-person effort, bait, cast, hook. You are the fishermen, the nets, the whole damn armada:

from the waist down, front knees pointing, sailing, a clipper ship; up top your own carved figurehead, a Valkyrie.

You will not get to be these things, of course, until your body earns them. First scrimmage, you pick your way to the line on the track—there are bodies all around you, the parts of them the closest all bulging and intimate: the parts, on a crowded bus, that you'd normally strain to avoid. You try facing, it seems logical, the direction in which you'll be skating, but feet snake between yours at awkward angles, it is a Jenga puzzle, Twister, your struts already hopelessly tangled. You begin shaking—first your tensed calf, and then it spreads up your body, upper half slightly out of sync with lower half, juddering. The whistle blows and it is total chaos—you run forward, try to run, are hit down in a quick business-like way, economically, before you manage a second step. You stumble up, no-handed, as practiced—better than expected—but already others are ripping past you, the whole pack is churning, and the point of your juddering, the instinctual message of it, is clear like it never has been before: you will be left behind. You are skating forward somehow, swimming toward safety, when you are walloped—there's no other word for it—clear off the track. A soft ribbon is driven from you, half a spoonful, maybe, of urine. You are up again, even faster—adrenaline expands all fuzzy and quantum—but you are hit to the ground, hard, again. And this is what it is—you know it now—to lose hope, to acquiesce, to give up your throat. The rabbit is quiet in the lion's mouth. Your body gives you no choice—the game is over, today, for you. Your juddering is an earthquake, the pit of your stomach so hollow and floating that you could be peeing on yourself again, who knows? You possess a snarled Swiss-Army knife of a body; you are Inspector Gadget experiencing a malfunction—you have at least three legs, telescoping arms, when the tool you were fumbling for was an extra set of eyes for the back of your head. You might not believe it is like this, the first time, for almost everybody. You might not believe that you'll ever want to do it again.

But you will. Want to. Want to master it—that limbic embrace. And as you skate longer and better, hidden geometries of the sport will slowly emerge. Circles (the desired path of a centripetal object), ovals (the shape of the derby track), and lines (the straight rows of wheels on your quad skate, which, no matter how you loosen the trucks, will never swivel the full way around). So, mastery: the crossover push that muscles a curve out of flat thrusts of direction, the plunging squat—"skater stance"—that holds your centripetal self to the earth. Euclid might like it: stark horizontals, verticals, all bent into manifolds—the sidetwisting "juke," tossing empty air in the space you occupied just a split second before; the various screeching stops, all of them frictional, forcing surfaces in directions they clearly don't want to go. It is a game that blooms in sudden absurd, transcendent moments—where you stick, belly to back, in your opponent's blind spot, waist sucked tight against her ass-smashery; where you plant a foot, at velocity, through a mass of other legs to shimmy yourself forward, the derby Hokey Pokey; where, if you are lucky, you can burst off the whistle straight through a line of shuffling blockers, thinking, or even yelling if you want to, "Stripper Birthday Cake Surprise!"

Roller derby is, after all, a sport that doesn't take itself too seriously. But its unpretentiousness (something different, more conscious and respectful, than the giggling camp of yesteryear) should not detract from its epic sweep. It has, always, a meaningful narrative structure. It plays as a drama, human and basic—two girls racing, the "jammers," to break through and past a pack of impeding "blockers." It is the X- and Y-axis of all rising action: the struggle against external obstacles, the compounding struggle to best a fellow struggler much the same as yourself. The screaming whistles, the orchestra-conductor motions, the whole Copernican apparatus of referees orbiting the rotating skaters on the track: that part is the theater of dramatic interpretation, of decisive but mortal action (agile footwork, jostling bodies, slippery track) tied immediately, with bluster and authority, to a choral meaning. With each turn of the wheel, some players are punished, exiled, "boxed" with a gesture like a master admonishing a dog. Others will see their opposition, even a formidable wall of them, evaporate, "out of play!" for being too far from the shifting pack: a theater of social alliance, of avoiding hubris and disdaining sloth. Meanwhile, the faster jammer, the one who first gains the clear road ahead, is a marked in mimeshow of manifest destiny: the referee locks on you, points, and stays pointing, tracing your path as you make a second pass through colliding blockers; the contrasting call, "you are not lead jammer," favors a man sweeping crumbs from his waist. That first jammer, lead jammer, wins the purest and most fitting right of all, the right to call the whole bloody race to a halt, to just plain stop, at least for that round.

And to persist in this sport, if you do—and you should—is, in the end, to see yourself transformed. Sure, the derby names get attention, and they deserve it: a genre unto themselves. There are the bawdy (Ivana Schoop, Queefer Sutherland, Susie Crotchrot), the boasting (Kim Mortal, Helsa Wayton, Hero Shima), the militant (Uma Bomber, Loretta Beretta, Matza Ball Breaker), the mordant (Celia Coffin, Ghoulita, Bloody Elle), the occupational (Busty Broke'Her, Scream Printer, Mia Bustya), the metafictional (Valerie of the Dolls, Sylvia Plaster, Sneer and Loathing), the pop-cultural (Maimy Winehouse, Rude E. Huxtable, Brawly Shore), the intellectual (The Apostrofiend, Lexistential Crisis, Freudian Tripp) and many, many more. And then there are the physical changes: ask the veteran skaters, now shaped like bells with robust, voluptuous clappers. You aren't a true member of the team until you split your pants getting up from a chair. Those legs are the reason Victorians put socks on their pianos: their quadriceps suck down like plungers; the word "ham" is not misapplied to their hamstrings. It is a bodily visage both stern and succulent (and you'll see a lot of it, know your friends' backsides much better than their fronts), a physique designed by R. Crumb, making thicknesses of us all.

And reputation for gratuitous violence aside (and unfounded—the mandates against punching, elbowing, or kicking are, in the modern ruleset, clear), roller derby is not a sport for genuine hotheads. It is far, far too regularly frustrating. Taken to technical perfection—both jammers perfectly held by opposing blockers—the game becomes only a sort of organized immobility, gridlock. Any sense of "play" in the play depends on the continual forcing of errors: sliding, falling, losing track of your teammates, mistaking the scorers' positions, a moment's complete inattention to the whole thrust of the jam. The laundry list of penalties that accrue in a typical bout are, in that sense, not for playing badly, but just for having played. And yet these errors, expected, even necessary, are diabolically easy to internalize. You cut the track, stepping illegally in front of another's advantage: in what other ways are you impetuous, hasty, do you cut corners? You shove clumsily into someone's back: how else are you a klutz, where else do you cause—or take—unnecessary damage? Why do you continually attempt to bullrush the outside line, the longest, and thus most strenuous route, when other paths, with a little more cunning and patience, might open for you? Must you always make a beeline, dumbly, for what you want, could you ever be convinced of the wisdom of a more circuitous route? How many times—final question—can you be knocked down and keep coming back?

So after all the poetic license and wordplay, the language you pile up, derby's biggest lesson is the confrontation with your own inner silence. One last new drill, perfect for new recruits, "fresh meat." Skate together in a tight pack, round and round the track, "but you must keep talking, you must communicate with your teammates. Say, 'the jammer is coming!' or 'on the inside!' or just, 'I'm here, I'm here, I'm here!'" You wobble on your toe stops, wipe the sweat from your upper lip; that sounds comparatively easy, no problemo, go. You start: and you are, as usual, surrounded by commotion, but you find you can't say a single thing. You gum your mouthguard, try, ummm, okay. Okay, okay! But nothing happens, it dies in the vault inside you.

You want to scream: No fair! Stop! Wait! I have it all here in my head! The whole game, all of it, all those impressions, conceptualizations: you jostle, roil, careen—you are crowded, then carried, one skate losing contact with the floor. Pushed from behind, whipped hard from the side, that strange moment of redoubling, taking on another's force, momentum: you lurch, stagger, and are through. You are something unwitting and raucous, the rampaging Wheelers of Ozma of Oz. You are relaxed, in that slightly lunatic way of a person exercising under conditions of constructed terror. But you still haven't made a sound. You are an offering, a sacrifice stuffed in the mouth of your own limitations. But "I'm here," you manage finally, "I'm here": not very loud, but at least, at last, in a way that doesn't only sound like a total lie.

INSIDE THE HIVE: THE EPIC PACK

TK-Oh!

"I GOT YOU, TK," A VOICE called from over my shoulder, somehow sensing I was afraid I'd fall behind the rest of the pack. There were around twenty of us clustered together keeping pace; this was...lap, what, ten? Twelve?

"That's six—you have nine minutes; pick it up!" the coach yelled over the hum of over one hundred wheels spinning, the *shhwhish...shhwishh* of bodies changing places, and the interspersed instructions of, "Inside!" and "Coming up center!" Lap six? Holy cow. Thirty-four more to go, and we were only getting faster. This drill was called the "epic pack"; the goal, forty laps in ten minutes or bust. Eff...

"That's seven; let's go! Let's go!" the coach called again.

"OK, push it. We're gonna get fifty!"

"Come on, ladies, we've got this!"

"Watch her, here—here...bring her up. TK, move into that hole!"

Ohmygod. I'd like to say that I took a moment here to contemplate the amazing hive-like mentality of the group, the apparent psychic connection of all the veteran girls, and how absolutely reverent the whole experience felt, but there in the fray, with the hum in my ears and the bodies jostling every square inch around me, for the first ten laps, I was terrified.

Wheels were locking every so often, and the girl next to me was suddenly whiffed out of existence—I mean gone, like some kind of phantom floor monster had just sucked her under. Who knew when it might come back for me? I raised up from derby stance for just a second at this thought and turned my head back to look for her to assure myself we were not all being systematically hunted by rink wraiths, but all I could see were waves of helmets undulating in every direction.

"Bring it down, TK. She's fine. Watch in front of you," I heard a voice say just over the pounding in my chest. I wasn't winded, was I? How could I be winded with all of them pushing me forward? And they were quite literally pushing me forward, imperceptibly pulling me around, turning my hips...I was part of a machine.

"That's twelve. Keep it up, you're ahead of pace!" the coach's voice came again from somewhere beyond the helmet ocean.

"Fifty! Let's go, ladies! Get this!"

"Take Danger—up there, go, girl..." a voice came over my shoulder again as one of my fellow recruits emerged at my side.

"Pull her in, TK. You can do it; I've got you," that same voice from before advised, the same one who assured me the floor monster hadn't eaten the girl who had fallen. Panic crawled up my throat. "I've got you! Pull her in!"

"Danger! In front of me! Here!" I heard my voice saying—saw my arm reaching. What? I didn't know how to put anyone anywhere, but my hand went around her hip and guided her in front of me. I felt someone do the same to me, pulling me back to make room, and suddenly, both Danger and I were absorbed into the middle of this buzzing hive again, shoulder to shoulder, wheels centimeters from other wheels, hearing the *hum, sshwisshh, hummmmmm* of what I can only describe as a building electrical pulse of people generating what would surely result in some kind of nuclear reaction after forty laps.

"Twenty! You're halfway there; move, move! You have six minutes!"

"Let's pick it up! Dig in!"

"Hang on!"

"Fifty! Let's get fifty!"

Faster? We were going to go faster!? The floor monster continued picking people off here and there, but I told myself not to look back. The sensors must have sounded in the part of the pack just behind me, though, because another voice found its way over my shoulder, and I felt a hand grip the outside of my hip in a gesture of what I instantly knew to be assurance.

"She's good. Breathe and stay low, TK; I've got you."

But how did they know I was panicking again? How could they read my mind like that? How did they somehow jump into my skin and make my arms reach for people and pull them in front me, pull them around, and if they were falling back, tell them to hang on to me? And before they said so, how did I know it was OK for me to do the same? I don't know. I didn't know then, and I don't know now. It was just what happened in the hive.

"Thirty-eight! Two minutes!"

"Let's go! Let's go! Egg... Egg... Egg!"

"TK, just hang onto me if you have to. I gotcha."

"Pull her in—pull her in!"

"Coming up the middle!"

"Pull her in!"

All the voices became one. The hum was louder, deeper; the shoulders were closer, and suddenly, all at once, we were lower and going faster. I knew the floor monster wasn't coming for anyone anymore. I wasn't afraid of being swallowed, I wasn't afraid of tripping someone else and sending them to the belly of that beast; I wasn't in my own body anymore. We didn't have individual bodies anymore.

I heard all of them inside my head saying, "Stay low, breathe. We've got you. Six more laps, come on—come on." I wanted to say thank you. I wanted to somehow express my appreciation for this impossible connection and tell them all how grateful I felt that they let me be part of it. But I didn't have any of these words, and even if I did, no one could have heard me over the *hummm* and the *sshhwishhh* and the coach calling out, "One minute! Do! Not! Stop! Until you hear the whistle!" and "That's forty-two, push it! Push it! You only have TODAY! RIGHT NOW!"

Amazingly, I belonged in this place. I was part of this telepathic sisterhood, this radioactive beehive machine. I was older than so many of these girls, but they were looking out for me. My whole life, I wanted an older sister or brother, someone to say, "I got your back."

Someone to go first, then look over and tell me it was OK. That I could do it, too… that they would make sure of it, so all I had to do was try. And here were twenty-something of them all around me, pulling, guiding, assuring, confirming, most of the time without even saying a word.

"TIME!" we heard after the whistle blew. "Forty-eight, ladies. Nice damn job. Skate it out."

"Wooo! Nice job!"

"Hey, fresh meat! Way to go!!"

Someone smacked my butt, someone else tapped my helmet.

"Good job, TK. Way to hang."

"Yeah, girl. That's almost double the twenty-seven in five!"

More smacks. More helmet taps. I could not stop shaking.

I wanted to talk. I wanted to tell them all how amazing they were, but everything locked up in my throat. I thought it. I thought it so hard in the hopes they could still hear me like they did when we were going warp speed to outrun the clock. My face felt hot, and all I could get out was how much it felt like we were all just energy for a while. They smiled at me, not in a patronizing way or even in an amused way, but in a way that told me they knew—and now, so did I.

I can, without hesitation, say that although I've felt completely moved by the poignancy of the last few miles of a triathlon or a marathon, and although I've felt the overwhelming connection of crossing finish lines with others who have lined up and waited for the horn at my side, I have never felt so completely wrapped up in the humanity of anything as I did that day during the epic pack. I've ridden in large groups of cyclists before, but if you fall behind in one of those, you just fall behind. No one can get you there. No one can guide you into the protective nucleus of the group and shield you from anything, except maybe headwinds, and while that is indeed a lifesaving respite when you're burned, you must continue pedaling. No one can physically carry you, and you can't physically carry anyone else. Not even for a little while.

There's something to be said, I think, for the tangible exchange of momentum. In an epic pack, you transfer a little of your strength to someone else who needs it, and in kind, when your time comes—and it always comes—before you can even think to ask, others mysteriously know to transfer a little of theirs to you. In this simple action, many become one, and the truly amazing part of it all is when the pack disperses and you're slogging down water or taking off your gear, you realize that somehow, you're still one.

You're more than a team. You're more than sisters. You're the same, and you believe all the way down to somewhere deep and low that nothing and no one can break this kind of bond. It has your back every time.

HURT IN A SKIRT

Melissa Faliveno, AKA Harlot Brontë

"In the depth of winter, I finally learned that within me there
lay an invincible summer."

—*Albert Camus*

THIS IS A STORY ABOUT REDEMPTION. It starts with a woman named
Hell Kat. I first met her more than ten years ago, at a goth dance club
in Madison, Wisconsin. It was called the Inferno. This detail feels
important, because at the time, I found myself wading through my
own personal hell. I was at the club for a theme night called "Leather
and Lace," awkwardly tottering around the dance floor in ill-fitting
leather pants and PVC boots, wildly drunk, and wondering what I
was doing with my life. I had just finished college and was living in a
city just thirty miles from my hometown. I was working a shitty job.
I was depressed. I was bored. I was trying new things—like dressing
up in leather and attempting to dance to The Cure, for instance—but
nothing felt right.

I grew up in a small suburban town. The kids I knew were mostly
blonde-haired, Catholic, and conservative, the kind who dreamed of
getting married, having babies, and buying a house down the street
from their parents. I didn't know what I wanted, but I knew for sure
I didn't want that. So it came as a much-needed shock to my system
when Hell Kat strutted her way into my life. The night we met, she
walked up to me in the middle of the crowded floor and told me she
liked my glasses. She had glasses of her own, with thick red rims,
and short black hair with a streak of pink in it. She wore a leather

corset, a studded collar, and knee-high combat boots. She looked like she could kick somebody's ass.

She leaned in close and yelled in my ear above the music.

"What are you doing next Saturday?" she screamed.

"Nothing!" I screamed back.

"I'll see you here, then!" she screamed again, extracting a flyer from her bag and stuffing it into my hand. *Mad Rollin' Dolls Roller Derby*, it said. *First bout of the season. Fast Forward Skate Center.*

I held the paper, bright pink or orange and glowing under the flashing red lights of the club. I was baffled. Not just because I was holding an advertisement for a sport that I had no idea even existed, but because of those last words: Fast Forward Skate Center. It was the roller rink I'd grown up in. Birthday parties, lock-ins, Friday night dates, Sunday afternoon open skates. The disco ball, doing the limbo, that weird numbers game with the huge fuzzy dice. The most perfect cotton candy, the sixty-four-ounce Cokes, and the arcade with the Skee-ball machine that had once eaten my quarters. I'd kicked it, hard, a couple of times, with my skates on and probably swearing, until one of the workers had run over and dragged me away, thrashing and clawing. He pulled me into the back room where the skates were stored, sat me down in a plastic chair, and ordered me to take a time-out.

"Think about what you've done," he said.

"Think about what *you've* done," I sneered. I was maybe seven.

He stalked away, slammed the door, and left me alone and seething, the muffled sounds of Gloria Gaynor and skates on polished concrete outside, and row upon perfectly ordered row of ancient brown leather skates with bright orange wheels eventually lulling me into something like serenity.

When I was a kid, it became abundantly clear from an early age that I had a problem with rage. No one called it that then—"oh, you know, she has a temper," they'd say, or "someone had a tantrum at school today." But let's call it was it was: I was an angry little kid, and having grown up in the heart of the Midwest, where no one learns to appropriately express emotion, I had no earthly idea how to handle it. When I furiously strong-armed the surface of my dresser one afternoon, sending a barrage of pewter dragons and porcelain cats sailing into the wall and exploding into tiny pieces at my feet, my parents realized there might be a problem. Thus, they did what any good parents in Wisconsin would do with an aggressive child: they enrolled me in ice hockey.

And so at the tender age of eleven, I strapped on some ice skates. I was nervous; I was excited. I was ready to hit some people. But on the first day of practice, I learned the horrifying truth about the state of women's sports in the early nineties, and one of my first real life-lessons about the inequities of being a girl: In women's hockey, at least in 1993, checking—for the lay, *hitting*—was illegal. It was hockey—the brawniest, brawliest sport on earth, whose history of knock-down, drag-out fights was as rich and culturally ingrained in Wisconsin as our age-old love affair with cheese—and we weren't allowed to hit. No rib-crushing blows to the boards, no gloves-off skirmishes—the things that, to me at least, as a fiery little thing looking for a fight, made hockey most appealing. I lasted five years—on ice in the winter and in Rollerblades on Fast Forward's outdoor track in the summer—and spent more time in the penalty box than on the rink. I once even managed to get ejected for sending my stick crashing across an opponent's back. While the experience did nothing for my anger, it did teach me one thing: I loved to skate.

But I never found an outlet for my aggression. As such, from age sixteen to twenty-four, I did what Midwesterners do best: I took it all out on myself. Sure, there were a few isolated incidents during which I completely lost it in public—including one occasion, in college, when I drunkenly destroyed a wicker chair on my quiet residential street at 2:00 a.m., shrieking obscenities into the night like a mad woman, the neighbors peeking through their mini-blinds before darting back inside the safety of their homes, where this insane creature—part post-adolescent girl, part subhuman rage-beast—couldn't find them and destroy *their* wicker furniture. But mostly, I expertly learned to turn my violent fits of rage inward. This involved various behaviors that therapists would later deem "self-harm"—mostly involving intimate dates between my forearms and kitchen knives—and the ridiculous rituals that accompanied them, such as drinking whiskey alone in my room, burning a ridiculous number of candles, and listening to Johnny Cash's cover of "Hurt" by Nine Inch Nails on repeat; or reading Sartre's *Being and Nothingness* and scribbling in my journal about things like ontological relevance and how overwhelmingly hopeless life really was.

Let's just say it was a dark few years, marked by long bouts of despair, a lot of booze, a few illicit drugs, and a bunch of scars on my arms. But then came the Mad Rollin' Dolls.

On a particularly freezing night in February, I made my way to Fast Forward for the first time in over a decade. As I walked inside, I was hit with such a wave of nostalgia that I thought for a second I might pass out. The place was completely unchanged—from the brown and orange skates and cotton candy machine to the arcade, including the offending Skee-ball machine, and the sickly sweet stink of sweat, sugar, and decades-old carpet. It felt like coming home.

I sat in the front row, on the floor, along the edge of the track, which was marked by blue gaffer's tape and a string of tube lights. I was transfixed in a kind of strange meditation: rock music blasting through the rink's blown-out speakers, the lights dim, punks and crunchies and kids and families pouring through the doors and packing the rink, a PBR tallboy in my hand. A man in a giant gorilla costume stampeded through the crowd, a kind of hype man for the outcasts. For most of my life, I'd felt like a bit of a freak—in my hometown, at school, among my family and friends. Suddenly, inside the rink, I felt like I was among my own. And then I watched in awe as a bunch of strong, fast, and fearless women, including Hell Kat— who somehow made even protective eye-goggles look good—skated hard and slammed the shit out of each other. They wore torn shirts and fishnets, and sometimes tackled each other to the ground (this was 2005, after all, when the derby resurgence was in its infancy, its roots still firmly planted in rockabilly, punk, and just plain weird). Hitting wasn't just allowed; it was encouraged.

I tried out the following season. Around the same time, I began seeing a therapist. I was diagnosed with depression, generalized anxiety disorder, and something called "intermittent explosive disorder," and was prescribed a colorful cocktail of meds. With a lot of work, I eventually learned what seems obvious now: that those years of rage and self-harm stemmed from deeply rooted feelings of helplessness, and that uncanny Midwestern penchant for self-loathing. Over time, the desire to hurt myself began to diminish. I had less time, after all, to brood about the unbearable futility of life. I had other things on my mind.

I showed up at the rink on a Saturday morning, along with forty other women, for a two-day tryout. I didn't know anyone. I felt sick. I thought about getting back in my car and driving away. But I swallowed a Xanax and stayed. And I skated. And I remembered how much I loved it: how high it felt to hit a stride; how sometimes it felt like flying. After the second day, I got a call: I'd made the first cut.

Practice pressed on through the summer. There would be a final cut in the fall. I bought skates and gear. I tore up t-shirts and sheared some stockings. I cut off all my hair. I got a tattoo. I toned down the drinking. I spent my nights studying the rules and obsessing over derby names rather than despairing. I skated three times a week, and worked out on the off days. I learned how to hit—hard, smart, and controlled. I felt strong; I felt stable. I started to feel healthy. The scars on my arms slowly began to fade.

And in September, I was drafted. I could almost feel the long-tortured Melissa fall away—and Harlot Brontë, a bookish badass on eight wheels, was born.

I skated for MRD for three years. At the end of my first season, I was named Most Valuable Rookie. I played for the Dairyland Dolls, MRD's All-Star team, and was among the charter members of Team Unicorn, the league's second travel team. I was even part of one of the first-ever Pants-Off Dance-Offs.

I sat on as many committees as I could. I developed muscles I didn't even know I had. At some point during my second season, I sat on a bench by myself, lacing up my skates for Sunday morning practice, and realized that I hadn't hurt myself (or any wicker chairs) in over a year. I got banged up, for sure: My knees were two semi-permanent swollen masses of purple, yellow, and green; I had bruises and scrapes and rink rash all over my body. Sometimes the pain was so bad it hurt to walk. But somehow, it also felt good. Through self-harm, I began to realize, I had been seeking some kind of release, but had only replaced pain with more pain. The pain that roller derby brought, by contrast, felt like actual catharsis—the release of something long-held—like I was purging myself of an ancient grief and replacing it with something new, something resilient. Each time I watched the color of a bruise begin to change, I felt a little stronger.

It's been eight years since I last hurt myself (intentionally, anyway). It's tempting to say that roller derby saved my life, but I don't think that's quite true. What it did was help change the course of my life at a time when I desperately needed redirection. I met the kinds of people with whom I could truly connect—including Hell Kat, who, despite the fact that we now live a thousand miles apart, is still one of the most important people in my life. Derby taught me the importance of being part of a community, particularly when you feel most alone. It taught me how to shore up confidence where there was once only self-doubt; that it's possible to find strength when you're at your weakest.

The tagline of the Mad Rollin' Dolls is "Hurt in a Skirt." I've never really been one for skirts, but the motto still sticks with me, though I've long since retired. Through roller derby, I learned not just how to channel aggression (for the most part, anyway: I still racked up a ridiculous amount of penalties), but I also found a sense of calm. I learned that it's possible to get back up when you get knocked down—even when you get a concussion, or tear a ligament, or end up with a skate-shaped bruise blossoming on your thigh and a chunk of someone's hair in your mouth. I learned that there's an unmatched triumph in resilience. I learned that recovery is possible. That the cuts and the scrapes and even the deepest fissures will all eventually heal.

PRACTICE

Emily Udell, AKA Vivi Section

YOU GO TO PRACTICE. YOU GO to practice and wobble out onto the track. You wobble out onto the track wearing skates that are a size too big for you, a fact you won't know until two years later when you buy new ones. You go to practice. You go to practice even though you can't do T-stops, even though you can only skate twenty-three laps in five minutes, even though you have no idea what people mean when they talk about "getting a goat." You go to practice even though you have no friends there. You shop for knee socks and go to practice.

You go to practice on a former ice-skating rink with an uneven floor in a dilapidated park-district building. You go to practice in an abandoned store in a shopping mall. You go to practice in a skating rink with rain coming through the roof, with overflowing toilets, with fountains spewing toxic-tasting water and a cotton candy machine that produces a sickening smell on the weekends. You go to practice and do pacelines and pack drills and hitting exercises. You go to practice and work on endurance and communication, and you try to master the basic skills. You go to practice and wonder if you're getting sick or are just out of shape. Still. You go to practice and pass your 27 in 5.

You go to practice and fall on your tailbone while scrimmaging. You go to practice and fall, shaving off the skin where your thigh connects to the floor. You go to practice and shave off the skin in the exact same spot on the other thigh. You go practice because for some reason you feel like you should go to practice, even though you mostly suck and are afraid you will have to jam. You are not sure you even like this roller derby thing. You go to practice and picture yourself coming out of practice on a stretcher. You wonder who on your league can drive stick-shift to get your car home.

You go to practice at a hockey rink off a highway exit with terrible traffic that has a delicious floor and air conditioning. You know your skates suck now but you keep going to practice. More things make sense now. You go to practice and see someone break an ankle, the first of several breaks you will witness in the coming years. The ambulance drives off and you keep practicing.

One day you go to practice and hit your head. Hard. You miss a few practices to heal your concussion, which helps you realize you might enjoy practice more than you thought you did. That it might be something sort of essential about your life now. You go to practice and start to feel a little more comfortable when someone hands you the jammer panty. At least it doesn't fill you with dread. It might even be fun sometimes.

Finally you get new skates and they hurt so much you nearly cry by the middle of practice. You get cramps so bad you have to stop skating and physically bend your feet out of a claw position. Maybe you do cry. You wonder if you will ever be even sort of good at derby again. You go to practice. You bout. You go to practice. You bout. You go to meetings. You do committee work. You go to practice.

During your third year, your league gives you an award at the end-of-season party, which shocks and humbles you. You put the award in a frame and go to practice. The days in which you imagine leaving practice on a stretcher have become few and far between.

You go to practice because your friends will be there. You go because you never know if something might click. You might do something good. You go because there might be beers afterward. You go because practice speeds the workweek along to the weekend. You go to prepare for a bout. You go after a bout, too, to work on whatever deficiencies made you lose or to try to capture the things that helped you win, to make them second nature before they slip away. You are dog-tired, but you go to practice.

When your boyfriend dumps you, you go to practice. You go to practice even though you might cry at practice. Then you go to practice because it's the only place you don't cry. It seems possible that you can sweat out the bad thing inside you. You skate like the world is ending.

You go to practice even when you don't want to go to practice. Derby has taken over so much of your life and you wonder if there will ever be a time where you don't have to go to practice. And sometimes you don't go. Sometimes you want to stop the feeling of being caught in an endless roundelay of practice, practice, practice. So you tell yourself: fuck it. You work late. You go to the bar. You lie around your apartment in your underwear, reading magazines and watching serial dramas on your laptop. You go back to practice.

You go to practice because there's no one waiting for you at home. Or maybe you go to practice because someone is waiting for you at home. You go to practice because what the hell did you do with all your free time before you went to practice? You go to practice because you feel like hitting someone. You go to practice because you feel like being hit. No one asked you to do anything else so you go. Someone asked you to do something you'd rather do, but still you go to practice. You go to practice because you're hungry to practice. You go to practice because you're never going to be any younger than you are right now. Because your body isn't broken yet or because it isn't broken anymore. You go because it's hard to imagine life before there was going to practice. You go to practice because you want to feel like you're flying. Over and over again.

You go to practice, you go to practice. Because that's what you do.

SOBER ROLLER DERBY

She-Wrex

APRIL 13, 2010. MY FIRST DERBY BOUT.

My attention was evenly split between two things: the beer vendors and roller derby. One was a current obsession, an old friend. It was a slow and sneaky passion that had made its way into my life like a shadow. The other was a brand new fixation that I would use to help me let go of the other. As I sat in the suicide seats, trying to figure out how I could get enough money for a beer, I had no idea that I was on my final run with alcohol. I had no idea the end was near—I didn't even think I had a problem. Alcohol was my solution.

I shifted around on the cold concrete floor, asking a million questions about the game, while at the same time antsy to get something to take the edge off. Beer was $5. I didn't have $5. This was a problem. My attention was split when I saw the Blue Ridge Rollergirls roll out onto the track. I knew immediately I needed to be one of them. I made up my mind that I would be. At that moment, I had no intention of ever stopping drinking alcohol.

Fast forward a month. Life had continually edged more and more to the right, and was heading straight downhill, all of it related to drinking. Blackouts, bad decisions, dangerous situations. One drink was never enough. A nice beer after work would lead to an all-nighter. Every night.

It didn't start this way. At first drinking was for parties and weekends. Then Thursdays. Then it was a great way to unwind after work. I'd drink to celebrate, to mourn, to deal with anger, to relax, to get pumped up. It was always a good time to drink.

In June, I had new skates and I was thirty days sober. Already, I was questioning the wisdom of joining a sport in which you can win an award for partying the hardest, but it was too late; I was head over heels in love. I had zero talent, but an infallible desire to make it. My evenings, formerly spent drinking margaritas at The Lucky Otter, beer at The Wedge, or wine at home, were filled with learning to stop, fall, and move on roller skates at an outdoor hockey rink. I was out of shape and hadn't played a sport in over ten years. Sobriety rocked my world. When it settled, there stood roller derby.

At ninety days sober, I was reaching out to my newly discovered "higher power," tentatively asking whether I could possibly hold on to this tenuous sobriety while at the same time falling even harder for roller derby. Even before becoming fresh meat, I juggled fitting in AA meetings with my meager skating time. One night, I Googled "sober roller girls" in the hopes of finding that this could, indeed, be done. (I didn't find much.) That same week, I found out a skater on my team who I admired was also in recovery. It was just what I needed—a small sign to keep on keepin' on.

Today, I am a few days past twenty-one months sober. I am a different person in so many ways. I still struggle to figure out how to fit it all in, and I am slowly piecing my messy life back together. I am a full-fledged Blue Ridge Rollergirl, with my first season under my belt. I go to AA meetings three to four times a week. I hit the gym two to three times a week. We practice three times a week, and I try not to miss even one, as I have a long way to go before I am good. Sometimes, I need to miss a practice and hit an extra meeting. My coach knows, and supports me wholeheartedly.

In the beginning, I went to the afterparties, but I have found that I am not comfortable there, as much as I really want to be. There is a sense of loneliness I get from not attending as many derby functions with my team, but I realize it is just a different path I am choosing. If I want to skate, this is what I must do. A bar is a dangerous place for a newly sober alcoholic, so why risk everything I have worked so hard to earn? For me, to drink again would be to lose roller derby.

These days, I eat healthfully and I work out—something I can thank sobriety and roller derby for. The other sober rollergirl on my team relapsed, and it is very lonely sometimes, but I wouldn't trade it for all the drinks and all the amazing afterparty stories in the world. Because I know that without sobriety, I would never have been given the gift of roller derby. And while the words "sober" and "rollergirl" aren't often seen together, that doesn't mean they can't be.

ROLLER DERBY AND THE COOL GIRL

Genevieve D. Berrick, AKA *Danger (ismymiddlename)*

I ADJUSTED THE SKIRT I WAS wearing, awkwardly.

For me, sixteen meant that most things felt awkward. I definitely wasn't yet used to the body with hips and thighs I'd grown into so abruptly, even though that particularly fast-growing year had happened nearly four years prior.

So I adjusted my skirt as I walked briskly, paying attention to the platform-heeled strides I was taking. Awkward is just awkward, but the fear of being late had to be measured against the potential for even further humiliation by failing to negotiate the cracked sidewalk in these shoes.

When I arrived at the bar, it was oddly empty. Our usual meeting point, this bar had a perfect combination of no-ID-checking policy and cheap drinks that no high schooler could turn down. I was expecting to see my usual posse of girls—all similarly clad, similarly awkward—clutching the evening's first drink in their hands.

But not this night.

I spied one girl I knew at the end of the bar—she wasn't one of the usuals, but we shared some classes. I approached her. But when she saw me, instead of the usual aloof greeting typical of such a casual acquaintance, I got a full-bodied hug.

As I pulled away, feeling a little flustered, the words that were to shape the rest of my high school experience filtered past the cranking music into my ears: "I don't care what they say, I think you're lovely."

And with that sentence, I learned that my friendship with that group of women was no more.

That wasn't the first day that I felt the sting of betrayal from groups of women. It wouldn't be the last, either.

In response to this new slight, I worked to cultivate a visibly uncaring attitude—rapidly, indiscriminately finding new friends and going out even more regularly, having the best time, all the time.

And skipping classes to lock myself in the bathroom where my chest-constricting panic attacks wouldn't be seen.

I was too cool for my old friends. Too busy to notice them. Too focused on my own stuff, which was more fun than what they had to offer.

My founded fears about groups of women from the repeated bullying I'd experienced throughout my life were now disguised, enclosed in glass behind my newly minted "Cool Girl" exterior.

I "just didn't really have anything to say to other women." I was definitely just one of the guys. Only hotter, and more dateable.

Standing with my hands gripping a bat, I all but re-enacted the tennis scene from the movie *Clueless*. I didn't care about this junior high gym class. What was successfully hitting a ball going to do for my grades? This moment was irrelevant to my life; I was way too cool for this.

I looked at the teacher, barely disguising the sneer on my face. I adjusted my hands incorrectly, and looked at him with a challenging stare: "You mean like this?" The class sniggered.

When I threw the bat down, leaving someone else to face the incoming ball, I projected all of the bravado I could. What a joke of a lesson!

I needed that bravado to keep everyone from seeing that the incorrect hold I'd done was unintentional. My inability to translate spoken instruction to physical movements meant that the teacher's instructions were totally incomprehensible to me.

But being unable to understand something wasn't something that a straight-A student in an academically competitive school could risk admitting to. So bravado was the answer.

And the teacher rapidly gave up on me anyway.

Just not quite as rapidly as I'd given up on myself.

Years later, a thing called roller derby happened to my life. It was rough and tumble. It was full of badass women. And because it was 2007, it had fishnets and short skirts and a punk/rockabilly aesthetic.

The Cool Girl I'd trained myself to be was ready for this. She'd never been so ready. Hard-drinking, hard-hitting, and totally cool, roller derby was the kind of sport a woman who definitely didn't need other women's approval could really commit to.

Overlooking the fact that this was functionally a sport that required working closely with other women both on and off the track was just something that everyone else seemed to be doing. None of us "needed other women" to be here. This was a place where other Cool Girls seemed to be at home.

So I dove in headfirst.

Roller derby changed around me as the years passed.

And I changed within it.

It kept being all of the things that contact sports are and can be—challenging, full of violent moments and chaos in all of the good and bad ways. But the rules were made by the people who play it, and so they recentered them around keeping on playing—safely, while still challenging themselves as players.

Meanwhile, my struggles understanding spoken instruction weren't changing, but initially because of the social kudos for the "cool" I gained from being a part of this community, and then because

I'd fallen madly in love with the sport and its community, I stayed. I didn't let my bravado sneak in. Well, not often, anyway.

And I learned that I could stay engaged in practices if I made sure I was standing on the sidelines watching when drills started. Or in the middle of the paceline. Or not the first line-up out on the track when a new strategy was introduced.

I watched, and I learned by mentally running myself through those movements. And I started to discover I might even be okay at this roller derby thing. Eventually, I began to feel like I could even ask my coaches to teach to my learning needs.

But as always, I'd lock myself in bathroom stalls when my chest got tight again. And again. But maybe just a little less frequently now.

After thirty or so years of negotiating this body and the world around me, including four years on my high-school swim team, I finally got compliments on my roller derby technique. It was the first time I'd ever been good at a sport. The first time a positive comment had been associated with these skills.

But one comment in a lifetime of negative self-talk and other critical voices wasn't enough. Even when it was followed by one more. And another. And another.

I had a period of too many chest-tightening escapes, and as much as I wanted to be on the track, I knew I needed to be away from it for a little while.

When I returned, my muscles were soft, I was struggling with one skill and then another. The words in my head, the ones that had made me give up on myself many years before, started to gather in my brain.

I was paired with another skater in a drill. She got frustrated at me—mad at my inability to skate low. I told her I needed a little time to get back, that I was working on it.

She turned to me and asked me if perhaps I'd considered that roller derby wasn't the sport for me.

A coach heard her and said nothing, and my chest tightened again, and my own head added, "She agrees. What are you doing here?"

So I left again.

But I couldn't stay away. Roller derby had gotten inside of me. I loved it with all of my heart, even if it was a complicated relationship.

Roller derby hadn't saved my soul.

It hadn't fixed me, it hadn't cured me, it hadn't made me an athlete from nothing. And it wasn't going to. It was always more complicated than that. It still is.

But something kept ticking inside of me, and always kept me returning.

I started writing about it. Volunteering to run bouts. Showing up to practices as much as I was able. Writing some more. Taught myself to Tweetcast. Signed up for as many jobs as I could. Showed up to every game, even most of the away ones.

And writing. Always writing.

So what am I trying to say here? Where is the point?

I think it's not so neat.

There is no punch line here.

But somewhere in the midst of my growing relationship with the sport of roller derby, I forgot to be cool. I left that bravado behind because it got in the way of the learning I had to do. And I discovered that I might actually one day get to be good at a sport. And how to try to learn.

And the community seemed to embrace my writing, and me.

But I wasn't always sure. I can't always be sure. All the memories of the times when I have not been quite embraced or been outright rejected, failed or not quite measured up, are still there.

Maybe one day I won't need to find bathrooms to calm my tightening chest. Maybe one day I'll have enough positive voices, including my own, that they'll drown out the ones that gave up on me all those years ago, and many times since.

My thirteen-year-old self looked into the mirror in front of her and smiled. The smile was genuine and unforced. It had a smattering of triumph and a tiny fist-pump in it.

Face flushed with exertion, this smile was the first time I'd openly confessed to myself that I really had wanted to ace that timed run.

It might have been a boring, necessary part of Physical Education classes that came around with a pressing inevitability each year, but this year, I'd actually managed to pound the sidewalks with the top runners in my class. Had managed not to feel embarrassed by the time the teacher's assistant yelled to me.

Though bad knees kept me from running, those quiet hours of roller skating I'd been doing in my neighborhood every day, not telling anyone why I was doing them, had silently ticked up together and amounted to something. I was fitter than my bookworm self had ever been, and I could look myself in the eye.

And somewhere in the midst of those daily measured strides, somehow without my even noticing, my body learned to trust its own knowledge of skating.

And though I never admitted out loud it to anyone, least of all myself, that was the first time I thought I could do this. This sport. The very thing that became my desire to play. To keep playing.

NUMBERS

Dara Fineman, AKA Hebrew-Ham Lincoln

NUMBERS HAVE ALWAYS HAUNTED ME. AS much as I fight it, I think they always will. My weight, my dress size, my height. Three years ago, I was my heaviest number, and I couldn't walk up the stairs without getting out of breath. I felt unhealthy and I knew I needed a change. Six months later, I finally built up enough courage to start roller derby.

Roller derby has never come easily to me. It took me a year and a half to pass my skills. After my first practice, I had to sit on a heating pad at work. I cried, angry with myself and this body, and how I had let myself go so far. Each skill was a mountain. There were some practices (thanks, Coach Dad) where I had to skate off and throw up, angry at myself for not being able to keep up. But I kept going.

The daydreams started. I was going to lose the weight and become Los Angeles Model–sized. I was going to be fit and get on Team USA and meet all of my derby heroes and my life was going to turn around!

I am so glad it didn't happen that way. Yes, I lost weight, losing fifty pounds and gaining a pants size (#derbyproblems). I've met, and even befriended, many of my derby heroes! But instead of getting model-skinny (and girl, if you are, that's awesome!) I've learned to appreciate what my body does for me. My size is great for hitting on the track. I've gotten fit. I can knock out a two- or three-hour practice and make it through endurance; and although I'm primarily a blocker, I've jammed in games before. My size is OK because I am healthy and strong and I am learning to love each bump and lump as long as it benefits me on the track. Yes, I have a ways to go, but I can feel the muscles grow and it makes me so happy. This year I accomplished my biggest derby dream and made the Garden State Rollergirls Ironbound Maidens, their WFTDA charter team, and was even rostered! How's that for someone who took a year and half to pass my assessments?

This year, we started a fresh meat program at the Garden State Rollergirls, and training these girls teaches me every day. The girls (and a few boys) have different shapes and heights, and all will be useful to the team in some way, because derby is a sport for everyone.

So today I will announce my numbers to the roller derby community and world at large. As I achieve my dreams and goals on and off the track, these numbers will change. I'll get older, bigger, smaller. I'll have great days, and bad bouts, I'll have skills I struggle with, and practices where I feel my best. I will own my numbers. I will feel the power of my body, and I will, in time, be happy no matter where I land.

I urge you, in life, to be healthy, be happy, and be confident, because we deserve it. If we define ourselves by our numbers, they will define us, but life isn't really about the numbers. It's about being with people we love, doing the things we love, and being a person who does good. So I urge you to announce your number and then let it go. Isn't it time to be happy?

My name is Hebrew-Ham (Hammy) Lincoln #56, I am 4 feet 11 inches, weigh 182 pounds, and wear size 12 pants and a size 6 women's shoe. I am 26 years old and have been playing roller derby for 3 years. I have played in 1 sanctioned bout (so far)... and I am not defined by my numbers.

SHEHECHEYANU

Caroline White, AKA *Mazel Tov Cocktail*

"**BARUCH ATAH ADONAI ELOHAYNU MELECH HA-OLAM** shehecheyanu v'kiyamanu v'higeeanu lazman ha-zeh." These are the words that make up the Shehecheyanu. It is the prayer said on the first night of Chanukah to thank God for keeping you alive to reach this moment, in this season. Those words sounded a little strained coming from the group of us huddled around an electric menorah outside the med room window of a locked psychiatric ward. The nurses peered at us through the glass as we screwed in the weak blue bulb (no matches allowed). Most of us in the group were on fifteen-minute check due to our recent suicide attempts. The girl standing next to me was in a back brace from throwing herself off a bridge. We had all tried very, very hard *not* to reach this moment.

I shifted my weight back and forth in my slip-on shoes (laces were considered dangerous for me). I stared down at my hands. They were shaking heavily, as they always did. They shook from the side effects of the strong medications I had relied on most of my life to try to ward off the dark moods and dark whispers that haunted me. They shook with my anger at the world and at myself for not having a place in that world. At age twenty-four, a time when many were starting families or careers, I had very little to show for my life beyond a long list of psychiatric diagnoses and a criminal record. I had failed at everything I had tried up until that point. School. Jobs. I was a disappointment. The clinicians on my treatment team agreed that if my mental health conditions did not improve, I would die, but I was failing miserably at all the treatments they had suggested.

And, yet, something *did* change for me. I did not die. But the path that led me out of that dark place was not outlined in any treatment plan or on any prescription pad.

Fast forward three years after that long hospitalization ended and I am looking down at my hands. They are shaking heavily again, but it is not from medication, for I have had no need of that for many months. I clack my wrist guards together to try to get rid of the nerves. Tonight, instead of dark whispers in my head, I hear only the roar of the crowd. Four thousand people have filled the Asheville Civic Center this bout day to see my team compete against the Texas Rollergirls, one of the world's greatest teams and the catalyst of modern roller derby. I have earned the right to have shoelaces again; they are tightly securing the Riedell She-Devils to my feet. I press the toe stop of one on the edge of the jam line. And in the excruciating moments while I wait for the double whistle to blow, I whisper a prayer. *Thank you for this moment.* Shehecheyanu.

There is a phrase I have often heard repeated: "Roller derby saved my life." I honor that truth for others, but I like to believe that I saved my own life. For me, it is important to acknowledge that I actively made that *choice* to live in a new way, because from the time I encountered the mental health system at the age of eight, I heard repeated messages that I was fragile and "ill," that I needed to listen to professionals whose clinical expertise could diagnose and save me. I had been told I had a broken brain and that I would need to take medications for the rest of my life to deal with my problems. For a long time, I bought into the idea of the answer being in a chemical substance, using prescription and, later, street drugs to cope. I also bought into the idea that I was "sick" and a "danger to myself" and often gave up when things got hard. It took roller derby to truly wipe away that myth of "fragility."

For, while roller derby did not "save" my life, it *did* give me a life worth fighting for.

The Blue Ridge Rollergirls took my identity of "mental patient," "bipolar," "borderline," and "addict" and—many, many hitting drills and double-knee slides later—transformed it into "Mazel Tov Cocktail," The Kosher Menace... faster than a spinning dreidel!

The name Mazel Tov Cocktail was actually suggested to me during my fresh meat days by a woman called Scarriet Tubman, who skated for the River City Rollergirls. Her number was "40+1", in reference to the promise of forty acres and a mule that has yet to be delivered to the survivors of slavery. I told Scarriet that I loved her name because it acknowledged two powerful identities in one—as rollergirl and as African-American woman. I told her that, although I lived in the staffed group home, I also had a volunteer job at the Asheville Jewish Community Center to provide structure to my days. This Jewish identity was the one thing I had pride in.

In fact, some of my fondest derby memories are the ones where my two identities intersected. The round challah I brought to practice on Rosh Hashanah. The custom Star of David helmet cover my Dad had made for me to wear in games. I always laugh about the time when, after I had earned a place on the training committee, I created a Seder-like practice for Passover. The jammer versus pack drill was changed into "Plagues vs. Pharaoh," with ten defensive skaters. I remember my teammate really getting a kick out of being "Death of Livestock," mooing with each hit. There was also a "Parting of the Red Sea" drill where skaters had to act quickly to move through a momentarily split pack. We had a blast, but it was also meaningful to re-enact a story of deliverance from Mitzrayim (the narrow place) with these women who had been critical to me finding my own freedom.

That day in the halfway house, when I registered the name Mazel Tov Cocktail on www.twoevils.org at Scarriet's suggestion, I chose to make my number 18. In Hebrew, each letter has a numerical equivalent, with the number 18 spelling "chai," the Hebrew word for life. Here I was, the person who had been suicidal for years and years, literally choosing "life." I committed to doing something different.

Choosing to live a new life, to step into a new identity, is never easy. Thankfully, roller derby gave me more than just a life worth fighting for—it also provided me with the tools to prepare for that fight: community, teamwork, physical strength, a sense of humor, financial responsibility, and even the re-interpretation of spiritual practices to make them my own. These tools served me better than any drug I had ever tried to help me deal with life. Roller derby also provided me with real, authentic support. Support that was not limited by my health insurance. It is a funny thing, but the greatest healers I have ever known have all knocked me on my ass. They had names like Sugar Magmaulya, Riot Crrrls, She-Wrex, Caslamity Jane, Moong Chi and Rigor Morticia. These women did not give a shit what my psychiatric diagnoses were and certainly did not walk on eggshells around me, as others in my life had. They provided healing by treating me like a fellow warrior.

When I first joined the team, so timid and ashamed about the fact that I lived in a staffed group home, these women were larger-than-life heroes to me. But then after joining their ranks, I learned a transformative lesson. The strongest women I had ever known were also deeply vulnerable. They had survived—*were* surviving—their own struggles. Addiction, deep feelings of worthlessness, prejudice, trauma, and debilitating physical conditions were some of the struggles that they, too, had been told were life-long. The best pivot on the team had once been told she would never walk again. They were not heroes because they were disciplined and fearless skaters: they were heroes because of what they had transcended and endured before they ever even stepped onto the track.

Most importantly, never once was I made to feel bad for falling. And I fell a lot. I fell over and over again, and not just in games, and not just in the literal sense. I made mistakes. But in roller derby, there is no shame or judgment in falling, for it is understood that some falls cannot be avoided. All that matters is how quickly you can get back up and re-enter the game. In roller derby, this ability to get back up from a fall is called "recovery." I can still hear the words echoing in my head sometimes, since I heard them so often in those early days: "Good recovery, Mazel! Good recovery!"

I still frequent the psychiatric units in the area where I live. Nowadays, I visit them in my role as peer advocate for the Western Mass Recovery Learning Community. I go to hang out with folks, build community, and facilitate groups for the "Hearing Voices Network" and "Alternatives to Suicide." I am open about the fact that these experiences, and psychiatric hospitalization, are part of my own story. I share my vulnerabilities and my strengths. I honor and affirm the strengths I witness in others. I do not use the clinical language of illness. No one arrives at long-term hospitalization because their lives have been easy, so together we look at the tools that have helped them survive until this moment and find ways to expand upon them. I am always adamant that I am not there to "save" anyone or tell anyone what they should do. The answers and the path are already inside of them, written upon their hearts. There is no shame in falling down. However, it is totally up to them to rise up again and to take the first step back in. Everyone is the jammer of their own life. I cannot score the points for you—I am just here to offer a few assists and maybe make a few holes for you to skate through.

I remember I even attended a roller derby newbie night with someone who I supported. This person was someone whose desire to take their own life had kept them hospitalized for long periods. Skating with them around that track, so far from a locked unit, was an amazing moment, an affirmation of life and freedom. Ultimately, this person's unique path out of the darkness was to join a rugby team and find a gender expression that resonated with their inner self. It was an honor to walk with this person for a while on their path.

Next week, I will once again light the first candle of Chanukah and say the Shehecheyanu. It will be the eighth Chanukah since the one I observed during that last long psychiatric hospitalization. I will smile and shed a few tears over all that has happened in my life that has allowed me to reach this moment. I will think of roller derby. And then I will light one small candle, to make this world a little brighter.

MUST BE THIS TALL TO RIDE

Boo LaLa

STEREOTYPICALLY, ROLLER DERBY HAS BEEN A sport where "larger-than-average" women are appreciated. Their ginormity is celebrated, and their confidence is built. What's really cool is, like so many things in derby culture, it goes both ways.

I'm tiny. I know a lot of women will say that about themselves, especially when surrounded by many derby players who could easily rival NFL linebackers; however, a woman of 5'2"—the high cut-off for RollerCon's Team Shortbus—towers above me. Weighing in at just over 100 pounds, I might possibly hit the five-foot mark with my size two skates and extra-small helmet on.

When I discovered derby, despite my friends and family telling me, "You're too little," and "You're going to get crushed," I decided to give it a try. I hadn't been on quad skates since I was five years old, but it seemed like a great challenge. Everyone in the derby world was so accepting of differences in age, sexuality, lifestyle, and everything else; size seemed to be no exception.

As a former gymnast and life-long athlete, I was already in decent shape. My endurance wasn't bad, and it didn't take me long to become pretty agile on my skates. I participated in scrimmages, and quickly became involved in my league. It was true that, when hit hard, I tended to fly farther than most—sometimes literally through the air. Hitting larger women was almost out of the question. Yet, coming up through subpool, I didn't feel impeded by my size.

My first season as a team player, I was pulled off the track every time my team skated short. I was told I was too small to be an effective blocker. My turn was skipped each time we had a power jam. I was told I was too small to be an effective jammer. Even so, by the end of the season, I learned to play a smart game, with blocking stats that rivaled many of my teammates, and I worked my way up to being one of the highest-scoring jammers on my home team.

I tried out for our All Stars. I didn't make the team. While inexperience was a factor, the number-one reason I was given for not making All Stars was that I was too small. Later in the year, I made the team. Under the same pretext of being too small, I was never played.

It was disheartening, to say the least. What could I possibly do about my stature? Getting taller obviously wasn't an option, and getting fatter didn't seem like a good plan either. Hearing "you're too small," began to take a huge toll on my mental game. Additionally, I became incredibly bitter toward everyone who could give me few other legitimate reasons for not letting me have a chance to play. Derby was supposed to be a place that was accepting of everyone without prejudice against things like age, sexuality, or size.

Instead of letting disappointment defeat me, I decided to stop feeling sorry for myself, channel my frustration, and become the derby player who couldn't be denied. I wasn't going to let being small mean I didn't deserve to be on the track. Aside from putting in countless hours on skates, I discovered cross-training. For many in the sport today, this might be an "uh, duh!" statement. But derby wasn't always about athleticism—not really. In fact, I had joined derby to avoid the gym. I thought it was enough to learn the skills and know the game.

I've been working out with a personal trainer three times a week on top of going to derby three to four days a week; I've upped my strength and endurance, and I've gained weight—mostly muscle, as my body fat percentage continues to drop. Jamming is still a lot of extra work to fight through walls of bigger blockers; however, I no longer go flying with every hit, I can push longer, and my recovery time has shortened substantially. Blocking is still challenging when going up against jammers twice my size, but now I am more solid,

I can hold blocking positions longer, and I can control my body in order to better control my opponents.

Of course, another year of experience to hone my skating skills and let the game sink into my muscles and brain has been beneficial. Cross-training has helped me regain some confidence, become a stronger skater, and be a better derby player. Many of those who said I was too small no longer skate with our league; however, a few of them have skated against me recently and have noticed a huge difference in my game.

I went from being pulled from every jam to skating more than fifty percent of the jams of most home-team games; from not getting to play any position to becoming a triple-threat; from being told I was the weakest skater on the track to earning multiple game MVP awards; from not being on a single game roster to being the captain of our All-Star team; from being told I would die against bigger women to being a co-ed starter; and from being told I was too small to be effective to making a national tournament All-Star team largely because I was able to use my small stature to my advantage.

I am still tiny, but now I take up more space on the track (and, I like to think, in life)—a little in my physical being, but mostly in the presence I exude.

Being little is only an issue if you let it be. It doesn't matter how young or old, how fat or thin, how tall or short you are; you've got to work hard, overcome your disadvantages, and learn to use your assets. Of course I still have a lot of progress to make and several more goals to accomplish, but nothing is impossible. In derby, even the smallest people can do big things.

THERE'S NO CRYING IN ROLLER DERBY

Brandy Rettig AKA Rettig to Rumble

I WAS STANDING IN THE MIDDLE of the derby track, frozen with fear. A tiny little sliver of an eight-year-old girl, clad from head to toe in blinding pink-ruffled cuteness, lay on the sport court ten feet away from me. She was crying. I had seen her fall, but it didn't look bad. I surveyed her from my safe distance. Her derby pads looked like inner tubes around her toothpick-sized elbows and knees, the giant white-water-rafting kind of inner tubes. I thought I might need to climb aboard those inner tubes to save myself from drowning as the rising river of her tears swelled my way.

"Do something, Rettig!" I demanded of myself. Up to this point, my experience with children had been limited to proudly displaying my superior bodily-function noise-making skills. Pressing my lips into the crook of my elbow and ripping out a mockery of a colossal wet fart never failed to crack up the little boys and slingshot me squarely into the "cool adult" category among them. But I had a feeling my best natural talent would not go over so well with the pink and pretty of this sobbing little fallen angel.

Then it popped into my head—the phrase I'd heard repeated hundreds or more times over the years: "There's no crying in roller derby!"

I almost did it. I almost hollered it out. But at the last second, I clamped my mouth shut, imprisoning my tongue behind the jail-cell doors of my teeth. I'm so glad I did, because in an instant, I had a shocking realization. That statement—that "I'm such a tough roller derby girl that I don't cry" declaration—is a lie. And all at once, the memories of my own derby tears came to me in a flash (flood).

I cried tears of joy at the weddings of two of my most dear derby teammates and friends. I cried tears of despair when I realized I could not attend the far-off wedding of another of my closest derby teammates. I then cried again when I saw how beautiful and happy she was in the photos.

I cried (secretly, at night, under the covers) at the pain in my throbbing knee where my mangled PCL poked and pulled on seemingly every raw nerve in my body. I cried more than once when the unimaginable heaviness of derby drama crushed down upon me from every conceivable angle. I cried when a former derby teammate and friend made the choice to end our friendship.

I cried when my teammate told me she was pregnant. And I cried again a few years later when her sisters told me the same thing. I also cried when all of their babies were born.

I cried when the team I captained won an intraleague championship. I cried when a girl so new to derby (and so frightened of it that she was almost literally green), stumbled up to me and stammered, "You're my derby idol."

I cried when a beloved derby friend, skater, and announcer described to me in the most raw and shockingly uncensored way how she was savagely attacked and beaten by a group of animalistic thugs.

I cried when I laughed so hard with my teammates that I could no longer make noise or even breathe, and all I could muster were the hot tears that streamed down my cheeks as we all rolled on the floor, gasping for breath.

I cried when I watched a team of my very best derby friends win the WFTDA Championship. I cried when my team went all the way to the WFTDA Championship game. Twice. I cried when my team lost the WFTDA Championship. Twice. I cried when I watched my teammate win WFTDA MVP. I cried when I tried to thank my coach for all the opportunities I had been given.

Like clockwork, every time my plane pulls away from the terminal after Nationals, I cry a little as I reflect back on the experience I have just shared with my derby family from around the country, and the sad knowledge that it will likely be another year before we get to do it all over again.

Some of the most joyful, most sad, most frustrating, most fulfilling, and most moving moments of my life have happened in roller derby. While I may have casually explained away the tiny droplets of water that escaped from my clenched tear ducts as the ever-present Seattle rain on my face, flecks of volcanic ash in my eyes, a rogue eyelash declaring war on my cornea, uncontrollable raging allergies, or an unfortunate reaction to those chopped onions on some hot dog I was eagerly shoving into my face, the truth is, I was probably crying. And it was probably because of roller derby.

Snapping out of my misty haze, I sucked in a deep breath and began to skate towards the wet-faced heap of a cutie-pie Tootsie Roller crumpled up on the derby track. But before I could reach her, something wonderful happened. Still crying, she rose up on her own, found the tiniest space of skin on her forearm between those hulking pads on which to wipe her nose, and quickly skated off (pink ruffles and all) sniffling, ready to get back at it again.

That little girl owned her tears. They made her tough. They helped her continue on. She showed me that, yes, there is crying in roller derby. And that little girl proved that crying doesn't make you any less of a badass.

A BOUT OF MIDLIFE

Linda Rice

OVER A YEAR AGO, I BECAME what is known in the derby world as "fresh meat." John McCain said, when he was called "The Comeback Kid" in the 2008 Republican primary, "At my age, I don't think I can be called the *anything* kid!" I don't often feel like a kindred spirit with old Republicans, but I get it, Senator. I found it difficult to think of myself as fresh anything at forty-six. But there I was, skating around the rink with a bunch of twenty-somethings.

In some ways, I had a leg up on them. Not so much my age, but my generation makes me more at ease on eight wheels. I first strapped metal skates over my Buster Brown shoes around age five. I spent Friday nights with the Camp Fire Girls at the Ballaroo skating rink in Medford, Massachusetts. When Rollerblades came into fad, I bought my first pair in 1992. Throughout the years, I found comfort and relaxation with wheels on my feet and ear buds in my ears. Even in Saudi Arabia, where the security of a self-contained compound allowed it, I would go out Rollerblading at 2 a.m.

I've never really had a "thing"—you know, something to challenge myself, a goal to work for. Exercise was moderately enjoyable, but mainly done with the incentive of not becoming fatter than I already am. My husband ran a marathon a few years ago. He decided to do it one day, read *Marathon Training for Dummies*, started with a few 5Ks and a half-marathon, then finished the Disney Marathon just after Chip. (Or was it Dale?) Over the years I've wondered, why isn't there a "thing" for Rollerblading? They have road races, bike races, and triathlons. I had always wished there was a 10K for Rollerbladers. Of course, I had heard of roller derby, but not as something I thought anyone could actually just do.

You gotta love Facebook. I know some of us are getting less social because of technology, but I'm a busy mother of two. There's no way I'd be able to keep in touch with everyone I'd like to in real life. One such person was Meghan, who shared one of those little photo/jokes you see on Facebook all the time. Now I can't remember exactly what it was, but I remember the words "roller derby" and "fishnet stockings." I messaged her, "Can just anyone do that?" When she said yes, I think I sent another one, "I mean really, just *anyone?*"

So there we were at the "Meat and Greet." We spoke to a few women from the league and skated in circles to Top 40 hits with the bass way too loud. As we were discussing, "What do you think?" "Should we?" a woman skated by us in booty pants and fishnet stockings. We looked at each other and simultaneously declared, "We are totally getting fishnet stockings!"

Since that night, my life has been filled with failed assessments, chronic pain, and a drawer full of fishnet stockings I've never worn. So why, you ask, after the glamour wore off, am I still here?

For months in the early days, my fellow fresh meats and I would gaze adoringly at the seasoned skaters doing hockey stops and two-footed jumps "Won't it be wonderful," we would think, while skating with the speed and stability of a young buck (if that buck were Bambi walking on ice), "when we can have that skill and confidence." Then one of the travel team players said something that took me by surprise. "The hardest thing about being at this level," she mused, "is that you have to try to find more challenges."

The experience and wisdom of age brings many gifts to the track. Speed is not one of them. At my first practice with the full league as a Level One, we did an exercise called a paceline. All skaters are in a line keeping up with the woman in front of her. There are various drills that can be run, such as having the back skater sprint to the front, or weave in and out of the other women. We were doing a "hitting" line, where the back skater weaves and hip-checks each woman in the line. Trying to keep up with the line was struggle enough. Trying to keep up while being slammed every five seconds was almost impossible. Every time I took my eye off the skater in front of me, I slowed down or veered off, creating a Grand Canyon–sized gap in the paceline. When it was my turn, trying to skate up in the line, losing momentum to hit and still passing the other women proved too much. I struggled to make it halfway before dropping out all together.

It was humbling at a time in life when I was starting to feel pretty comfortable. I've been a midwife for sixteen years, and while dealing with human beings is always a new experience, I don't break a sweat at the start of every call shift anymore. I am mercifully out of the dating scene, and done with the turnstile of new men for whom I suck in my stomach and pretend I don't fart.

I still feel like a terrible mother most days, but I would argue that being a "good mom" is an unattainable goal. Before all the moms out there threaten to stab me with toddler-safe forks and splash me with non-toxic craft paint, let me explain. You can be a good mom, but you never get to feel good about your parenting skills. When my son was born, I had the typical fear of dropping him. What's funny about that is I have held hundreds of babies over the years, sometimes with one hand, often sloppy wet. I got the diaper-change, breast-feeding thing down, and guess what? He started eating solids and sitting up. Every time we would screw up with Evan, we would take solace in the fact that we'd get it right for the next one. Then, after fumbling through parenting for twenty-two months, along came Lily: the second child, not the practice model. After a few months, we made the most horrific discovery—she was like this whole different person! So although motherhood keeps me on my toes, it doesn't feel like such an extraordinary challenge because it's an experience of humility and self-doubt that I share with most women on the planet.

So yes, for the first time in a while, outside my home, I feel like a complete moron! Why would I want to put myself through this? I guess for the same reason I eat vegetables and drive the speed limit (or the Boston version thereof). It doesn't always feel good, but it's good *for* me. Besides the benefits of physical exercise, researchers found that trying new things and having a variety of experience makes one retain positive memories and minimize negative ones. Another article I found said that taking in new information actually makes our brains perceive time as going slower. Not a bad benefit to have at a time when I not only feel over the hill, but racing down the other side at break-neck speed.

I'll let you in on another secret of feeling comfortable: insecurity is rare, but so are meaningful victories. I've climbed to the top of the ladder I had designed for myself—I became a midwife, got married, and had kids. There may be more to life for some, but when I was mapping out my goals, this was the "win" space on my game board. Roller derby has helped me discover that I'm not ready to stop playing the game yet.

One more word about the over-forty crowd in derby. I've spoken about my struggles and gains, but why would a league want to train a middle-aged, overweight mother of two with the hopes of getting a player who may work her way up to mediocre? Besides regaling the young girls with stories of the roller-disco years gone by, what do I bring to the track? I've asked myself that many times. My only answer is: I'm there. I mean really *there*. I don't have the luxury of taking a break from derby and coming back when it's more convenient. I know there are over-fifty players, but as a realist, I know I won't be one of them. Every practice, every scrimmage, and every bout is precious time. I'm not the best player, but I'm all in. No one on your track will huff and puff through the next blocking drill or paceline with more enthusiasm than the woman who knows her next injury will likely be her last.

Over the last year, I've been trying to read stories and watch movies about over-the-hill achievements. There's a line in *Cinderella Man* that I say to myself every practice. It's not from the latter half of the movie, when the character is in the midst of a victorious comeback. It's in the middle, when he's competing at a small-time fight, and his coach asks, "Anyplace else you'd rather be?" My answer is always the same: "Not tonight."

ROLLER DERBY SAVED MY SOUL: OVERCOMING DEADLY CYNS

Katrina Swirko

"ROLLER DERBY, HMM?" MY ONCOLOGIST LOOKED up skeptically from his laptop.

"Yeah," I replied, shrugging. "It's fun. It's something to do."

It was the fall of 2008, and I was sitting in an office at a cancer center in New Hampshire, discussing my recent diagnosis—a rare blood disorder called PNH. I had just graduated from college, I was unemployed, and now I was looking at a future of sterile rooms, IV tubes, and little white pills. When you've reached that kind of rock bottom and you're handed a roller derby recruitment flyer, you say "What the hell?" and give it a shot.

My oncologist, on the other hand, wasn't thrilled when I told him about my new hobby. "You get knocked around a lot?"

"It's full-contact, so yes. Kind of similar to hockey."

"Well, we won't be able to put a port in your chest if you're going to get all…knocked around," he said it patronizingly, gesturing with one hand while typing notes. "They'll have to poke around in your arms every time you come in for an infusion."

"That's OK."

"Are you sure? A port would be much easier. But you'd have to stop the roller derby."

"I'll deal for now. As soon as it gets to be too much, I'll quit and we'll put in a port."

"You're doing really well right now with the treatment," he told me. "That's normal. But statistically, it won't last. Over time, things will get harder."

He didn't have to tell me—I knew all the facts well. What little was known about the rare disorder fit onto the small pamphlet my oncologist had handed me after months of biopsies and blood tests. It read like an animal fact brochure from the zoo. The average life expectancy for a PNH patient is ten to fifteen years after diagnosis. Since it seemed it would only be a matter of time before my body succumbed to the disease, roller derby was a way to amuse myself in the meantime.

Despite the cool reception from the doctor, I went back to practice the following Saturday morning. I was unsteady on my loaner skates—white artistic boots with bright pink outdoor wheels. We didn't have a real practice space on the weekends, but that didn't deter us; we did blocking drills in empty parking lots and learned our stops on the rough pavement of the millyards. Generally speaking, we had no idea what we were doing.

Our coach and league owner did seem to know. Standing there in roller skates and a mink coat, she was the perfect embodiment of the sport at the time. "All right, girls," she said, cigarette pursed between her lips, "it's time for some blocking drills."

I was paired up with a teammate who had brought her two boys along, a normal occurrence in a sport that accepted middle-aged mothers as well as ill twenty-somethings. I crouched down nervously, bracing myself for a block, but she stopped suddenly to scream across the parking lot, in the way only a mother can, "WE DON'T URINATE ON THE TRAIN TRACKS!" She shook her head, rolling her eyes, and offered me a quick apology before laying me out on the ground.

Thirty percent of PNH patients die within the first five years of diagnosis. I was sprawled on the ground, feeling a combination of after-effects from the hard hit and the weight of medical statistics that always lingered in my mind, especially when I fell down in derby.

In the doctor's office, in the pamphlets, they told me all the things I could no longer do. They spelled out my future for me and wrote their orders for medication. But roller derby was different. Roller derby knocked me down to the hard concrete, stood over me, and said, *Now what are you gonna do?*

The skin on my thigh stung from the pavement, and all my muscles ached from fatigue. I felt the autumn air heaving in and out of my lungs. I felt a single drop of sweat travel down the side of my face. I felt my blood pulsate through my veins. I was alive, despite the disease. But it was not PNH I was fighting; it was cynicism. It was the statistics and the experts and the peanut gallery that I needed to overcome. I figured if I was going to stubbornly believe in something, it may as well be conducive to living a full life.

At that moment, I made the choice to stand up. I would continue to make that choice for seven more seasons and counting. I would go on to play for other leagues, against some of the best teams in the sport. When I didn't have the odds or the doctors in my favor, I had roller derby to give me courage and resolve. And when I felt tired or symptomatic on the track, I had PNH to remind me why I needed to play.

"Are you OK?" my teammate asked as I brushed myself off.

"Yeah," I replied. "Let's try that one again."

EAST COAST DERBY EXTRAVAGANZA: A LOVE LETTER

Jasmine Facun AKA *Sweet N. Lowdown*

I STARED AT THE BIG BLUE plus symbol, half-expecting it to disappear. It just stared back.

Pregnant. Again?

How could this happen? Well, I knew how it had happened, but really—*How could this happen?*

A familiar knot bubbled up into my throat as I tried to unravel a thousand tangled emotions.

Am I happy?

Well, yes, I suppose I am. Levi will share his childhood with a sibling. Another baby to hold in my arms. Oh, I just know it's a girl...

Yes, yes, I am happy.

C'mon, admit it, even if it's only to yourself: Aren't you just little disappointed? Just maybe?

Sigh. Yeah. The timing could have been better. The interleague season is just starting and I'm going to miss all of it. I wonder if my team will still want me as their captain...

Don't be silly, Jasmine; it's just derby. But this... this is a new life.

But we have a bout coming up and then there's that new invitational in Philly in a few weeks! Hmmm... I must only be four weeks along and just happened to catch it early. Most women wouldn't even know by now. Maybe I can still bout just for a little while...

No, no, you're right. I can't do that. Stupid idea.

A baby! Again!

It took me all of a minute to get over the shock and then fly downstairs to tell my husband the news.

The next month was easy enough. In fact, it was almost too easy. I still didn't have any morning sickness and hardly even felt pregnant. My team took it well and decided to keep me on as the All-Star captain and League Head Coach even though I was out of commission. We won our bout, and I learned that coaching from the sidelines is really just code for jumping up and down and whooping like a maniac. Sure, I was bummed about not skating, but my absence was an opportunity for a brand new rotten meat, T. Rex YaFace, to don the jammer star, and the girl showed a ton of promise. The excitement of having another baby had taken over and I was already falling in love with that little morsel of cells growing inside me.

It was the morning of Friday, February 9, 2007, when I noticed a familiar stain of red. I stared at it for a few minutes, taking more time than necessary to process the very obvious fact that I was bleeding. I stifled the panic creeping into my thoughts and calmly called my doctor. I was eight weeks pregnant and my first appointment wasn't scheduled until the following Monday, but the doctor told me to come in. My husband and I breathed a sigh of relief when the doctor found our baby on the ultrasound and we smiled as we listened to her little hummingbird heartbeat for the first time.

I made a quick post on my league's forum when I got home and they assured me that bleeding in pregnancy is common and offered anecdotal evidence of perfectly healthy babies being born after not-so-perfect pregnancies. I felt somewhat assured, wanting to hope.

But the bleeding didn't stop.

I cried through the weekend, and through my doctor's visit Monday morning when that cold jellied wand searched across the skin of my womb for a miracle, only to find nothing.

Empty. And just like that, she was gone.

I took the day to mourn and thanked my friends and family for their awkward condolences. *Well, at least you weren't further along... It's just nature's way... I am so sorry...* They were all well-meaning but what does someone say in a situation like this? The baby was gone almost as quickly as she—it—had come. More than anything, I wanted to erase the memory, the pain. I deleted all mention of the pregnancy on social media and assured my friends that I was fine, that yes, it was early in the pregnancy, just one of those things; it happens, after all, and that I was ready to continue with my own life. Just, please, I can't bear the pity.

Saturday morning at the rink was colder than I had remembered. In fact, it was freezing. I kept my giant winter coat on over my pads and joked self-deprecatingly with friends as we started warm-ups. *See? I'm okay!*

To my disappointment, I felt sluggish and out of shape. Tired. I hadn't realized how much the pregnancy had already taken its physical toll on my body in two short months. In the weeks before the pregnancy, I had been working on breaking a personal time-trial record and was only one second away from my goal. Now I feared it would take much longer than two months to catch up again. This thought was terrifying, not because I would have to rebuild my endurance but because I didn't think I could handle the daily reminders of a body that was recently pregnant, and then wasn't.

I stuffed those feelings down and struggled through practice.

One week later, I received a call. My husband, Rich, was in the ER. He had hurt his foot skateboarding and didn't know what the damage was yet, only that it was bad.

We soon learned just how bad. This was no six-week ordeal. He had dislocated all five metatarsals of his left foot and broken four of them. He would need at least two months of bed rest, several surgeries, and eight months on crutches. He would need constant care. If he wanted a drink, someone would have to fetch it. If he wanted food, someone would have to make it. If he wanted to move at all, someone would have to help him.

Until August.

When I would have been due to have my baby.

I wanted to laugh at the ironies of life and how darkly appropriate it was that instead of caring for a baby around the clock, I would instead be caring for a full-grown man.

The world was spiraling out of control and I needed air fast.

So I left.

It was the weekend of the first-ever East Coast Derby Extravaganza in Philadelphia, then affectionately known as "ECE." Our league, the Dominion Derby Girls, had originally planned to play sanctioned games, but ever struggling with numbers, we were forced to pull out of our bouts and instead opted for a single challenge bout with another team. Before the pregnancy, I had planned to attend ECE—er, "ECDX"—and had even been invited to compete in a few challenge bouts, including one with Team Awesome. Of course, I had since declined all my derby obligations, but I made a last-minute decision to travel to Philadelphia with the team and skate in Dominion's one challenge bout.

It was mid-March and unseasonably cold. In fact, the farther north our van inched, the more treacherous the journey became. Ice and snow blanketed the highway and we traveled at a snail's pace, finally reaching the designated derby hotel several hours later than expected. Tell-tale signs of derby littered the otherwise-nice hotel: women at every turn, in the elevators, in the bar, in the lobby, all donning derby. We had arrived.

I had been put into a room with another skater who had decided to come along at the last minute—T. Rex YaFace—and we bonded over our shared hotel-bed sleep number. She proposed to me a month later and we've been derby wives ever since.

The next morning, the venue was relatively quiet. Teams were still trickling in or completely stuck in travel because of the snowstorm. There were warnings not to walk under the outside awnings because of icicles and falling snow. An entire row of cars in the parking lot was demolished by snow that avalanched down from the venue's roof. There was tension in the air and some fear that the weekend would be a bust.

We skated our challenge bout with eight skaters and lost. As I was removing my gear on the sidelines, someone frantically tapped my shoulder and asked if I could fill a spot in a challenge bout. Half of Team Awesome was still stuck in transit and they needed skaters—now. I hurriedly put my skates back on with a twinge of adrenaline coursing through my veins, grabbed a jersey from the pile of no-shows and smiled. Roxy Rockett. She wouldn't mind.

It was chilly in the venue and it felt good to sweat. By the end of the two bouts, I felt...better? It was as if my heart, which had been left as cold and cracked as the weather outside, was thawing with each lap and every hit.

And so I skated.

The rules for joining challenge bouts were lax that first year and I happily admit that I fully exploited them. I hopped from one challenge to the next all day, not caring what team I was on or whose jersey I wore, whether I jammed or blocked. I just wanted to roller skate. I hadn't known it until then, but I was furious and I was going to leave it on the track. There were very few fans or skaters in attendance that weekend, but I was skating for no one but myself. With each jam, the events of the previous month were swept away under my wheels, sweated out in buckets of perspiration, delivered into each johnny crash. That weekend was my therapy, my absolute catharsis.

As I write this, my pads are in the washing machine, and I'm making mental notes on what I need to pack. We're heading to ECE—er, *ECDX*—tonight. I've returned almost every year since that first one, and each year I'm awed by the growth of both the event and the sport. It truly is something to behold. And even though the organizers have (wisely) moved the weekend to June, with pool parties and food trucks, and even though the event has become more and more professional, and even though the skating has become so much more spectacular, I don't think any year, for me, will compare to that first year in 2007, when a weekend in Feasterville, Pennsylvania, gave me something I couldn't give myself—healing. So thank you, East Coast Derby Extravaganza. You will always have a special place in my heart. I'll see ya soon.

A WALK IN THE MOUNTAINS

Kamikaze Kitten

OUR LIFE IN ROLLER DERBY HAS always reminded me of a walk in the mountains. A challenging journey that takes us above the humdrum world. An all-encompassing adventure. We can look around on this journey and see others walking alongside us, some ahead, some behind, some on other mountain slopes altogether. Our friends and our enemies all walking together, and a thousand others we don't even know.

Some have been walking for years. They walk because they simply want to walk.

Some have just started their journeys and are jogging to get as far as they can, to catch up to those they see ahead of them, full of fresh energy and not yet settled into their steady pace.

Some drop in two miles ahead of us and it doesn't seem fair.

Some run a few paces, then have a little rest, then run a few more, flip-flopping between wanting to get to the top and doubting it's worth the effort.

Some hang out by the lodge, not really on the journey at all, but enjoying the company of those setting out or heading back.

There are those who walk because they have to get to the top, only to crest every peak to be met with another, higher and threatening more effort than the last. Each milestone becoming disappointment at not reaching the top yet, rather than a benchmark of achievement.

There are those who find that they've been walking for so long that they don't know how to do anything but walk. Their beards have grown long, they have nothing but the mountain left and they don't even know if they like walking anymore—it is just who they have become.

There are those who chase the walkers ahead, desperate to be where they are.

And those who help the walkers behind so that their journey will not be a lonely one.

There are those who stumble on the mountain and get hurt, and can no longer walk any further.

And those who decide to set up camp right where they are because right there is the best it will be.

There are those who walk the shortest distance but with the biggest heart, and truly double in stature.

There are those who find themselves, and even those who lose themselves.

But the big secret is that there isn't a top, there is just the journey. We're all on it for different reasons, and we'll all end it when it is time, and start a new walk over on those other mountains in the distance.

NEVER SKATE WITH SCISSORS AND OTHER ADVICE FOR SURVIVING ROLLER DERBY

Brandy Rettig, AKA Rettig to Rumble

FUTURE ROLLER DERBY SKATERS, IF I had only one piece of advice to offer regarding your upcoming derby career, it would be this: Invest in a good bra. Regardless of the size of your chest or budget, do yourself this favor and indulge. Like a loyal friend, a good bra will support you when you need it most, it will lift you when you're feeling down and it will help you stand firm in the face of your adversaries. Treat this bra with care. Never put it in the washing machine. Do not sleep in it. Some day, when you look back on the photos of yourself skating, you'll thank me.

As for the rest of it, advice for the world of derby, I only have a random selection of miscellaneous pieces of guidance that I have been able to cobble together over the thousands upon thousands of laps I have skated. Some of these "pearls of wisdom" were learned the hard way, some were given to me by others (whether I wanted them or not), and some I admittedly stole from those much wiser than myself. But, my young derby sisters, what is mine is yours. Like a heaping pile of discarded garments at a clothing swap, feel free to take the sparkly ones that catch your eye and throw back those that don't quite fit.

Without further ado, and in no particular order:

Enjoy this experience. It will be over far sooner than you can imagine. Hold fast to the friends you make. Even though you can't conceive of it now, they will be there for you once you no longer compete. One day in the not-so-distant future you will sit with them and absentmindedly twitch your feet as if you are skating as you recount the lovingly embellished "remember the time when..." stories.

Make an effort to get to know your teammates. They will become like family for this brief period of your life. Like family, regardless of your differences, they will have your back and you will have theirs.

Do not judge yourself based on the abilities of others; it's not fair to anyone. Your talents are unique and every bit as important to this sport as everyone else's.

Push yourself. The amount you are able to achieve will shock and amaze you.

Don't limit yourself. If you need to throw up, do it. Then get back on the track and finish your laps.

Help out the new girls. You do not need to act superior to them—they already idolize you.

Get low.

Accept compliments. But don't let them swell your head. Insults will come your way. They will probably bother you for a little while. That's normal. Do not brood over them longer than is necessary. Throw them out with your old stinking wrist guards. Never pick either of them back out of the garbage.

Balance is key, on and off skates. Be a little wild sometimes, but remember—whether you like it or not, you are a role model. Be a little responsible sometimes, but never act your age.

Listen to your coach. The good ones know much more than you do.

Talk less, skate more.

Read the rules. You may not agree with them, but knowing what they are and what they mean will give you a natural advantage over those who haven't.

Come to practice severely hungover one time. That will be enough to teach you never to do it again.

Remember about twenty sentences ago when I said to "get low"? Well, you probably aren't skating low enough yet. Get lower.

At some point, you're going to screw up, both on and off the track. When you do, apologize. Mean it. Make every effort not to do it again. Forgive yourself and others will forgive you, too.

Volunteer to coach a junior derby league at least once. The experience will change you as a person and it will make you a better skater.

When your body is so tired that you feel like you can't take another step, skate two more laps before you quit.

Be respectful of the refs. They are human beings. Bad calls will happen. You will get pissed off. Assume the best of intentions. Forgive and move on.

You can never thank a volunteer too much. Risk sounding ridiculously repetitive by telling them how much you appreciate them every time you see them.

Call your mother. She is your biggest fan. She takes pride in your achievements in a way that you will probably never fully comprehend. A ten-minute phone conversation every now and again won't kill you and it will make her more happy than you can imagine.

When you're giving high fives after the bout, take the time to bend down to gently slap the hand of a child who has been cheering you on. It will mean the world to them to connect with a real live roller girl and they will likely remember the experience well into their adult lives.

Keep an eye out for the biggest, meanest, most skilled, scary bitches out there. Immediately recruit them onto your team. You do not want to play against these women. Trust me.

Do not be overconfident—anything can happen on bout day. Never doubt your abilities; you are stronger than you think.

Never check your skates on a flight. Carry-on only.

Do something nice for an injured skater. At some point, this will be you and you will appreciate the favor returned way more than you can know while you're healthy.

Don't blame yourself. Don't blame others. Blame doesn't solve anything and it won't change the outcome of a bout.

Buy a photographer a drink. Although you likely don't realize it now, they are giving you a gift that you will cherish long into old age. They will allow you to see yourself in a way that is not possible on your own—through somebody else's eyes. Their work will show you that you are slimmer than you think and that you are more beautiful than you give yourself credit for. If you don't see this right away, wait ten years, then look at the photos again. Call me if I'm wrong. I don't expect to hear from you.

When you ask someone for advice, actually listen to their response. When you are asked for advice, be kind, start with a compliment, and tell the truth.

Wow, you're doing great at getting low. Now relax your shoulders.

You may get divorced, you may suffer a breakup, and you may fall in love. Do not let any of these things take you away from skating. Only quit when you're ready, and only on your own terms.

Be your own cheerleader. Do this quietly inside your head. Encourage yourself. Do not berate yourself. Be a cheerleader for your teammates. Do this out loud and frequently. Others may not have the inner positivity necessary to embolden themselves and they will thrive on your encouragement.

No matter how hard you try, not everyone is going to like you. Accept this now and your skating experience will be much easier. Show me how to do this.

Never leave your skates in your car. It will be very difficult to forgive yourself if they are stolen. It's not worth the risk.

You can come back from injury. It will not be easy. Have patience.

Don't take yourself too seriously.

Always shake your opponent's hand. Even the total bitches. Do this sincerely.

After each bout, thank the fans. It will be just as rewarding an experience to you as it is to them.

Well, that's it. That's all I've got. Whether this haphazard collection is worth the paper it's printed on, I honestly can't say. But the advice about the bra, I'm telling you—that's worth its weight in gold. Still don't believe me on that one? Go back and look at those pictures again.

ENDNOTES

1 www.derbylisting.com

2 www.derbylisting.com

3 Turner, James, and Michael Zaidman. "The Development of Skates." *In The History of Roller Skating.* Lincoln, Neb.: National Museum of Roller Skating, 1997.

4 http://amhistory.si.edu/sports/exhibit/removers/plimpton/index.cfm

5 http://curbed.com/archives/2014/10/23/history-of-the-roller-rink.php

6 "The Controversial First Days of Roller Skating Rinks, Lowell - 1885." Forgotten New England. March 1, 2013. Accessed April 24, 2015. http://forgottennewengland.com/2013/03/01/the-controversial-first-days-of-roller-skating-rinks-lowell-1885/.

7 http://www.skatingfitness.com/RollerSkating-History-of-Roller-Skating.htm

8 http://www.historylink.org/index.cfm?DisplayPage=output.cfm&file_id=5534

9 http://www.historylink.org/index.cfm?DisplayPage=output.cfm&file_id=5534

10 Coppage, Keith, and Baron Wolman. *Roller Derby to RollerJam: The Authorized Story of an Unauthorized Sport.* Santa Rosa, CA: Squarebooks, 1999, 4.

11 Coppage, 8.

12 Coppage, 12.

13 Coppage, 11.

14 Coppage, 13.

15 Coppage, 6.

16 Coppage, 17.

17 Coppage, 20.

18 Coppage, 36.

19 Deford, Frank. *Five Strides on the Banked Track; the Life and times of the Roller Derby.* Boston: Little, Brown, 1971.

20 www.hellonwheelsthemovie.com

21 www.twoevils.org/rollergirls or www.derbyrollcall.com

22 JRDA junior names database http://www.juniorrollerderby.org/junior-derby-names-listing

23 wftda.com

24 www.mensrollerderbyassociation.com

25 www.juniorrollerderby.org

26 www.teamusa.org/USA-Roller-Sports/Resources/Rules/Roller-Derby-Rules

27 www.rollerderbycoalitionofleagues.com/rules

28 www.skatemade.org

29 www.wearehellarad.com/2011/01/definition-derby

30 www.juniorrollerderby.org/jrda-tournaments

31 mrdwc.com

32 statewarsrollerderby.com

33 https://www.facebook.com/Vagtastic

34 rdjunkies.tumblr.com

35 www.chopra.com/ccl-meditation/21dmc/mantra.html

36 Bernstein, Elizabeth. "'Self Talk': When Talking to Yourself, the Way You Do It Makes a Difference." *The Wall Street Journal*, May 5, 2014. Accessed April 29, 2015. http://www.wsj.com/articles/SB10001424052702304831304579543772121720600.

37 www.npr.org/blogs/health/2014/10/07/353292408/why-saying-is-believing-the-science-of-self-talk

38 lifehacker.com/how-and-why-to-develop-your-mental-toughness-1619305771

39 www.inc.com/jeff-haden/7-habits-of-people-with-remarkable-mental-toughness.html

40 This article gives a full discussion on concussions, and there is a short, on-the-field evaluation form as well as a longer evaluation form for initial evaluation and follow-up. The whole document is available at http://www.cces.ca/files/pdfs/SCAT2[1].pdf in the *Journal of Athletic Training*, 2009:44 (4):434-448.

ADDITIONAL RESOURCES

These are some of the resources I've drawn on while researching for this book, along with other books, films, and articles that might be of interest to a derby lover.

Books

Bay Area Roller Derby
Jerry Seltzer and Keith Coppage

Down and Derby: The Insider's Guide to Roller Derby
Jennifer "Kasey Bomber" Barbee & Alex "Axles of Evil" Cohen

Five Strides on the Banked Track
Frank Deford

The History of Roller Skating
James Turner in collaboration with Michael Zaidman

No Mercy: Roller Derby Life on the Track
Jules Doyle

Roller Derby: The History and All-Girl Revival of the Greatest Sport on Wheels
Catherine Mabe, Foreword by Ivanna S. Pankin

The Roller Derby Athlete: A Skater's Guide to Fitness, Training, Strategy and Nutrition
Ellen Parnavelas

Roller Derby Classics and More!
Jim Fitzpatrick, Foreword by Ann Calvello

Roller Derby for Beginners: Get Out of the Bleachers and on the Track
Frisky Sour

Roller Derby to Rollerjam: The Authorized Story of an Unauthorized Sport
Keith Coppage

Roller Derby Rivals
Sue Macy

Roller Girl
Victoria Jamieson

Rollergirl: Totally True Tales from the Track
Melissa "Melicious" Joulwan

Scars & Stripes: The Culture of Modern Roller Derby
Andréanna Seymore

A Very Simple Game: the Story of Roller Derby
Herb Michelson

Whip It (originally titled *Derby Girl*)
Shauna Cross

Films

Blood on the Flat Track: The Rise of the Rat City Rollergirls (2007)

Brutal Beauty: Tales of the Rose City Rollers (2010)

Hell on Wheels (2007)

Kansas City Bomber (1972)

Rollergirls (TV Show, 2006)

This is How I Roll (2012)

Whip It (2009)

Articles

"The Dude of Roller Derby and His Vision" by Michael Brick, *New York Times*, December 17, 2008
http://www.nytimes.com/2008/12/18/sports/othersports/18devildan.html

"The Roller Derby" by Frank Deford, *Sports Illustrated*, March 3, 1969
http://www.si.com/vault/1969/03/03/558511/the-roller-derby

"Roller derby revival a draw" by Leigh-Ann Jackson, Cox News Service, published in *The Chicago Tribune*, October 30, 2002
http://articles.chicagotribune.com/2002-10-30/features/0210300081_1_novice-skaters-kansas-city-bomber-lace

"Roots of the Roller Derby Revival" by Michael Corcoran, originally published 2007.
http://www.michaelcorcoran.net/archives/2668

"You Just Can't Keep the Girls from Jamming" by Paul Wachter, *New York Times Magazine*, January 29, 2009
http://www.nytimes.com/2009/02/01/magazine/01Derby-t.html

SKATE SHOPS

Here is a good selection of skate shops around the US and the world. It's definitely not a complete list by any means. For more information about roller derby shops and businesses, visit www.derbyowned.com.

USA

Apex Skate Shop
Hatfield, PA
apexskateshop.com

Bruised Boutique
Nashua, NH
www.bruisedboutique.com

Cruz Skate Shop
Berkeley, CA
cruzskateshop.com

Derby Star Pro Shop
Frederick, MD
derbystarproshop.com

Derby Supply: Hampton Roads
Norfolk, VA

Derby Supply: High Altitude
Colorado Springs, CO
derbysupply.net

Derbyville
Denver, CO
derbyvilleonline.com

Fast Girl Skates
Seattle, WA
www.fastgirlskates.com

Five Stride Skate Shop
Brooklyn, NY
www.fivestrideskateshop.com

Krunch Skate Shop
Spokane, WA
krunch-skate.com

Leadjammer Skates
Bremerton, WA
Leadjammerskates.com

Long Beach Roller Sport
Long Beach, CA
www.longbeachrollerskate.com

Medusa Skates
Austin, TX
www.medusaskates.com

Next Level Skate Shop
Columbus, OH
nextlevelskateshop.com

Powerhouse Skates
Atlanta, GA
powerhouseskates.com

Sin City Skates
San Diego, CA

Sin City Skates DEUCE
Las Vegas, NV
sincityskates.com

Square Cat Skates
Hermosa Beach, CA
www.squarecatskates.com

Turn Two Skate Shop
Portland, ME
www.turntwoskateshop.com

Vital Skates
Indianapolis, IN
vitalskates.com

Wicked Skatewear
Los Angeles, CA
wickedskatewear.com

Canada

EOC Skates
Regina SK
www.eocskates.com

Nerd Roller Skates
Calgary AB
www.nerdskates.com

Rollergirl.ca
Vancouver BC
Rollergirl.ca

Europe

5th Blocker Skates
Glasgow, Scotland
www.5thblockerskates.co.uk

Derby Store
Sheffield, England
www.derbystore.co.uk

Double Threat Skates
London, England
www.doublethreatskates.co.uk

Jam in the Box
Helsinki, Finland
www.jaminthebox.com

QUAD Roller Skate Shop
Berlin, Germany
quadrollerskateshop.com

SCKR PNCH Skate Shop
Gent, Belgium
sckrpnch.com

Turn Left Roller Derby Shop
Eindhoven, The Netherlands
www.turnleftderby.com

Australia & New Zealand

Aotearoller Derby Gear
Wellington, New Zealand
aotearoller.co.nz

Sydney Derby Skates
Newtown, Australia
sydneyderbyskates.com

CONTRIBUTORS

Boo LaLa (#215lbs) hails from Red Wing, Minnesota, home of Riedell Skates. She has long been in the habit of speeding around on all sorts of wheels. Since discovering modern roller derby in 2011, Boo has been playing both banked and flat track with the San Diego Derby Dolls.

Brandy Rettig (AKA Rettig to Rumble), a former skater with the Rat City Rollergirls and the Oly Rollers, lives in Seattle and works in the field of Transportation Engineering. Her interests include pit bulls, power tools, heavy music, hip checks, and horror movies. She plays drums in her basement and writes stories in bed with her snoring puppy curled up next to her.

Carla Smith (AKA Booty Quake) is an eight-season veteran skater with Terminal City Rollergirls in Vancouver. Booty Quake founded Roller Derby Athletics in 2012 to provide fitness resources to all derby skaters. She preaches "pre-hab" work for injury prevention; effective and sport-specific cross training; and training smarter not harder. Roller Derby Athletics provides training programs to leave skaters feeling unstoppable. You can learn more at www.rollerderbyathletics. com, www.facebook.com/rollerderbyathletics or @bootyquake.

Caroline White (AKA Mazel Tov Cocktail) channels her strength from three years as a Blue Ridge Rollergirl into re-envisioning mental health supports in her work with the Western Mass Recovery Learning Community and the Hearing Voices Network. She lives in Holyoke, Massachusetts, with her partner Chris and their two cats, Schprintzi and Leonard Elizabeth Cohen.

Danielle Flowers (AKA OMG WTF) grew up running cross country, track, and playing soccer. She competed in the 1992 Track & Field Junior Olympics in Auburn, Alabama, in the 1500m and Discus Throw. She later went on to receive a scholarship to Cal State University Fullerton to play NCAA Division 1 soccer in 1997. After a brief stint away from athletics, she found roller derby while living in Montreal, Quebec, in 2008. That year, she moved to NYC to join Gotham Girls Roller Derby, where she has played since. With four WFTDA titles, she is known for her derby smarts and mastering how to use her small size to her advantage.

Dara Fineman (AKA Hebrew-Ham Lincoln) was originally from a beachy city in Southern California and moved to New York City over two years ago. Dara does comedy, acting, and singing. She began skating three years ago with San Fernando Valley Roller Derby and currently skates for the Garden State Rollergirls.

Dave Wood is a roller derby photographer, coach, and part-time official for the Rocky Mountain Rollergirls in Denver, Colorado. He started photographing roller derby in 2010 and joined the team on the bench in 2013. You can find him online at davewoodphotography. com.

David Dyte is an Australian-American, a former Gotham Girls Roller Derby NSO, and a part-time sports photographer with higher aspirations.

Dr. James Ramsay (AKA Papa Doc) retired from pediatrics and has been with the Windy City Rollers for ten years. He was introduced to roller derby by his daughter, Varla Vendetta. He has written a first aid manual for roller derby and participated in both the WFTDA Safety Squad and Derby Injury Prevention Network. He has worked on every home game and tournament for the Windy City team as well as at Champs and the 2nd World Cup.

Emily Udell (AKA Vivi Section) started playing roller derby in 2009, and plays for the Naptown Roller Girls. Off the flat track, she works as an editor for an award-winning digital publication based in Indianapolis. She holds degrees from Northwestern University and the University of Chicago. Find her at callthejam.com and @callthejam.

Genevieve D. Berrick (AKA Danger (ismymiddlename)) discovered roller derby in 2007 with the Victorian Roller Derby League. Resident tweetcaster, bout recap go-to, and a league skater with Angel City Derby Girls, she has written about all things derby, including being a founding and managing editor of Derby Central, and writing for *Hit & Miss Magazine*, *fiveonfive*, WFTDA, and *DNN*. She's an Associate Producer of *In The Turn*, a documentary about the queer roller derby community of the Vagine Regime, and the city founder and director of Hollaback! LA, a non-profit against street harassment. www.genevievedberrick.com

Jasmine Facun (AKA Sweet N. Lowdown) is a biology student currently living in Virginia Beach, Virginia, with her husband and two children. She began skating with Tucson Roller Derby in 2005 as "Space Racer" and transferred to the Dominion Derby Girls in 2006 as "Sweet N. Lowdown." She retired from roller derby in 2014.

Jonathan deSoto (AKA Julius Freezer) is a Non-Skating Official who started his career after researching and writing his Masters thesis on the rise of flat track roller derby. He is the Head NSO of the Long Island Roller Rebels, and an official for the New York Shock Exchange.

Jonathan Rockey (AKA Jonathan R) is a childhood competitive artistic roller figure skater who began coaching for Gotham Girls Roller Derby in 2005. In order to play roller derby, he founded the New York Shock Exchange and helped bring together the Men's Roller Derby Association. He currently serves on the MRDA Board of Directors. He skated on the first-ever men's roller derby Team USA and was named MVP of the 2014 Men's Roller Derby World Cup. He is also the Gotham Poet Laureate. Find him at jonathanr@nyshockexchange.com or on Twitter as @JonathanRockey.

Juan Paden started photographing Roller Derby on March 14, 2010, as HARD took on the D.C. Rollergirls, and got serious about it in

June 2012. He's been hooked ever since. You can see more of his work on Facebook under JPaden Photography.

Jules Doyle (AKA Axle Adams) has been photographing roller derby for a long time, and has shot skaters at every level of the sport. His work was showcased in his book, *No Mercy*, and you can also find him at @AxleAdams or www.type2bphoto.com.

Kamikaze Kitten skated with London Rollergirls for seven years and retired following the 2014 Roller Derby World Cup. The final jam of the final game was also her final jam of her final game. She captained London Brawling through some of their greatest achievements within international roller derby, but got just as much pleasure from learning new tricks or coaching keen rookies.

Kat Selvocki (AKA Lemony Kickit) played for Gotham Girls Roller Derby until 2008. After retiring, she discovered a class called Yoga Fight Club, where she learned that she could do yoga AND hit people—in the same room. Sold! Since then, Kat has completed 200+ hours of training and taught around the globe in her adventurous, mindful, unpretentious style. She specializes in teaching athletes and is the queen bee at Flat Mat Roller Derby: Yoga for Skaters. Now based in Seattle, you'll often find her rolling with PFM Roller Derby. www.flatmatrollerderby.com.

Katrina Swirko first strapped on skates in 2008 and currently jams for the Boston All-Stars. When she's not skating or writing for her derby website, www.kswirko.com, Katrina plays concertina in the competitive polka band Bellows of Fire, which played in the 1975 Polka World Championships (they lost to Argentina, though).

Kimberly Harding (aka Polly Gone) loves the feeling of gliding, which is why ice hockey, sailing, and roller derby are her sports of choice. She started playing derby with Gotham Girls Roller Derby in 2008, and has played with Maine Roller Derby's Port Authorities, Texas Rollergirls' Texecutioners, and Team USA. She's from the Jersey shore, where she enjoys surfing and eating lobsters and spaghetti. When her skates aren't on, she is a landscape architect.

Laura Wombwell (AKA Lilith NoFair), a certified Precision Nutrition coach and Roller Derby Athletics' "Derby in the Kitchen" contributor, wants to help you develop healthy habits that will carry you through a lifetime. In addition to her nutrition credentials, she is a personal trainer, kettlebell specialist, and skater with Tri-City Roller Girls in Kitchener, Ontario. She runs the blog and fitness training business How We Roll Fitness at howwerollfitness.com.

Linda Rice (AKA Stirrup Trouble) is a Nurse Midwife and blogger at www.midwifelindarice.com. After traveling the world, she broke all laws of convention by marrying, of all things, a Yankees fan. They now live with their two beautiful children in a small town north of Boston, blissfully happy in every month but October.

Manish Gosalia is a visual artist who photographs music & sports. His likes are b&w film, masala chai, and whiskey. He loves mostly behind a camera. You can find his work on Instagram and Twitter at @ManishGosalia, or www.manishgosalia.com.

Melissa Faliveno (AKA Harlot Brontë) has skated with the Mad Rollin' Dolls of Madison, Wisconsin, and Suburbia Roller Derby of Yonkers, New York. A writer, editor, and book reviewer, she holds an MFA from Sarah Lawrence College and her work has appeared in *DIAGRAM*, *Green Mountains Review*, *Isthmus*, *Kirkus*, *Lumina*, and *Poets & Writers Magazine*, where she is the associate editor. She lives in Brooklyn.

Nicole Matos is a Chicago-based writer, professor, and retired roller derby skater with the Chicago Outfit. Her work has appeared in *American Short Fiction*, *The Rumpus*, *Quiddity*, *Salon*, *XOJane*, *The Classical*, and many others. Her second chapbook of poetry, *The Astronaut's Apprentice*, is forthcoming with Dancing Girl Press.

Nicole Williams (AKA Bonnie Thunders) spent her childhood ice skating in pretty dresses during the winter and pushing girls around on the soccer field all summer. During college, she competed with an ice synchronized figure skating team, the Syracuse Orange Experience. After moving to New York City in 2005, Bonnie traded in her ice skates for roller skates. Bonnie is now known as one of the best jammers in the sport. She is celebrating her 10th season of roller derby, and has won the WFTDA Championship five times. She is co-owner of Five Stride Skate Shop in Brooklyn, New York. Outside of roller derby she enjoys spending time with her French Bulldog, Freddie, and caring for feral cats. www.fivestrideskateshop.com

Richie Frangiosa (AKA Judge Knot) is a WFTDA Level 5 Official currently with Philly Roller Derby. He started officiating in 2006, and has performed as a skating official in the last seven WFTDA Championships, as well as dozens of Regional/Divisional tournaments. He was a member of the WFTDA Rules Committee and helped shape past and present rulesets. He is currently Chair of the WFTDA Tournament Officiating Selection Panel, as well as a WFTDA Clinic Instructor. He is a fan of being creatively heckled, preferably with signs.

Scald Eagle found derby in the summer of 2010 and has never looked back. She's beginning her fifth season with the Rose City Rollers' All-Star team, the Wheels of Justice. She's been named DNN's 2011 Rookie of the Year, 2011 Western Regionals MVP, and RCR's 2012 & 2013 MVP of the Year. She is incredibly honored to be a member of the 2014 Team USA and has loved traveling the globe teaching roller derby.

Sean Hale (AKA Hale Yeah) is a photographer based out of the New York City area who has captured the sport of roller derby since 2009. His work has graced local newspapers, international magazines, and the side of two buildings in NYC. It can also be seen on seanhale. zenfolio.com.

She-Wrex skated with the Blue Ridge Rollergirls from 2010-2014. She retired as an All Star after suffering a head injury playing in Sacramento at BRRG's first trip to WFTDA Division 1 Playoffs. Originally hailing from Maine, she loves dogs, rocks, photography, and roller skating. She will have five years sober in May 2015.

Suzy Hotrod joined the sport in 2004 with New York City's Gotham Girls Roller Derby after being an athletically dormant art school student who spent her free time playing in a punk band. Her skating background consisted of attending birthday parties at the roller rink. After eleven years of hard work and determination, Suzy has become one of the most recognized skaters in flat track roller derby. In 2011 she was honored to represent our sport as the first roller derby skater to be included in The Body Issue of *ESPN Magazine*. Find her on Twitter or Instagram at @suzyhotrod55, or www.facebook.com/ suzyhotrod55 or www.suzyhotrod.com.

Swede Hurt has covered a lot of ground in her eight years in the sport: she began her roller derby career with Jet City in 2007, and has since skated with Rat City, Gotham Girls Roller Derby, the Crime City Rollers in Malmö, Sweden as head coach and captain, Stockholm Roller Derby as coach and captain, and recently returned to New York as a skater for Gotham and a manager for the New York Shock Exchange. In addition, she's been a critical member of Team Sweden since 2011, and skates for compilation teams like Team Legit, Team Vagine, Wolfpack, and others. She has coached in fourteen countries, and helped produce The Battle of the Nordic Light, the first tournament in Scandinavia.

Thor Olavsrud is serving his eighth consecutive year-long sentence as track manager of Gotham Girls Roller Derby's home team, the Manhattan Mayhem. During his tenure to date, Mayhem have reached the GGRD championships four times and won twice. Thor is also the track manager for the Gotham Girls Roller Derby All Stars. @Mimir9

TJ Chase is a Vancouver-based sports photographer and an official shooter for the Terminal City Rollergirls. He photographs the Vancouver Canucks, BC Lions, Vancouver Whitecaps, and is known for his unique style of athletic portraiture. You can see more of his work at tjchasephotography.com.

TK-Oh! (TK for short) is a mother of two middle schoolers, wife, English teacher, and writer from the rolling Midwest. She skates with the South Bend Roller Girls' Bonnie Dooms team as a blocker. Before joining the team, she trained and competed in triathlons, running the Madison Ironman race twice.

Wild Cherri started on skates at age two because of a pigeon toe. After trying shoes on the wrong feet, braces between shoes, and casts, the doctor recommended roller skating and she was hooked. She started figure skating at age eight for a total of ten years. In 2005 she started skating with Tampa Roller Derby before moving around a bit to Brandentucky Bombers, Gotham Girls Roller Derby, and now Atlanta Rollergirls. In 2014 she opened a skate shop called Powerhouse Skates in Atlanta, Georgia. She currently skates for Team USA, Atlanta Rollergirls Dirty South Derby Girls as their All-Star captain, the Denim Demons (home team), and SASS. Find her at www.powerhouseskates.com or @powerhouseskate.

ACKNOWLEDGMENTS

Like roller derby, making a book is a team effort, and that has been especially true for this one. There are so many people to thank—for their hard work, their encouragement, their inspiration. I can't hope to properly thank everyone who has helped me along this journey, but here's my best shot.

Thank you to Suburbia Roller Derby for giving me my start, and Gotham Girls Roller Derby for giving me a home.

To my derby wives: Dinah Party, Straight Razor, and Full Metal Jackie. To Ginger Snap for her kindness and for embodying the hard work, dedication, and humor that make this sport great. To Thor Olavsrud, Cruel Hand Luke, Sweet Sherry Pie, and everyone else on Manhattan Mayhem for pushing me to be the best skater I can be.

To my beta readers for their thoughtful reading and early comments, which helped me make this a better book. Special thanks to Jonathan deSoto, Corinne Lenk, Sharon Atwell, Ali Lemer, and Meredith Lawrence. Additional thanks to Nancy Atwell, Jessica Gay, Bridget Downey, Ted Thomas, Sara Dorchak, Karen Fittinghoff, and Margaret Hart.

To the Derbylife.com and *Derby News Network* teams, who built something incredible and gave me my first chance to write about roller derby. Mercyless, Hurt Reynolds, Lex Talionis, Fox Sake, Gnosis, Justice Feelgood Marshall, and many others deserve credit for creating something great for the derby world, against all odds, and out of sheer love of the sport.

To everyone who has provided publishing help along this journey: Ali Lemer, for savvy and eagle-eyed proofreading, Manish Gosalia and Sean Hale for generously sharing their gorgeous photos even before the book was a reality, Josh Sterling Bragg for contributing video footage, Megan Trank for general advice and enthusiasm, and Zak Deardoff for designing the cover, postcards, and anything else that needed to be designed along the way, among many other roles. To Tammis Day and Rose Ellen Epstein for teaching me some of my first lessons about publishing.

To my family and friends for their love and support. They have remained enthusiastic about this project even when my own enthusiasm occasionally waned.

And finally, to my Kickstarter Backers. These acknowledgments would be incomplete without my profuse thanks to all of the incredible people who supported my Kickstarter project. You didn't just provide the financial resources to create the book; your enthusiasm and shared desire to see this book get made provided me with confidence, excitement, and strength throughout the writing and publishing process. I could not have done this without you. Thank you.

Anonymous

Gail & Ted Roman

Kathleen Scheiner

Wayne Atwell

Emilie C Samuelsen

Bobby Narco

Meredith Lawrence

Sharon Atwell

Aunt Nancy Atwell & Uncle Doug McDaniel

Jessica Gay

Bridget Downey

Ted Thomas

Sara Dorchak and Jonathan deSoto

Lily Fittinghoff / Quest Shove

Xena Paradox

Thor Olavsrud

Wayne Atwell

Hot Quad

Andrew Atwell

Lori

David Dyte

Morgan

Nancy and Ken Duffy

Yogi HazMat

Jenn Hubbs

Ginger Snap!!

GalXC

Ed & Laura Hunkele

Massiva Hamiche

Tobi Reinhard (aka T. Ruth OrDare)

Andy & Michelle Santoro

Adam "Gireffe" Goucher

Seth J Bradley

Beverly Marshall Saling

Stephen

Duncan Fordyce

Little Mary Switchblade

Joules, #3Nm

Full Metal Jackie

Catherine "Suki Tawdry" Smith

ambush 202

Fatal Exception

Sadie Stingray

Gillian Speace

Val Capone

Alex von der Linden

srs biznis

Bada Bing Bada Boom

Mani-Ax

Mike "Ref In Peace" Fiedler

Michael Tax

George Starks

Tieg Zaharia

Maris Kreizman

Cruel Hand Luke

Angela Slamsbury

Don Jimatos

Mattie "Miss American Thighs" Kennedy

Zak <3

Jeffrey Doker

Natalie Ung

Tom Igoe

Rebecca "Chopsaw" Robbins

Byers Remorse

Grand Theft Autumn

Cedric Howe

Alexander Cox

Maddie Lux aka Delux Madness

Elly Blue

Amiee Tucker

Jim and Lynne

Carly Bogen

Danielle Sporkin (aka: Spork Chop)

cab

Ivanna S. Pankin

Esther!

Katie Dowling

Ana Bollocks

Dr. Joel and Joan Mark

Jess "Jez Rebelle" Planos

Justin Jones

Kat Selvocki

Doogie Howitzer

Jamie McIntyre

Fisteria

Marissa

Kat Napper #333

Mur Lafferty

Garth BeMiller

Rollerdad

Sarah Russo

Genn Oden (aka Roxie Wrecked-Her)

The Rogers Family

Misfit Kitteh

Dan O'Mahoney-Schwartz

Mike SumNoyz, NSO, Angel City Derby Girls

Sarah Kilts

Amie "JK Elemenopee" Aragones

R. M. Fretz

Stephanie Allen

Pinky Swears

sharon j abbott

Lindsay A Carbone

This American Strife

Kyala Stewart

Julian Yap

Camille, Helen & Joel

DiTolvo

Andrea Pierce

Stacey Earley

Butterscotch Cripple/Holly Freundlich

Yancey Strickler

JWagner

Arson Tina

Mandy Moreno

Lindsay R Hartman

Kate O'Shea

Kate Milford

Smacky

Fox Sake

Dr. Andrew Serota, Ph.D., Esq., BAMF

Buddha

Tom Spencer ("Deep V Diver")

Tai and Jess

Keith Woodson

GypsyBones

Moxxxie and HELLARAD

Melissa "Harlot Brontë" Faliveno

Jeremy Buller

Lauren Ward (Tiny Apocalypse)

Fountain City Roller Derby, Kansas City, Mo.

Jeremy Kerr

Kit Kittle

Nell Eckersley

grace green

Max Schmid

Lauren Alexandrea

Jess & Carlos Pelaez

Martha Atwell

Bitches Bruze

Mr. & Mrs. Hotrod

Megan Carbine

Donna

Lab Rat

Impure Blonde

xnonymous

Hayley Rosenblum

Jamie Tanner

Jon Leland

JNK

George Schmalz

David Peter

Emma Tangoren

Lukas Myhan

Liz Cook

victoria rogers

alfie

Terry Hope Romero

Julio Terra

Mike Lonesky

Johnny Promqueen

Silence in the Library Publishing

J.M. Martin

Morgan Levy

Ally Shwed

Nicola C

Kelly "PAC-JAM" Wetzel Talesnick

Emily Felger

Alison Benowitz

DerbySkinz.com

Craig

Lauren Swagerman

Megan O Cross

Limpin Lily

Kristin W.

Tracy Dawicki

salem

James Turnbull

Alex Shvartsman

Betsy Nails

Kevin Clark

Ken Nielsen

Lioness

Sarah Jacob

Cara Snellen

Laura Pruett

Jude E Boom

Julian Mercuri

ehma gardiner

Melanie Schaffner

Trent Stokes

The Commissioner

HorrorTalk.com

Jeremy Bent

Rob & Liz Howell

Philip Sandifer

Owen Rowe

emiLy "Winter is Coming" Quick

Chris Connett

Jeffrey Yamaguchi

Daryl Concha

Sam Skipsey

R. Sovertits

Isaac "Will It Work" Dansicker

Emma James

Catie Myers-Wood

hank doyle

Ames to Maim

Ferociraptor

Jeremy Cragg

Nicole He

Eric Mersmann

Aurora Thornhill

David F. Gallagher

Amanda Niu

Anonymous

Stephanie Pereira

Jeremy Salfen

Melissa Wong

Nick Yulman

Alex Hudson

Mark K.

Will "Pops" Bungarden

ABOUT THE AUTHOR

Margot Atwell has been playing roller derby since 2007 and skates under the name Em Dash for the world champion Gotham Girls Roller Derby league. She's the co-founder and editor-in-chief of derbylife.com and has written for publications such as *Derbylife, Derby News Network, Derby Central, fiveonfive magazine,* Moviefone.com, the *Huffington Post, Publishers Weekly, Publishing Perspectives,* and others. She is the co-author of *The Insider's Guide to Book Publishing Success* (Beaufort Books, 2013). She lives in Brooklyn with her tiny dog, Schlitz. You can find her online at @emdash8212 or www.margotatwell.com.

Photo by Sean Hale

Made in the USA
San Bernardino, CA
13 December 2019

61414266R00180